DISCARDED

Reversing Course

Reversing Course

Carter's Foreign Policy,
Domestic Politics,
and the Failure of Reform

David Skidmore

VANDERBILT UNIVERSITY PRESS
Nashville and London

Copyright © 1996 by Vanderbilt University Press
Nashville, Tennessee 37235
All Rights Reserved

First Edition 1996
96 97 98 99 00 5 4 3 2 1

This publication is made from recycled paper and meets the minimum requirements of American National Standard for Information Sciences—Permanence of Paper for Printed Library Materials ∞

The publisher wishes to thank the following copyright holders for permission to include portions of the following publications in this work:

> David Skidmore, "Explaining State Responses to International Change: The Structural Sources of Foreign Policy Rigidity and Change," in *Foreign Policy Restructuring: How Governments Respond to Global Change,* edited by Jerel A. Rosati, Joe D. Hagan, and Martin W. Sampson III (Columbia, S.C.: University of South Carolina Press, 1994).
> David Skidmore, "Carter and the Failure of Foreign Policy Reform," *Political Science Quarterly* 108, no. 4 (winter 1993–1904).
> David Skidmore, "Foreign Policy Interest Groups and Presidential Power: Jimmy Carter and the Battle of Ratification of the Panama Canal Treaties," in *Jimmy Carter: Foreign Policy and Post-Presidential Years,* edited by Herbert D. Rosenbaum and Alexej Ugrinsky (Westport, Conn.: Greenwood Press, 1993).
> David Skidmore, "The Politics of National Security Policy: Interest Groups, Coalitions and the SALT II Debate," in *The Limits of State Autonomy: Societal Groups and Foreign Policy Formulation,* edited by David Skidmore and Valerie M. Hudson (Boulder, Colo.: Westview Press, 1993).

Library of Congress Cataloging-in-Publication Data
Skidmore, David, 1959–
    Reversing course : Carter's foreign policy, domestic politics, and the failure of reform / David Skidmore.
        p. cm.
    Includes bibliographical references (p.) and index.
    ISBN 0-8265-1273-9 (alk. paper)
    1. United States--Foreign relations--1977–1981. 2. United States--Politics and government--1977–1981. 3. Carter, Jimmy, 1924– .
    I. Title.
E872.S556   1996
327.73'009'047--dc20   95-45293
                                                                                 CIP

Manufactured in the United States of America

*for my parents, who taught me
independence of mind*

CONTENTS

Acknowledgments ix

Introduction
The Politics of Decline xi

1 Explaining State Responses to International Change 3
2 Interpreting the Carter Administration's Foreign Policies 26
3 The Sources of Policy Change 52
4 The Search for Policy Legitimacy 84
5 Interest Group Politics and National Security Policy 104
6 American Foreign Policy under Reagan, Bush, and Clinton 149
7 A Structural Approach to Foreign Policy Analysis 174

Notes 182
Bibliography 215
Index 229

ACKNOWLEDGMENTS

IN ITS IDEAL FORM, scholarship is a collective enterprise. Over the years, I have been fortunate to benefit from association with many friends and colleagues who are committed to closing the gap between this ideal and the day-to-day practices of academic life. This book would never have come to fruition without their assistance and support.

This study began as a dissertation undertaken at Stanford University. For their helpful guidance, I owe a large thanks to the members of my dissertation committee, including my thesis supervisor, Stephen Krasner, as well as Alexander George and Robert North. My fellow graduate students at Stanford also provided much inspiration, solace, and friendship during a challenging period of my life.

Throughout my work on the book, two individuals served as critical sources of insight and encouragement. Thomas Lairson and James Nolt each helped me work through many intellectual tangles connected with this project. They have been good friends as well as important intellectual influences in my life. Others who provided constructive criticisms and suggestions include John Vasquez, Ole Holsti, Jerel Rosati, James McCormick, Robert Pastor, George Moffett, William Jordan, and several anonymous reviewers. I am grateful to each. I alone, however, am responsible for the ideas and interpretations found in these pages.

I also appreciate the efforts of Charles Backus, Director of the Vanderbilt University Press, who embraced this project and guided it toward completion. Barbara Dietrich Boose, Timothy Poe, and Drew Gentsch each provided crucial help in preparing the manuscript for publication. I would also like to acknowledge financial support from Drake University's Humanities Center.

My largest debts are to my family, who daily enrich my life in a multitude of ways. My wife, Charlene, and my children, Sonia and Sarah, freely offered their love, support, and patience through the many trying times that accompanied my work on this study. Finally, I would like to dedicate this book to my mother and my late father, who together taught me independence of mind, among many other valuable lessons in life.

INTRODUCTION

The Politics of Decline

THE SEVENTIES were a period of aborted change in American foreign policy. The pervasive post–World War II consensus among foreign policy elites crumbled under the weight of the Vietnam War and international economic turmoil. New policy paradigms such as détente and liberal internationalism not only prompted debate but in many instances provided the basis for marked policy departures. The Nixon administration was the first to challenge past orthodoxy openly when it took bold steps toward improving relations with both the Soviet Union and the People's Republic of China.

Yet the influence of new schools of thought on American foreign policy was most evident during the early stages of the Carter presidency. Heralding a new era, Jimmy Carter and his advisers brought to office a belief that many of the traditional rationales that had guided American foreign policy for more than a generation were now outmoded and inappropriate to altered world realities. Carter's first year brought a flurry of liberal initiatives intended to shift the general direction of America's role and strategy in the world. Carter promised to overcome America's obsession with communism, adopt a skeptical attitude toward the utility of military force, and loosen the country's embrace of Third World dictators. Carter's international agenda would be shaped by sensitivity toward the forces of change sweeping the Third World, a desire to deepen détente with the Soviet Union, and a willingness to seek cooperative solutions to pressing global problems. Of Carter's early enthusiasm for reform, Gaddis Smith has observed that "the sheer level and range of activity, if not the results, suggested a foreign policy equivalent of Franklin D. Roosevelt's New Deal."[1]

Yet by the end of Carter's reign, this new liberal agenda had been largely abandoned in the face of rising domestic criticism. U.S.-Soviet relations had deteriorated markedly, military spending and arms sales were on the rise, Carter's early emphasis on human rights was muted and rapid deployment forces were being readied for possible Third World intervention. Confirming this turnabout, the Reagan administration soon reversed what few policies survived the liberal interlude of the seventies.

The Carter administration's initial enthusiasm for and eventual abandonment of liberal internationalism[2] raises interesting questions for students of American foreign policy. Carter's early critiques of past policies, while by no means radical in nature, were systematic and far reaching. Similarly, the policy changes attempted by his administration were wide-ranging and interdependent. When Carter eventually chose to retreat from these reforms, he did so not in a piecemeal fashion, but across a range of policies. While the timing of these reversals varied from issue to issue, the overall pattern of change suggests a paradigmatic shift in the administration's orientation. Comparing Carter's first year in office to his last, one discovers not only broad policy changes, but also marked shifts in rhetoric and even personnel. The scope of Carter's attempted reforms in American foreign policy was matched by the breadth of his retreat from these initial ambitions. This suggests that the rise and demise of liberal internationalism under the Carter administration must be viewed not as a series of independent, unrelated initiatives, each failing for special reasons, but as an aborted shift in the intellectual regime underlying American foreign policy as a whole.

This book attempts to explain the failure of foreign policy reform during the Carter years. Others, of course, have addressed this topic. Yet previous interpretations generally fail to provide complete or satisfying explanations for Carter's experience. Most suffer from a common flaw: the lack of an explicit theoretical underpinning. Without the guidance of theory, observers tend to fall back upon ad hoc or normative patterns of explanation. Carter's failure then appears idiosyncratic, unconnected with the broader trends or forces shaping American foreign policy either before or since his term of office.[3]

This trap can be averted by grounding one's interpretation of the Carter era in a broader model of continuity and change in American foreign policy. Explaining the reversal of Carter's reform strategy requires the construction of a more general theory of foreign policy formulation that could, in principle, be applied not only to other periods in American history but to other national settings as well. The following discussion lays the groundwork for this task by detailing some of the assumptions underlying the subsequent analysis and providing a bare sketch of the argument.

The Structural Context of Foreign Policy Decision Making

The theory proposed here is structural in design. It focuses most heavily, in other words, on the way in which enduring, though not immutable, features of the international and domestic environments structure the political incentives confronting foreign policy decision-makers. The first step in understanding how the structural context of decision-making influences the substance of foreign policy is to locate central decision-makers within this structure and to posit some plausible assumptions about the interests that motivate them.

U.S. foreign policy is generally crafted at the highest levels of the state by the president and his principle advisers. The positions occupied by these officials require them to consider two potentially contradictory sets of interests. On the one hand, the president is uniquely vested with responsibility for pursuing policies that further broad national interests. Unlike bureaucrats, members of Congress, or private lobbyists, the president speaks for a national constituency and is therefore less likely to become the captive of special interests when formulating the broad objectives and strategies of U.S. foreign policy. While this role does not automatically endow the president with special wisdom, it does provide him with a broader perspective than other actors when judging American interests and selecting policies to advance them.

Given this role, presidents must be concerned with the task of adjusting American foreign policy to changes in the international distribution of power and interests. Presidents have an incentive, in other words, to monitor the compatibility between U.S. policies and the structure of the international environment. This concern manifests itself in efforts to maintain a rough equilibrium between the national resources devoted to the pursuit of foreign policy objectives and the commitments that constitute claims upon those resources. The performance of American foreign policy will suffer when negative trends in the distribution of international power and interests lead to a growing gap between resources and commitments. These conditions present top officials with external incentives to close this gap by either expanding resources or restricting commitments.

The president is also, however, an elected official with political interests in re-election, in the prospects of his party, in maintaining good relations with Congress, and in sustaining a reservoir of popular support for his policies. In this dimension of his role, the president must be attentive to the underlying domestic political legitimacy of his overall foreign policy program. The president must not only cope with potentially powerful interest groups, but also defend his policies when challenged on broad ideological grounds. He must establish the legitimacy of his view of the nation's interests and demonstrate that his policies are based upon a correct interpretation of the principal challenges facing the United States abroad. Finally, both the ends and means of policy must be consistent with widely shared cultural values and normatively appealing to the public at large. Domestic and international structures each, therefore, serve to constrain the range of politically viable foreign policy options.

These tasks, the balancing of power and commitments abroad and the pursuit of policy legitimacy at home, place potentially contradictory constraints and demands upon top foreign policy officials. There is little reason to assume an automatic convergence between domestic and international incentives, and there are bound to be times when the strains between the two intensify. When efforts to reconcile these conflicting objectives fail, a president is likely to find domestic constraints more compelling.

This assumption is based, in part, upon the argument that foreign policy legitimacy is a prerequisite to the pursuit of any coherent and consistent external strategy. Moreover, continued controversy over a president's foreign policies, if sufficiently deep and broad, may prove damaging to his broader political interests, including the viability of his domestic policy goals or even his hold on office.[4]

The weakness of the American state offers additional reason to suspect that domestic political interests will be given priority over external interests when the two are in conflict. The fragmented authority of the state as well as the many potential points of access for societal groups place the president in a politically vulnerable position when faced with sustained societal opposition.[5]

This simple model specifies the relevant features of the external and internal environments that influence the general direction of American foreign policy. Top foreign policy officials try to balance resources and commitments abroad while maintaining political legitimacy for their policies at home. When conflicts between these imperatives arise, domestic legitimacy will be accorded priority.

The Influence of International and Domestic Constraints

To apply these propositions usefully to the analysis of American foreign policy, one must develop ways of describing changes in the relevant features of the international and domestic environments and the relationships between these trends over time. The crucial feature of the international environment influencing U.S. foreign policy during the post-World War II era has been the relative power of the United States as compared with other countries. The most important domestic factor has been the degree of consensus surrounding U.S. policies.

Different sets of literature address each of these issues. Flowing from the realist tradition in the study of international relations, a large and expanding body of scholarship has emerged on the decline of hegemonic states. The United States, most agree, achieved hegemony, or international dominance, after World War II when it possessed economic, political, and military resources that, together, dwarfed those of any competing state. The theory of hegemonic decline attempts to explain why hegemons, such as the United States, tend to lose relative power over time and suggests a basis for judging the appropriateness or effectiveness of various strategies available to hegemonic states for responding to external decline. This literature provides us with a broad perspective on the international challenges facing American decision-makers during the seventies.

There is also a considerable literature on changes in elite and public foreign policy opinion in the United States during the post-World War II period. Most analysts have concluded that the broad consensus characterizing opinion during the fifties and sixties broke down in the wake of Vietnam. By comparison with their predecessors in earlier decades, policy-makers during the seventies were left to cope with a much more contentious domestic political environment.[6]

Each of these bodies of literature contains valuable insights that can aid in understanding the evolution of policy-making during the Carter administration. Yet neither provides a complete and adequate explanation for the rise and demise of liberal internationalism. Based solely on changing external incentives, the theory of hegemonic decline offers predictions regarding how the policy-makers of a hegemonic state will respond to declining power. This proves most useful in understanding the emergence of Carter's early reform program, which generally matched the theory's predictions. As argued below, Carter's early foreign policy strategy represented an effort to close the gap between U.S. resources and commitments caused by declining relative power. This may be referred to as a strategy of adjustment. Yet the theory of hegemonic decline tells us little, if anything, about why the Carter administration abandoned these efforts. The literature on changes in domestic opinion during the seventies sheds light on the challenges Carter faced in building domestic support for an adjustment-oriented program of liberal internationalism. Yet it does not explain why Carter's efforts to sway opinion failed so dismally or why the conservative coalition opposed to Carter's reforms proved so resilient.

The problem with these literatures on the external and internal contexts of American foreign policy is that each has evolved in relative isolation from the other. Analysts in both traditions have been slow to explore the possible linkages between the two.[7] Moreover, there is often a tendency to explain policies and policy changes solely in terms of contemporaneous developments. Little attention is given to the possibility that today's policies may be constrained by the legacy of decisions taken yesterday. And yesterday's decisions may, in turn, be traced to the previous interactions of internal and external forces.

This study argues that domestic constraints played the most important role in explaining the failure and abandonment of Carter's adjustment strategy. Public skepticism and elite opposition to reform raised the political costs of policy change to intolerable levels, prompting the administration to retreat from its initial liberal internationalist orientation. Each of these constraints can be traced back to the domestic politics of the Cold War era. The combination of state weakness and hegemonic ambition prompted policy-makers to oversell the Cold War in hopes of winning public support for an active U.S. role abroad. The very success of this effort raised the domestic barriers to policy change when the Carter administration later sought to break with Cold War routines. Just as importantly, the expansion of the post–World War II national security state led to the accumulation of groups with material or ideological vested interests in status quo policies. Carter's challenge to existing priorities prompted an elite backlash as these interests mobilized to stymie serious efforts at policy reform during the seventies. Theoretically, this argument emphasizes the special obstacles that undermine the ability of hegemonic states to respond in a rational and timely fashion to declining power. The next section of this introduction summarizes the argument in greater detail.

Summarizing the Argument

The theory of hegemonic decline suggests that structural characteristics of the international system will contribute to the weakening of hegemonic power over time. Declining power will create pressures for the hegemon to adjust its policies to account for its weakened position. Adjustment involves the adoption of policies that will slow the process of decline and contain the costs of defending the hegemonic order. A declining hegemon should be expected to shed peripheral commitments abroad and seek ways of expanding resources internally. Failure to adjust previous policies will lead to a pattern of escalating costs and declining benefits.[8]

The theory of hegemonic decline accurately predicts the loss of American power over the past several decades but does less well at explaining the slowness of U.S. policy adjustment to this development. Although the United States emerged from World War II in a position of dominance, American hegemony relative to its economic and political rivals steadily waned over time. By the late sixties and early seventies, this process began to seriously complicate American efforts to defend the international commitments and arrangements the United States had sponsored during the early post-war period. At this point, the domestic consensus within the United States favoring of a strategy of hegemonic dominance began to crumble, and many foreign policy elites came to advocate policies of adjustment.

Contrary to realist expectations, however, changes in American power did not insure the success of compensating adjustments in policy. Indeed, although the Nixon/Ford administrations and, even more so, the Carter administration initiated various attempts at adjustment during the seventies, these were all but abandoned by the end of the decade.

The failure of these administrations to sustain a strategy of adjustment reveals the inadequacy of simple power-based models for understanding policy change. Liberal internationalism, the Carter administration's paradigm of adjustment, was frustrated by domestic constraints on policy change. Realist theory, with its emphasis on state responsiveness to international change, does little to illuminate this experience. Only when it is recognized that hegemony has domestic as well as international effects does this paradoxical pattern of policy rigidity in the face of changing international constraints become comprehensible.

The experience of hegemony contributes not only to the diffusion of international power but also to the rigidification of domestic structures within society and the perpetuation of policies constrained by these structures even after the international basis for their effectiveness has evaporated. Relatively speaking, a hegemon is freer of international constraints than are less powerful states. This allows hegemonic powers to pursue particularly ambitious goals that are beyond the reach of normal states. It also frees hegemons from the competitive discipline normally associated with participation in the international system. To protect their basic interests, middle-level powers have little choice but to continuously adapt their domestic structures and foreign policies in ways responsive to international change. Hegemonic states, by contrast, have sufficient power and resources to allow them to avoid the necessity of adapting to international change. Freed from competitive pressures by enormous power, the policies and the supporting domestic structures of the hegemon become rigid and fail to adapt to changes in the international environment.

As the process of relative decline proceeds, the hegemon will face an increasingly competitive environment. Unable any longer to rely simply on its gross capabilities, the hegemon will begin to experience the same internal pressures that plague ordinary states. Yet adaptation to these new circumstances will prove difficult. The rigidification of domestic structures and policies that takes place during the long period of ascendance hamper the adjustment response capabilities of the state and contribute to the perpetuation of policies that are no longer suited to the new international context in which the hegemon must compete.

In the case of the United States, the experience of hegemony and the preexisting weakness of the American state combined to provide decision-makers during the early post-World War II era with both the opportunities and the incentives to promulgate an ambitious set of foreign policy goals based as much upon ideology as upon interests. The intersection of international with domestic structure made it both internationally feasible and politically desirable for decision-makers to adopt strong and exaggerated ideological appeals in their attempt to build domestic consensus around an activist American role in the world.

Their success in this effort left a powerful domestic political legacy that frustrated the process of policy adjustment during the Carter administration. Vested interests, along with the constraining effects of state weakness and the ideological legitimation of old policies, left the Carter administration with little maneuvering room in which to institute policy changes and forced the abandonment of many initiatives that, however desirable as responses to external change, could not garner sufficient domestic political support. Thus, despite external incentives for adjustment, the domestic structural consequences of past hegemony inhibited efforts to legitimize an internationally viable alternative to the rigid, universalistic formulations that controlled American foreign policy during this country's period of hegemonic ascendance.

The line of reasoning suggests that realist theory, which attempts to predict responses based upon changing international incentives, is inadequate to explain the behavior of hegemonic states experiencing decline. Even once decline has set in, the hegemon may resist the external imperatives of adjustment as long as the domestic political costs of policy change continue to outweigh the external costs of delayed adjustment. Shielded by enormous power from the necessity of adjusting to external change for so long, domestic structures become institutionalized and insure the persistence of rigid or sticky policies long past the point when they are internationally efficacious.

Under these conditions, contradictory pressures produce a great deal of conflict over policy and insure that the sustenance of a coherent, consistent set of policies will prove extremely difficult. The nature of the constraints on policy consistency will vary, however, depending upon the policy orientation of the administration in power. A president, such as Jimmy Carter, who pursues a strategy of adjustment will face obstacles primarily from the domestic side. These domestic constraints will provide an incentive to abandon reform in favor of more traditional policies. A president, such as Ronald Reagan, who resists adjustment will, by contrast, face frustrations that are primarily external in origin. A strategy of resistance to changing external realities, even if popular at home, will result in international failures and growing costs. This may force reconsideration of such a strategy. As Kenneth Oye has argued, this is precisely what occurred in the case of the Reagan administration.[9]

Thus, American foreign policy was, during much of the seventies and eighties, trapped in a structurally determined pattern of vacillation and inconsistency. Strategies of adjustment met with critical levels of domestic opposition. Domestic obstacles eventually forced a reversion to traditional strategies of resistance. Yet a strategy of resistance could not succeed internationally, compelling policy-makers to consider the introduction of at least some elements of adjustment. This argument helps to explain the perplexing and often frustrating indecisiveness and lack of consistency that has characterized the foreign policies of recent administrations. As we suggest in chapter seven, the dramatic international and domestic changes that have accompanied the end of the Cold War may succeed in breaking this debilitating cycle in U.S. foreign policy. The structural conditions necessary to support a sustained strategy of foreign policy adjustment are more favorable now than in the past. Whether Bill Clinton and his successors will possess the foresight and wisdom to take advantage of these new opportunities remains unclear at this point.

Research Strategy and Organization

Policy-makers may pursue adjustment through two means. They can choose to expand internal resources or restrict external commitments. Since the former is a long-term task requiring a reallocation of domestic resources to revive economic growth and productivity, policy-makers must look to the latter option when seeking short-term means of resolving critical gaps between resources and commitments. As Carter's energy program attests, the administration was not oblivious to the necessity of addressing the long-term problem of domestic resource constraints. Yet the primary burden of adjustment was placed on efforts to restrict external commitments, shift burdens to allies, and develop less costly means of achieving American objectives abroad. This study will mirror the priorities of the administration itself, focusing on policies addressed to external commitments rather than those dealing with domestic resources. In particular, U.S.-Soviet relations, defense issues, and U.S. policies toward the Third World receive the closest attention.

The empirical sections of this study will rely upon case studies, survey data, public speeches, historical studies, and articles by and about Carter's domestic opposition in our analysis of the domestic constraints on American foreign policy during the Carter presidency. The objective is not to provide a chronological history of American foreign policy during these years, but to identify the principal sources of policy change.

Chapter 1 lays a theoretical foundation for the subsequent analysis of policy change under the Carter administration. Policy-makers must choose between two alternative strategic responses to declining power and international change: adjustment and resistance. States possessing a combination of hegemonic power abroad and state weakness at home will be poorly suited to carry out timely and appropriate policy adjustments to declining power. Instead, resistance is the more likely response.

Chapter 2 reviews various interpretations of Carter's initial foreign policy program and concludes that Carter's policies constituted a coordinated set of responses to hegemonic decline. Carter's reforms were rooted in a strategy of adjustment broadly consistent with the international incentives accompanying decline. Gradually, however, these initial orientations were abandoned over time. Carter generally failed in his efforts to engineer relatively permanent changes in American foreign policy and, by his last year in office, pursued a more traditional foreign policy agenda.

Chapter 3 attempts to locate the primary sources of policy change. A careful examination of Carter's retreat from liberal internationalist policies in various key issue areas demonstrates that the impetus for change was primarily internal rather than external in origin. In other words, domestic constraints were more imposing barriers to reform than international constraints. Yet against the general pattern of change and failure, a number of cases can be identified where the Carter administration could claim success for its strategy of adjustment. These successes occurred, however, in areas that were, for various reasons, sheltered from the domestic pressures responsible for failure elsewhere. This analysis makes it possible to specify certain restricted conditions under which policies of adjustment may succeed.

Chapter 4 examines the difficulties the Carter administration experienced in trying to gain domestic legitimacy for its new policies. Carter's program was the victim of contradictions between the imperatives of external adjustment and the requirements of internal legitimation. The legitimating routines institutionalized during the earlier period of hegemonic ascendance stressed simple, consistent, doctrinal appeals based upon ideological symbolism and the exaggeration of external threats. Carter's strategy of adjustment revolved around pragmatic, flexible policies designed to accommodate rivals and reconcile conflicting interests in a complex and rapidly changing world. This program was not easily translatable into the kind of appeals consistent with the legitimating routines outlined above. Thus, Carter found it difficult to explain or rationalize his efforts in terms that could command public support.

Chapter 5 explores elite and interest group constraints on Carter's reform program. Carter faced opposition from an active, organized, well-financed and ideologically united coalition of individuals and groups with strong ties to the institutions and policies of the Cold War era. This coalition pursued a populist strategy designed to sway elite and public opinion by using techniques and appeals drawn from the successful legitimating strategies of the Cold War years. These groups proved successful at filtering popular perceptions of external developments and establishing control over the agenda of foreign policy debate. Besides a general discussion of the interest group environment, this chapter provides a detailed look at the debates over the Panama Canal and the SALT II treaties.

Chapter 6 examines the structural constraints that have shaped U.S. foreign policy during the period since Carter left office. The efforts of Presidents Reagan, Bush, and Clinton to reconcile conflicting international and domestic pressures are explored. Consideration is given to the lessons that can be drawn from the experience of recent presidents as the United States faces the prospect of carrying out continued adjustment to a rapidly changing global environment.

The concluding chapter considers the broader theoretical implications of the book's analysis. It offers some guidelines for applying a structural approach to the study of foreign policy in the U.S. and elsewhere.

Reversing Course

CHAPTER ONE

Explaining State Responses to International Change

HOW SHOULD we expect hegemonic states to respond to declining power? Indeed, how do states generally deal with international change? Does state responsiveness to external change vary across cases in predictable ways? These are important questions about which there is disagreement in the relevant literature. This chapter offers a model of state response to international change that encompasses the existing theoretical alternatives. This argument suggests that states differ in their abilities to adapt to international change, depending upon their particular combinations of international power and domestic state strength. The following analysis throws into bold relief the special problems that hegemonic powers such as the United States, as compared with more modestly endowed states, experience in coping with relative decline and international change.

The dependent variable, state response, can be pitched at various levels of abstraction. At the highest level, a state may either resist or adjust to international change. Resistance is the refusal to alter policies poorly suited to cope with the new incentives and constraints posed by an altered international environment. Adjustment, by contrast, involves policy changes designed to render state behavior more consistent with present or emerging international constraints and incentives.[1]

The choices facing a declining hegemon, in particular, can be described less abstractly.[2] The loss of relative power leads to a growing gap between resources and commitments. A strategy of resistance reinforces this tendency by stubbornly binding a hegemon to the defense of previous commitments while neglecting measures that might stimulate accelerated resource growth. A strategy of adjustment, in the context of decline, entails policy changes designed to close or narrow the gap between resources and commitments by either increasing resources, curtailing commitments, or both.

Existing theories about the relationship between international change and state response are typically pitched at the highest levels of abstraction. They offer predictions, sometimes implicitly, about how states should respond to international change, without distinguishing among various types of states or the nature of the international circumstances they face. There exist two alternative models of policy response: the first, an evolutionary model springing from realist theory, predicts policy adjustment; the second, a sporadic model drawn from an institutional framework, predicts resistance or, at a minimum, considerable lags in adjustment.

Neither of these models, however, is adequate to predict the policy responses of all types of states. Each applies under differing circumstances, depending upon the combinations of state strength and international power characteristic of the case in question. Hegemonic powers, particularly those with weak states, will be apt to resist the implications of international change and declining power. Their behavior will follow the sporadic pattern of policy change predicted by institutional models. States combining modest power abroad and state strength at home, on the other hand, are more likely to carry out appropriate policy adjustments in response to international change, just as realist theory would lead one to expect.

Models of Policy Response: Evolutionary Versus Sporadic

The concepts of adjustment and resistance distinguish between broadly different strategic orientations toward situations of decline. As Robert Gilpin suggests, hegemonic powers face increasingly difficult resource tradeoffs over time stemming from a tendency for the proliferating costs of consumption and protection (or defense) to crowd out productive investment.[3] A strategy of adjustment uses policy change as an instrument for redressing this imbalance by shifting resources toward investment, while a strategy of resistance aggravates the dilemmas of decline by defending the very domestic and international commitments that continue to rob resources from investment.

Adjustment, while preferable in the abstract, confronts policy makers with difficult choices. Although, in principle, a gap between resources and commitments can be narrowed by increasing resources while protecting existing commitments, there are practical obstacles to this path. In the short run, increased resources in support of commitments abroad can be attained only by enhancing the extractive activities of the state at home (i.e., higher taxes or borrowing). Given the costs this will impose on societal groups, such a course may entail political risks. In the long run, increased resources can be obtained by shifting resources from consumption to investment, using natural resources more efficiently and promoting technological innovation. These measures, however, may be difficult to implement and, since the results are likely to be long in materializing, do little to overcome the immediate consequences of a gap between resources and commitments.

Shedding commitments offers a quicker method for narrowing the gap, although not without costs. Since commitments are made in order to defend actual or potential sources of benefit, shedding commitments will increase net benefits only if the costs avoided as result of shedding the commitment exceed the benefits to be preserved through its defense. Before commitments are abandoned, hegemonic powers are likely to seek less expensive ways of meeting them. This can be accomplished, for instance, by shifting burdens to allies or substituting, where possible, less expensive economic or diplomatic means of leverage for relatively expensive military forms of protection. Where these efforts fail or prove inadequate, some degree of retrenchment must form part of a strategy of adjustment. Retrenchment is likely to begin with peripheral commitments, where benefits are marginal and costs are excessive. If declining power persists, the number of commitments that can still be defended at a cost lower than the benefits at stake will shrink. In other words, growing numbers of commitments will come to be viewed as marginal in relation to the expense of maintaining them.

A strategy of adjustment is not always an appropriate response to declining power. Where the sources of decline are transitory and contingent rather than long-term and structural, far-reaching and relatively permanent adjustments in policy are likely to be unnecessary and undesirable. In such cases, a strategy of resistance is better suited to the circumstances. The discussion that follows assumes circumstances involving long-term, structural decline where policy adjustments are likely to be necessary and appropriate.

In considering which strategic orientation a hegemon is likely to adopt, it quickly becomes apparent that two conditions must be met before a strategy of adjustment may emerge: 1) the hegemon must be sufficiently sensitive to environmental conditions to recognize the fact of decline, its sources and its implications, and 2) the leaders of a hegemonic state must have the political freedom and capacity to manipulate policies in such a way as to manage a strategy of adjustment.

Realism, the reigning intellectual model within the discipline of international relations, assumes that these conditions are easily met. Because realism posits a tight linkage between environmental conditions and policy responses, it leads logically to an evolutionary model of policy change. Given the premises of realist theory, one should expect state leaders to adjust policies in an incremental and adaptive way to international change.[4]

Realism depicts states as if they were "unitary rational actors, carefully calculating costs of alternative courses of action and seeking to maximize their expected utility. . . ."[5] In a realist world, states constantly adjust their policies in response to perceived changes in the international configurations of power and interests. As Robert Keohane explains: "The link between system structure and actor behavior is forged by the rationality assumption, which enables the theorist to predict that leaders will respond to the incentives and constraints imposed by their environments."[6] The assumption of rationality, which Keohane describes as "essential to the theoretical claims of Structural Realism," allows the analyst "to attribute variations in state behavior to variations in characteristics of the international system" rather than "the calculating ability of states."[7] Realism abstracts away from the domestic politics of foreign policy making on the assumption that little explanatory power is lost in the process.

According to realist theory, hegemons are not unique in their capacities to adjust to international change. They differ from other states only in the nature of the constraints they face during a period of declining power. If one understands the sources and implications of decline, then one can predict the likely policy responses of the hegemon without acquiring knowledge about the domestic or institutional context in which such decisions are to be made. Hans Morgenthau explains that realists put themselves "in the position of a statesman who must meet a certain problem of foreign policy under certain circumstances, and we ask ourselves what the rational alternatives are from which a statesman may choose . . . and which of these rational alternatives this particular statesman . . . is likely to choose."[8] Keohane refers to this method of analysis as "rational reconstruction."[9] This reasoning rests upon the notion that decision makers have virtually infinite flexibility in choosing among various policies. Realism tells us that they are constrained only by the resources at their disposal and the environmental conditions they face.

Institutional approaches challenge this assumption. Contrary to realist theory, institutionalism treats the constraints on rational adaptation as severe and predicts, therefore, a sporadic rather than an evolutionary pattern of policy change. The suggestion that social change is more often discontinuous and abrupt than continuous and gradual has been championed by many authors in a variety of fields.[10] Among these, the work of Stephen Krasner is particularly relevant to the present study. Borrowing from theoretical developments in the field of evolutionary biology,[11] Krasner builds a model of policy change around the concept of "punctuated equilibrium." This model suggests that policies do not adapt incrementally over time in tandem with environmental conditions. Instead, policy change occurs only intermittently and often in large leaps.[12]

Policies remain rigid due principally to the stickiness of institutions and the domestic structures in which they are embedded. The first source of rigidity is that policy change is costly, requiring the creation of new analytical models and organizational routines corresponding to altered realities. The intellectual and organizational costs that go into the creation of new policies mitigate against future change. Change is also rendered difficult because policies become enmeshed in domestic interests that have a stake in their perpetuation. Krasner suggests: "State decisions taken because of state interests reinforce private societal groups that the state is unable to resist in later periods."[13] Vested interests can use their political power to rob policy makers of the flexibility required to manage a process of steady, gradual adaptation.[14]

As a result of these constraints, policies become "stuck," leading to a growing gap between static policies and changing external realities. The increasing dysfunctionality of existing policies eventually leads to a crisis that may finally succeed in shaking up domestic routines. As Krasner puts it: "Once policies have been adopted, they are pursued until a new crisis demonstrates that they are no longer feasible. States become locked in by the impact of prior choices on their domestic political structures."[15] Policies change only when crises impress upon policy makers the external costs of maintaining old policies and galvanize the state to challenge vested interests and adopt new policies more congruent with international conditions.

Toward an Integrated Model of Policy Response

Despite appearances to the contrary, these contrasting models of state response can be reconciled with one another. When the assumptions underlying both evolutionary and sporadic theories of policy change are treated as variables rather than as givens, it is possible to show that each applies under different conditions. This allows for the rather obvious fact that some states adapt well and readily to international change while others do not—an observation that, given their blanket predictions, neither theory, taken alone, is prepared to acknowledge or explain.

The implicit independent variables underlying both the models described above are 1) the degree of external compulsion and 2) the degree of domestic constraint. Where external compulsion is high, policies are likely to adapt. Where external compulsion is low, policies are likely to remain rigid. Similarly, domestic conditions affect the likelihood and degree of policy rigidity. A strong state—one where authority is centralized and that can act relatively autonomous of domestic interests—is potentially capable of implementing policy change at reasonably low domestic costs. A weak state will be too divided and encumbered by domestic interests to manipulate policies so easily.

Realist theory, in other words, is best suited to explaining the behavior of states characterized by modest power abroad and great strength at home. Policy adjustment to international change is most likely where international constraints are tight (as is the case for middle-level powers) and domestic constraints are loose (as is the case for states that are domestically strong and autonomous). Realist theory should predict well under these conditions because states facing them clearly have stronger incentives to respond to international than to domestic constraints.

Recalling the prerequisites for adjustment mentioned above, middle-level powers will come closest to meeting the condition of sensitivity to external change. Due to their limited international power, they face a competitive and compelling set of international constraints. States possessing considerable strength and autonomy in relation to societal actors at home will come closest to meeting the condition of policy flexibility because they will have the capacity to act relatively free of domestic constraints when it becomes necessary to adjust external policies in response to international change. States combining both characteristics will meet the conditions of sensitivity and flexibility relatively well and might be expected to respond quickly and easily to international change, just as realist theory predicts.

An institutional approach, on the other hand, is much better suited to explain the behavior of states characterized by a combination of great power abroad and state weakness at home. Policy adjustment to international change will be difficult where international constraints are loose (as is the case for hegemonic states with surplus power abroad) and domestic constraints are tight (as is the case for states that are weak and permeated by societal interests at home). Under these conditions, which fit the assumptions underlying the sporadic model of policy change, incentives are biased in favor of policy rigidity or resistance to international change rather than adjustment.

Due to their great power, hegemonic states face a less competitive and compelling set of international constraints than middle-level powers. They are likely, therefore, to be less well attuned to underlying international changes and less compelled to respond to them. States characterized by domestic weakness in relation to their society may, even if they recognize the desirability of foreign policy change, lack the capacity or domestic freedom to manipulate policies in response to external change. States characterized by both hegemonic power abroad and relative weakness at home will be most poorly suited to meet the requirements of sensitivity and flexibility. They are likely, therefore, to adjust relatively slowly or inadequately, if at all, to international change or decline. Contrary to the predictions of realist theory, such states might well pursue strategies of resistance, despite the excessive external costs such a strategy entails. They can better afford to ignore international change than to ignore the vested interests or ideological constraints that favor existing policies.

Figure 1.1 illustrates the relationships discussed in the preceding paragraphs. The next two sections elaborate upon the structural sources of the differential capacities of states to adjust to international change.

International Constraints

The realist assumption that states are responsive to changes in their international environment and that policies evolve incrementally is based upon the image of an unforgiving international system in which mistaken choices are quickly punished. The ability of states to safeguard vital interests, such as territorial security, political independence and economic prosperity, is placed in constant jeopardy by the anarchic, competitive nature of the international system. Realism likens international politics to a Darwinian process of natural selection. States failing to adapt to changes in the global distribution of

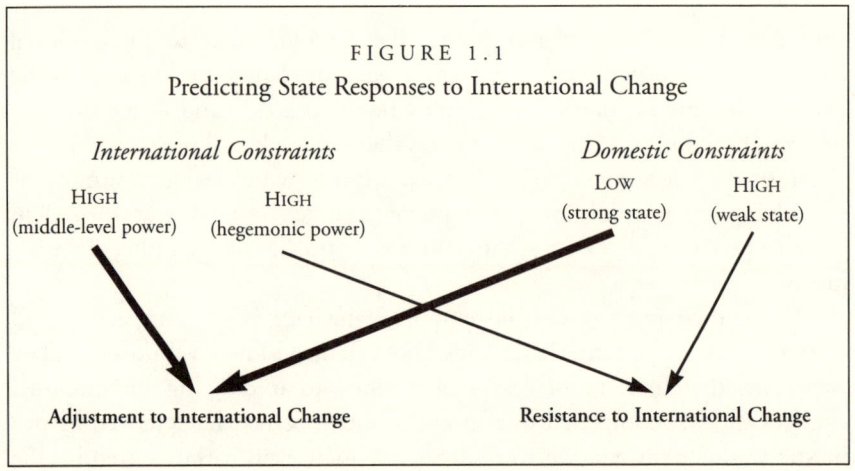

FIGURE 1.1
Predicting State Responses to International Change

power and interests soon discover their basic values and even their sovereignty at risk. Such a world enforces, through constant feedback and external compulsion, a realpolitik logic of power and maneuver upon participating states. In the words of Kenneth Waltz: "Structures encourage certain behaviors and penalize those who do not respond to the encouragement."[16]

This model approximates, at least crudely, the realities facing middle-level powers. Such states, as Keohane has noted, "do not have the luxury of deciding whether or how fast to adjust to change. They do not seek adjustment. It is thrust upon them, because they are not powerful enough to control the terms through which they relate to the international . . . system."[17] Middle-level powers can ill afford to absorb the costs of defending policies and domestic structures poorly adapted to the international environment. The deleterious consequences of such policies are quickly felt and the search for corrective adjustment is prompt. Not only day-to-day policies but also basic institutional structures are affected by this adaptive process.[18]

Traditional realist theory, which posits an evolutionary model of policy change, is likely to apply best under these conditions. If policies become rigid and fail to adapt, crises will emerge quickly, not after a long time lag. If the international system is itself in flux, then so too must be the state's policies for coping with it. An environment where policy change is the norm rather than the exception will prove inhospitable to the growth and maturation of vested interest groups. Even where state leaders are faced with a choice between serving their domestic or international interests, they may choose policies that favor international interests if the external threat is compelling enough.

Very powerful states, on the other hand, are likely to experience a quite different relationship to the international system. Due to their great power, hegemonic states are largely free of the external constraints faced by middle-level powers. Basic interests such as independence, security and prosperity can be achieved with only a portion of their wide-ranging resources. As a consequence, changes in the international environment will not so readily compel changes in policy. The costs of resisting external incentives are more easily managed by hegemonic powers than middle-level powers. The former live in a world of freedom while the latter must make due in a world of constraint. As Keohane observes, "Powerful countries can postpone adjustment; and the stronger they are, the longer it can be postponed."[19] To be sure, the costs of refusing to adapt policies to international change will eventually accelerate hegemonic decline. This process is, however, likely to be gradual, its effects may not become immediately apparent, and such costs may be actively hidden by domestic groups that have developed vested interests in perpetuating old policies.

This unusual freedom from the competitive discipline that dictates the behavior of most states has two important effects on the choices of hegemonic state elites. First, hegemonic powers may choose to pursue ambitions beyond the reach of middle-level states. While middle-level powers must struggle simply to defend interests imposed from without, hegemonic states may seek to reshape their international environment in ways consistent with internally generated ideological preferences.[20] Resources beyond those necessary to protect basic material interests may be externally deployed on behalf of an imperial vision. The extravagance of such ventures is hidden by the hegemon's ample economic, political and military superiority over other states.

Once the power of the hegemon has declined to the point where it begins to face a more competitive environment, one approximating that experienced by other states, then the costs of these far-reaching ideological goals may be felt more acutely. At this stage, it behooves the hegemon to begin shifting resources from imperial ambitions to the protection of more basic interests. An imperial ideology, however, can be difficult to shed once it has permeated the political culture of the dominant power. As suggested below, this is particularly likely to be the case if the resort to ideologically based appeals has become part of the means by which officials of a domestically weak state seek to bolster the political legitimacy of their management of the nation's foreign policies.

Second, a state with the power and freedom to pursue foreign policies not closely conditioned by the international environment is much more likely to be subject to the kinds of domestic constraints on policy flexibility foreseen by institutionalists. Domestic groups with vested interests in the continuity of existing policies are only likely to succeed in forestalling policy adjustment when international conditions change if the pursuit of increasingly maladaptive policies does not quickly lead to crisis. This is, of course, seldom the case for middle-level powers. Where a state's power is sufficient only to defend its basic interests, the making of policy is likely to be subordinate to the competitive discipline of the international system. Policy makers will find international incentives for policy change more compelling than domestic incentives for policy stability. If, by chance, state managers of a middle-level power do fail to make the appropriate policy adjustments, the result is unlikely to be a long period of policy rigidity but instead a quickly felt crisis that punishes the mistake and compels corrective action.

A country enjoying a surplus of power, on the other hand, may find it possible to absorb the costs of defending inappropriate policies and thereby put off the day of crisis. The leaders of a hegemonic state are likely to judge the pressures arising from vested interests more compelling than the international incentives for policy adaptation, particularly, as seems likely, if decline takes place gradually rather than quickly. Moreover, the longer policies remain rigid, the more dense the network of domestic interests that grow around them and eventually come to oppose their alteration.

It may be relevant here to recall Mancur Olson's argument that distributive coalitions, or groups organized to seek economic rents through collective action in the economic or political spheres, are more likely to proliferate in large nations than in small ones. This is due to the fact that such coalitions thrive only where they face little effective international competition; a condition more likely to be found in large states, where trade tends to account for a smaller proportion of economic output, than in small states. As distributive coalitions put their narrow interests ahead of those of the society as a whole, they tend to reinforce social rigidities and to oppose innovations that threaten to disrupt existing patterns of resources allocation. Since hegemons are usually characterized by large-scale domestic markets, as well as technological or organizational superiorities that yield cost advantages as compared with international rivals, they will face a less competitive international economic environment than rival states during the phase of hegemonic ascendance. These conditions favor the growth of distributive coalitions as well as the social, economic and political rigidities to which they give rise.[21]

While in the long run continuing external pressures may eventually lead to policy change, particularly if the failure to adapt results in one or more major crises, policy is likely to be dominated by internal pressures for stability during the initial stages of decline. Unlike states that have always experienced the international environment as highly competitive, a declining hegemon will remain attached to patterns of behavior developed during its period of ascendance that are now inappropriate given altered realities. Founded upon intellectual and interest-based moorings, these policy patterns may loosen only slowly under the influence of external pressures.

Domestic Constraints

International power is, however, not the only variable affecting a state's capacity to respond flexibly to international change. As suggested above, hegemony contributes to policy rigidity by relaxing the external pressures on policy makers to respond to international change while also allowing the growth of ideological and interest group pressures for policy stability at home. Whether the latter set of obstacles to adjustment prove decisive depends to a significant degree on the institutional strength and autonomy possessed by central decision makers in relation to contending bureaucratic and societal forces. Strong states concentrate decision-making authority in the hands of a few officials within the government. They are also relatively autonomous from the influence of societal groups. Weak states are characterized by dispersed or shared authority and lack autonomy from societal influences.[22]

Why should state strength make a difference in the ability of a hegemon to adapt to decline? Conceptually, strong states loosely approximate the realist ideal of the state as a rational, unitary actor.[23] Weak states, on the other hand, more closely share the characteristics posited by Krasner in his model of punctuated equilibrium, where it is assumed that domestic interests encumber the ability of central decision makers to manage policy except during times of crisis. Strong states will be more sensitive to changing external incentives than weak states and better capable of formulating and implementing a consistent, rational and appropriate strategy of adjustment to decline. Thus the stagnating effects of hegemony on policy depend in part by the domestic strength or weakness of the hegemonic state.

State weakness contributes to policy rigidity in several ways. It is more likely that continued attachment to an imperial ideology will become a source of policy rigidity during a period of decline if the hegemonic state suffers from domestic weaknesses. This stems from the fact that weak states are more dependent upon gaining widespread public legitimacy for their policies than are strong states. By definition, strong states experience relative autonomy from societal influences. They therefore have the capacity to pursue policies that are unpopular or poorly understood by the society at large. Lacking this autonomy, weak states are compelled, to a greater degree than strong states, to seek societal consensus behind their policies.

With reference to the U.S. case, Alexander George has stressed the importance to political leaders of this kind of deference to the wisdom and desirability of their long-range plans: "In the absence of the fundamental consensus that policy legitimacy creates, it becomes necessary for the president to justify each action to implement the long-range policy on its own merits rather than as part of a larger policy design and strategy. The necessity for ad hoc day-to-day building of consensus under these circumstances makes it virtually impossible for the president to conduct a long-range foreign policy in a coherent, effective manner."[24]

This dependence upon public approval makes it difficult for officials in a weak state to pursue a rational, calculating, flexible, interest-based approach to dealing with the international environment. The need to acquire widespread policy legitimacy leads weak state policy makers to rationalize favored policies in terms of popular cultural and ideological values that have broad societal appeal.[25] The pressures of legitimation may also lead to a reliance upon doctrine as a means of organizing policies around broad, principled and easily explained rationales.[26] Political leaders will experience incentives, as Theodore Lowi has noted, to resort to the exaggeration of threats and the oversell of solutions as mechanisms for bolstering legitimacy. The manufacture or exaggeration of crises allows leaders to rally the public around their policies and helps to bypass elite opponents by isolating the latter politically and pushing decisions upward toward the apex of the state.[27] Each of these legitimacy bolstering tactics biases foreign policy making away from a rational, calculating approach to evaluating and coping with international change. As the search for legitimation drives the insertion of ideological content into the nation's foreign policies, those policies become less an expression of national interest than the means by which national values are projected into the world.

Ideology, doctrine and exaggeration/oversell also rob decision makers of future flexibility.[28] Katarina Brodin argues that efforts to shore up support for present policies through the resort to broad foreign policy doctrines can "create commitments which serve as barriers against sudden or sharp changes of policy. . . ." Future decision makers "[tend] to be tied down by the . . . commitments and public statements made by [their] predecessors."[29] Similarly, Lowi notes that "A great danger in oversell . . . is that the president's own flexibility may be further reduced at a later point when he may like the crisis to be over."[30] B. Thomas Trout best summarizes the overall effects of the vigorous pursuit of domestic legitimation on policy flexibility:

> Because of legitimation, policy-makers tend toward relatively fixed positions which are extended to include broad areas of policy. This creates inertia with important consequences. If projected responses to specific conditions fall outside the scope of the available legitimative structure . . . [then] the domestic costs of restructuring the image of the international situation may exceed foreign policy gains.[31]

A highly ideological strategy of legitimation is most likely to be adopted by weak state leaders where the state also possesses great power abroad. The leaders of most states will find the international constraints on the pursuit of broad ideological goals too severe to allow resort to this sort of legitimation strategy for gaining public support. Policy makers in a state combining domestic weakness with external strength, by contrast, will find such a strategy not only attractive and necessary from a domestic point of view, but feasible internationally as well due to the freedom afforded by the state's hegemonic status. In the case of states possessing both internal weakness and external strength, therefore, the exigencies of legitimation are all the more likely to lead to policies based upon simple declarative rationales and generalized ideological doctrines. Policies constructed and rationalized in this manner will be relatively insensitive to situational change or to differentiation across time and place. Public identification with the legitimative routines upon which the weak state becomes dependent leads to continuing ideological constraints on policy adjustment and change.[32]

The United States, during the post-World War II period, possessed each of the traits associated above with policy rigidity and resistance; namely, hegemony and state weakness. This combination of traits may help account for the highly ideological character of American rhetoric and policies during the Cold War period. The ideological content of U.S. foreign policy as well as associated characteristics such as heavy reliance upon doctrine, oversell and moralism can be attributed to the pressures weak state leaders experienced in seeking consensual legitimacy for America's new leadership role as well as the freedom afforded by great power to pursue particularly ambitious ideological goals. The combination of state weakness and hegemonic power, in other words, provided policy makers with both the internal incentive and the external opportunity to pursue an ideologically imbued foreign policy.

Alexander George offers the foreign policy legacy of the Truman administration as an example of the way in which the efforts of U.S. policy makers to bolster legitimacy led to policy rigidity:

> In striving to attain policy legitimacy with Congress and the public for its Cold War policies the Truman administration was led into a considerable rhetorical over-simplification and exaggeration of the Soviet threat, one that rested on a new "devil image" of the Soviets and a new premise to the effect that U.S.-Soviet conflict was a zero-sum contest. The struggle to maintain policy legitimacy or the Cold War led in time to considerable rigidification in the supporting beliefs and an unwillingness of American policy-makers to subject them to continual testing.[33]

The Truman Doctrine, of course, best illustrates this phenomenon. In his famous speech to Congress, Truman justified aid to Greece and Turkey by declaring "it must be the policy of the United States to support free people who are resisting attempted subjugation by armed minorities or by outside pressures." In reality, however, the Greek Communists had strong indigenous support, and they received little aid from the Soviet Union. Moreover, the civil war pitted Communists not against democrats but against right-wing monarchists. Thus Truman's rhetoric bore little resemblance to the realities of the situation in Greece. According to Stephen Ambrose, George Kennan, among others, "was . . . upset at the way in which Truman had seized the opportunity—to declare a world-wide, open-ended doctrine, when what was called for was a simple declaration of aid to a single nation. Truman was preparing to use terms, Kennan later remarked, 'more grandiose and more sweeping than anything that I, at least, had ever envisaged.'"

The universal scope of Truman's rhetoric was, however, quite deliberate. Policy makers believed that emphasizing the ideological aspects of the Cold War played a crucial role in winning domestic legitimacy for their overall policies. Ambrose notes that Truman was unhappy with early drafts of the speech that he did not consider tough enough. Truman later recalled "I wanted no hedging in this speech. This was America's answer to the surge of expansion of Communist tyranny. It had to be clear and free of hesitation or double talk."

The purpose was, as Arthur Vandenberg put it, to "scare hell out of the American people." Historian John Lewis Gaddis quotes Clark Clifford, who characterized Truman's speech as "the opening gun in a campaign to bring people up to (the) realization that the war isn't over by any means." Gaddis himself calls the Truman Doctrine "a form of shock therapy: it was a last-ditch effort by the administration to prod Congress and the American people into accepting the responsibilities of . . . world leadership." Another historian, Marshall Shulman, sees this episode as part of a more general pattern that had lasting consequences for U.S. foreign policy: "In the effort to loosen congressional purse strings to fund military programs, the Greek Turkish aid programs, and the Marshall Plan, U.S. officials exaggerated and oversimplified the Soviet challenge as an ideologically driven effort to conquer the world. Anti-Communism became the American ideology, the central principle of U.S. foreign policy."[34]

Two examples, among the many that could be cited, illustrate the argument that the demands of legitimation distorted the political rhetoric of American leaders throughout the Cold War years. The author of a State Department memo written in 1951 argued that it was "necessary for the administration to oversimplify Soviet intentions in appealing to congress and the people for support of the defense program."[35] During the Eisenhower administration, Secretary of State John Foster Dulles candidly explained

"Our people can understand, and will support, policies which can be explained and understood in moral terms. But policies merely based on carefully calculated expediency could never be explained and would never be understood."[36]

The resort to doctrine, universalism, moralism and oversell as techniques for legitimating America's Cold War strategy proved largely successful. Yet, as the Carter administration's experience attests, this very success served to raise the domestic political costs facing future leaders who sought to fundamentally redirect U.S. foreign policies to bring them into alignment with changing international circumstances.

The accumulation of vested interests around old policies provides another source of policy rigidity. The interest group environment that influences present or future decisions is seldom autonomous of previous policies. If interest groups affect policy, it is equally true that policies affect the formation and strength of interest groups. Policy innovation reallocates resources among groups and generates new groups representing institutions involved in or affected by the implementation of the new policies. The interest groups that grow out of or become attached to existing policies can serve as powerful obstacles to policy change.

Weak states are especially prone to this sort of rigidity. They will be less capable of resisting the pressures brought by societal groups which lobby on behalf of old policies. They will also be vulnerable to bureaucratic resistance to change. Bureaucracies constitute institutional embodiments of past policies and, more often than not, resist fundamental policy reform. Commenting on the obstacles to change and adaptation in U.S. foreign policy, Charles Hermann points out that:

> The Cold War provided a framework that for more than forty years served as a structure indicating to the U.S. government's foreign policy organizations what situations to monitor and what meaning to attach to problems that arose. These highly established search routines and interpretative processes may now become increasingly dysfunctional, not directing monitoring activities or situations that could pose new kinds of dangers or opportunities, or imposing an inappropriate Cold War definition on a detected problem.[37]

Bureaucratic resistance will prove more difficult to overcome in a weak state than in a strong state, because weak state bureaucratic institutions are given a greater grant of independence and autonomy from centralized control. Indeed, this problem is complicated by the fact that, as Hermann suggests, highly independent bureaucratic organizations will "search for and sustain public constituencies that support their general world view and specific interpretations of policy problems."[38]

In weak, hegemonic states, ideological and interest group pressures may interact in complex ways and reinforce one another. If the leader of a weak state attempts the wholesale adjustment of old policies as a response to declining power, he or she may stimulate equally broad and comprehensive forms of ideological and interest group resistance. Ironically, the popular ideological appeals once used by the state to mobilize public support for previous policies may now be used by the state's opponents to mobilize popular resistance to policy change. Groups with vested interests in old policies are likely to depart from the usual pattern of isolated, behind-the-scene influence wielding and instead seek to build all-inclusive coalitions of interested parties that fight change through broad-based ideological campaigns. Rather than disparate groups lobbying to protect the narrow interests of their members, one may find more encompassing associations of groups and individuals making public appeals based upon grounds of national interest. These appeals will be addressed broadly, to linked sets of issues, rather than narrowly, to single issues in isolation.

The hypothesis that weak states will be less responsive to the need for policy adjustment in the face of hegemonic decline leads to two seemingly paradoxical corollaries. First, although policy stability is often viewed as a sign of governmental strength while change is taken as an indicator of incoherence and weakness, the preceding model suggests that, under some circumstances, just the opposite may be true. Policy stability or rigidity in the face of external change is indicative of a weak state unable to mobilize the political resources to respond appropriately to shifting environmental conditions. Such a state lacks sure control over policy. In a shifting international environment, policy change or adjustment signifies political strength rather than weakness and incoherence. Change requires a state strong enough to challenge the intellectual and institutional forces that support the status quo.[39]

Second, the ambitiousness or scope of a declining hegemon's external commitments or goals cannot be positively associated with the domestic strength of the hegemonic state. If the above hypothesis is correct, it should be the weak state, not the strong one, that pursues a more aggressive and ambitious external agenda during a period of decline. A weak state will persist in the pursuit of old policies that defend the status quo even if this results in a net excess of costs over benefits. Only a strong state will be able to manage the difficult politics of retrenchment.

Other Combinations of State Strength and International Power

Although not directly relevant to the case study that follows, it is useful to round out the foregoing theoretical discussion by indicating how the argument advanced thus far can be adapted to consider other combinations of state strength and international power. A state may combine hegemonic power abroad with state strength at home or moderate international power with domestic state weakness. While these hypothetical cases do not generate entirely clear predictions of adjustment or resistance to international change, some speculation is possible. A state possessing both hegemonic power abroad and great strength at home will experience few compelling constraints on its freedom from either the international or domestic spheres, making predictions about its behavior difficult. It seems likely, however, that while such states will pursue ambitious strategies abroad as ascendant hegemons, they will adjust to decline more quickly than hegemonic powers with weak states. International constraints will, as they tighten, come to outweigh the relatively low levels of domestic constraint.

The situation is reversed for states characterized by modest power abroad and state weakness at home. Facing serious constraints from both their international and domestic environments, they may well vacillate between adjustment and resistance. The choice between these two strategies is likely to vary across issues and over time in response to subtle shifts in the relative strength of international and domestic constraints. Overall, responses to international change are likely to be inconsistent, incoherent and ineffective.

What of small powers? In principle, they, like middle-level powers, experience strong incentives to adjust quickly to international change lest their failure to do so lead to serious negative consequences. In practice, however, small powers are unlikely to adjust readily due to failures of both capacity and will. Middle-level powers, while they may lack the surplus power necessary to pursue ambitious goals abroad or to postpone adjustment, nevertheless possess sufficient means to defend their sovereignty and independence, except under extreme circumstances. Small powers, on the other hand, can survive as separate entities only by sacrificing important elements of sovereignty. They often serve as only nominally independent satellites to larger powers. Their domestic political systems may be permeated by external forces. As a result, very weak nations do not calculate their own interests or deploy their own resources as autonomous actors. Larger powers not only constrain their policy choices but sometimes also influence who holds governmental power in such countries. Under these circumstances, the political elites of small powers may act less as defenders of their own nation's interests than as collaborators serving the interests of a dominating external power.[40]

The ability of a small state to act independently is, of course, further undermined by domestic weakness. Yet where a small state is strong at home, one might expect opportunistic adjustment. Strong state elites, despite external weakness, have the domestic authority to mobilize available internal resources in occasionally successful efforts to exploit cracks in the edifice of external domination. The opportunities to do so will still depend heavily, however, upon international factors. Opportunistic small power elites are most likely to find the space to exercise independence if, for instance, their country is geographically removed from any great powers, the attention of nearby dominating powers is temporarily distracted by other pressing matters, or the issue at stake is peripheral to the dominant state's concerns.[41]

The United States Experience

A brief look at how U.S. policy makers have responded to hegemonic decline and international change supports the theoretical argument posed above. The outcome of World War II catapulted the U.S. into a position of unprecedented international power. The early post-war years also witnessed the rapid expansion of America's external commitments as the U.S., abandoning its previous isolationist posture, set out to reorganize the global political and economic order and to counter the threat that the Soviet Union posed to this system.

Yet the material basis for America's commanding role in the post-war order soon began to erode. The recovery of Western Europe and Japan brought growing economic competition. The expansion of Soviet military capabilities left the Soviet Union in a position of near parity with the U.S. by the early seventies. Decolonization multiplied the number of independent and highly nationalistic states in Third World regions, further complicating the task of world order management for U.S. officials. These trends quickly altered the underlying foundations of American hegemony. In Robert Gilpin's words, "History affords no more remarkable reversal of fortunes in a relatively short period of time than the reversal the United States experienced in the decades following World War II."[42]

With declining power came tighter external constraints, higher costs, and a growing gap between resources and commitments. These trends can be traced back to the late fifties and early sixties; a period when, as Robert Keohane remarks, "the United States contracted the disease of the strong: refusal to adjust to change."[43] The Vietnam War both reflected the growing limits on American power and worsened the resource trade-offs facing American leaders between domestic and international goals and among various types of the latter. The war also highlighted U.S. policy rigidity and the consequences of failing to adjust to changing international circumstances.

By the mid-seventies, the need for adjustment was recognized by the incoming Carter administration and incorporated into its early policies. Yet, as our theoretical analysis would predict, the domestic obstacles to reform proved formidable. Carter and his advisers failed to develop a legitimation strategy capable of enlisting public support for policy change. In addition, the administration faced an asymmetrical interest group environment. Supporters of reform lacked the size, resources and political clout possessed by opponents. These domestic constraints forced the administration to abandon its initial strategy of adjustment. The politics of resistance embraced by the late Carter and early Reagan years marked a return to policy rigidity in the face of continuing decline and exacerbated the gap between U.S. resources and commitments. Paul Kennedy could therefore correctly observe, in 1987, that "the United States today has roughly the same enormous array of military obligations across the globe that it had a quarter century ago, when its shares of world GNP, manufacturing production, military spending, and armed forces personnel were much larger than they are now."[44]

The British Experience

Although this study focuses on the United States, a brief look at the experience of turn-of-the-century Great Britain bolsters the contention that the combination of hegemony abroad and state weakness at home will delay adaptive responses to declining power.

In his study of British foreign policy decision making during the decades prior to World War I, Aaron Friedberg concludes that "Britain reacted to the early evidence of relative decline with a handful of partial, and only partially coordinated measures.... Even the nation's diplomacy ... was largely ad hoc and opportunistic."[45] While conceding that British efforts did, to a degree, succeed in narrowing the immediate gap between resources and commitments which plagued Britain's global posture, Friedberg nevertheless argues that "the policies pursued at the turn of the century simply ignored or papered over serious underlying weaknesses in Britain's position or, in solving certain problems, created new and perhaps more dangerous ones."[46] Options which might have more fully slowed British decline were either overlooked or rejected.

Friedberg focuses on British responses to decline in four areas of national power: industrial, financial, and land and naval forces. British leaders, with the exception of Joseph Chamberlain, largely ignored or explained away indices of the relative decline in British industrial and commercial power. Growing financial strains were met with partial and inadequate economizing measures. New taxes were too limited, and came after too great a delay, to place the country on a sound financial footing. The British responded more vigorously and successfully to the loss of naval supremacy; simultaneously modernizing the fleet and concentrating it in European waters. Yet, even here, officials did not fully face up to the consequences of naval redeployment for the security of the British empire. Finally, although the British did take steps to increase army efficiency after British troops performed poorly during the Boer War, officials resisted the introduction of conscription or other measures which might have better prepared the British army for a major war. Britain paid a heavy price for this oversight during the early stages of World War I.

Among the reasons Friedberg gives for the shortcomings of Britain's response to decline, two are pertinent to the present argument. Ideological presuppositions formed during and inherited from Britain's period of hegemonic ascendance desensitized British leaders to evidence of decline, even when manifested in the form of foreign crises. Ideology also distorted the debate concerning appropriate policy responses by ruling out potentially viable options when they either fit uncomfortably with traditional formulas or were deemed contrary to public sentiment and thereby politically unaffordable.

The British clung to the notions of limited government, low taxes, free trade, a volunteer army, and the two-power naval standard long after changing circumstances dictated some reexamination of these cherished ideals.

The weakness of the British state also, according to Friedberg, served as a source of policy failure. Bureaucratic decentralization and fragmentation both impeded policy coordination and allowed vested interests the opportunity to inhibit threatening alterations in policy.[47] From this evidence, Friedberg deduces more generally that "countries in which power is concentrated, both in the states and inside the national government, seem . . . to have a better chance of responding in a coordinated, centrally directed way to early inkling of relative decline. . . . The more widely distributed decision making is within a political system, the more likely it is that a nation's initial response to relative decline will be fragmented."[48] Friedberg's treatment of the British case thus reinforces the proposition that hegemony and state weakness may serve as barriers to prompt adjustment in the face of international change.

Conclusion

A realist approach to international politics is inadequate to the task of understanding the dynamics of hegemonic decline and adaptation. Realism posits a close relationship between international change and policy response. This linkage is, however, not always so tight. Adaptation to environmental change is conditioned by two key variables: external power and internal state strength. In particular, hegemonic powers characterized by state weakness at home are especially prone to policy rigidity during periods of declining power. For such states, the process of adapting to international change is anything but smooth or automatic. A sporadic model of policy change, informed by institutional analysis, applies best to such cases. Realist theory's prediction of evolutionary change remains superior, however, with respect to cases where modest power abroad is combined with state strength at home. The model outlined in this chapter thus encompasses both major existing theoretical alternatives by specifying the conditions under which each is likely to apply.

The conclusion to this study examines the broader implications of this theoretical approach for the study of foreign policy change. The intervening chapters, however, take up the task of demonstrating how the structural model specified thus far aids in explaining the failure of policy reform and adjustment during the Carter administration. The next chapter begins constructing this argument by examining the initial purposes and policies of the Carter administration and the ways in which they evolved over time.

CHAPTER TWO

Interpreting the Carter Administration's Foreign Policies

THE DEBATE among historians, political scientists and journalists over how to interpret the Carter administration's foreign policies has centered around three questions: 1) Did the administration ever possess a coherent world view? 2) If so, what were the central tenets of this world view? 3) And, lastly, how did this world view change over time? This chapter reviews the ways others have answered these questions before presenting and defending an alternative interpretation of Carter's foreign policies and the intellectual rationales that accompanied them. According to the latter view, the Carter administration took office in 1977 with the intention of pursuing a relatively coherent strategy of adjustment to hegemonic decline. Over the next several years, however, this basic policy paradigm gradually gave way to an alternative strategy of resistance, which crystallized in a coherent form during Carter's last year in office.

Framed alongside a review of the existing literature, it quickly becomes apparent that this interpretation of the Carter administration's foreign policies is frankly revisionist. Conventional wisdom portrays Carter's early policies as either incoherent and confused or intensely moralistic. Policy change, represented by the abandonment of liberal reformism, is most often attributed to international constraints. Neither view is persuasive. Carter's team crafted a reasonably coherent strategy of adjustment to U.S. relative decline during the administration's first year in office. While these early policy initiatives were largely discarded over the ensuing years, the sources of this turnabout lay primarily in the domestic arena, rather than the international sphere. Explaining policy change is, however, a task reserved for the next chapter. First, it is necessary to examine Carter's initial policies and how they evolved over time.

Existing Interpretations

Interpretations of the Carter administration's early foreign policies commonly fall into one of three general schools of thought. Some see only incoherence and inconsistency in Carter's initial policies. The administration's confusion is usually attributed to its failure to develop a central world view, though Carter's own inexperience as well as divisions among his advisers are also often cited as either independent or related factors.[1]

Others credit the administration with a coherent yet naive and ineffective world view founded upon the president's own misplaced moralism.[2] In the view of some, Carter's Wilsonian idealism was matched by his exaggerated and intellectually faddish obsession with a variety of transformative forces in world politics. This preoccupation with change led Carter to ignore the traditional and continuing relevance of power to statecraft.[3]

A third and final view, popular on the left, held that the Carter administration was neither confused nor naive. Instead, its policies represented a sophisticated strategy designed to serve the interests of transnational capital. Radical commentators placed great emphasis on Carter's ties to the Trilateral Commission, a private organization composed of American, European and Japan elites from the fields of business, politics and academia. The Commission, according to this view, constituted "the executive advisory committee to transnational finance capital."[4]

Virtually all observers agree that the Carter administration's foreign policies changed over time, though disagreement exists over the degree and nature of this shift. Some argue that Carter's retreat from his administration's initial policy orientations emerged gradually over the course of his four years in office. Others portray substantial continuity across the first three years of Carter's term, followed by a wrenching shift in tone and policy in the aftermath of the Iranian hostage crisis and the Soviet invasion of Afghanistan. The great majority of observers depict the direction of policy change in similar terms (though there remains some dispute over how complete was the transformation): the administration abandoned Carter's initial inclinations toward liberal reformism in favor of a traditional Cold War containment strategy. The most widely accepted explanation for this evolution holds that Carter's increasingly tough approach toward the Soviet Union and national defense was dictated by a harsh and threatening international environment that undermined Carter's earlier optimistic assumptions and forced the administration in more conservative directions.[5]

While each of these interpretations offers useful insights into some aspects of the Carter administration's international behavior, none provides an adequate overall understanding of the basic purposes underlying Carter's foreign policies or the reasons why these policies changed over time. A closer examination of each of these interpretations will reveal their respective limitations.

Those who argue that the administration lacked a coherent world view fail to distinguish between coherence and complexity. Carter and his advisers believed that a bipolar view of the world failed to account for the increasing complexity of the international system. The diffusion of international power and the growth of interdependence both created the need for a more subtle and differentiated approach to U.S. foreign policy. Many observers have mistaken the complexity of Carter's world view for confusion or incoherence. Yet many of the apparent inconsistencies to which others have pointed disappear when Carter's policies and beliefs are interpreted as related aspects of a complex strategy of adjustment to hegemonic decline.

Some observers trace alleged policy incoherence to failures of leadership and policy coordination. While there is little doubt that these sorts of problems hampered the conduct of Carter's foreign policies, it is easy to exaggerate their significance. The intellectual and bureaucratic complexities of managing the multifaceted foreign policies of a great power are always considerable. While presidents have varied in their political and management skills, one can find bountiful examples of bureaucratic bungling, personal rivalries and mismanagement in even the most successful of administrations. For such factors to be considered decisive in the Carter case, one would have to accept as plausible the notion that a more politically skilled president might have achieved considerably greater success with the same general program pursued by Carter. Although Carter certainly lacked in leadership skills, this argument nevertheless misses the substantial structural impediments that would have plagued any adjustment-oriented administration.

Moreover, an emphasis on Carter's poor management and political skills does little to explain the direction of policy change under Carter. An argument stressing Carter's haphazard management style might lead one to expect random fluctuations in policy. Yet the direction of change in Carter's policies, across a variety of issue areas, veered consistently from a liberal strategy of adjustment toward a more conservative strategy of resistance.

Some who allege incoherence and poor management trace these problems specifically to divisions among Carter's top advisers. The clash between Carter's dovish Secretary of State, Cyrus Vance, and his more hawkish National Security Adviser, Zbigniew Brzezinski, is often treated as a critical source of policy inconsistency. The attention given the Vance/Brzezinski split in many accounts is understandable. The struggle between these two figures became increasingly public as time went on and inevitably provided a convenient focal point for outside observers.

Yet the divisions exposed by the Vance/Brzezinski clash were more a symptom than a cause of Carter's foreign policy problems. Despite the underlying differences in outlook between Vance and Brzezinski, little serious disagreement plagued the inner circle of the Carter administration during its first year in office. In this period, Carter relied most heavily upon Vance while Brzezinski took a rather low public profile. Subsequently, however, as conservative attacks on Carter's liberal policies escalated and the president's public approval ratings declined, Carter began to backtrack from important elements of his initial foreign policy agenda. In doing so, Carter turned increasingly to Brzezinski for advice, heightening the internal struggle within the administration over the direction of policy. Brzezinski's more hawkish outlook and reputation, especially on U.S.-Soviet relations, provided a better fit with the increasingly conservative domestic political climate than did Vance's preference for patient diplomacy. Also, Carter hoped that Brzezinski might have stronger credentials with the right and thus serve as a bridge to help mollify the administration's critics. In sum, Brzezinski's growing influence and Vance's receding role reflected Carter's gradual move away from his early liberal foreign policy orientation in response to domestic pressures. While Brzezinski undoubtedly worked to hasten this shift, he should be seen as less the source of policy change than its fortunate beneficiary. Those who exaggerate the significance of the Vance/Brzezinski conflict confuse cause with effect.[6]

Other observers correctly attribute a coherent world view to the administration but err in treating Carter's foreign policies as uniquely a product of the president's own admittedly moralistic personality. Despite the idealistic rhetoric in which Carter chose to wrap them, virtually all of his administration's initial policies reflected ideas widely advocated among liberal foreign policy specialists on purely pragmatic grounds. Furthermore, as discussed below, Carter's moralistic embrace of human rights was motivated not only by his own intense moral convictions but also by the belief that these sorts of appeals would bolster his own political fortunes and win support for his foreign policy reforms. An overemphasis on the Carter administration's idealism is, therefore, misplaced.

It is equally misleading to suggest that Carter ignored the role of power in world politics. Carter believed that American power was not as predominant as it once had been and that the relative efficacy of various instruments of power had shifted over time. Economic power, for instance, was considered relatively more effective while military power had declined in utility. These changes required a greater appreciation for the limits of American power and a rethinking of some of the means by which influence could best be wielded. Yet neither of these beliefs implied the rejection of power as an instrument of the national interest.

Radical accounts of the Carter administration's foreign policies are also flawed. Many stress, with some justification, the co-optive character of Carter's policies toward the Third World. Yet these critics exaggerate the repressive character of this process while ignoring the considerable degree of reformism and retrenchment that stood out in the writings of the Trilateral Commission and the early policies of the Carter administration.[7] It is, for instance, misleading to portray Carter and his liberal allies as advocating an "offensive against revolutionism" in the Third World.[8] Early in his administration, Carter advocated the normalization of relations with revolutionary countries such as China, Cuba, Vietnam and Angola. At the same time, the administration considerably distanced itself from a number of pro-American regimes over disagreements relating to human rights and other issues. Radical accounts are peppered with other conceptual and empirical flaws as well. The notion of an international ruling class, for instance, is based upon an unrealistic assumption of unity among industrial country political and economic elites.[9]

A Strategy of Adjustment

If the interpretations reviewed so far are lacking, then how should Carter's policy reforms be understood? The presidents of the seventies, Carter in particular, were principally concerned with adjusting U.S. foreign policy to account for declining American power. Their policies were aimed at addressing what Huntington has called the "Lippmann Gap": the growing imbalance between dwindling resources and static commitments.[10]

This imbalance emerged naturally as rival states gradually narrowed the enormous military and economic lead enjoyed by the U.S. during the early post-World War II era. Its existence was made apparent to many foreign policy elites during the seventies by the elusiveness of victory in Vietnam, the growth of Soviet military power, the weakness of the dollar, and the rise of OPEC. These indicators of America's relative decline and strategic overextension signaled the emergence of a more constraining international environment.

Since reversing the dynamics of decline is a difficult task, the operative problem for policy makers becomes that of narrowing the gap between resources and commitments to manageable proportions. As Huntington points out, "Unlike the decline in relative power, the imbalance in policy can be corrected."[11] This may be accomplished by either reducing commitments or finding less costly and risky ways of maintaining them. Kenneth Oye notes that: "A degree of retrenchment is the first element of a strategy of adjustment."[12]

The Carter administration was not the first during the seventies to recognize and respond to the "Lippmann Gap." The Nixon administration, followed by that of Gerald Ford, initiated a number of important policy adjustments designed to protect U.S. interests abroad through less costly means. Among these were the improvement of relations with the Soviet Union and Communist China, the reduction in the number of wars the U.S. would prepare to wage at any one time from two and one-half to one and one-half, and the de-escalation of U.S. involvement in the Vietnam War along with the "Nixon Doctrine," which stated that, in the future, the U.S. would seek to strengthen threatened U.S. allies in the Third World through aid and advice rather than the active commitment of U.S. troops

Carter sought to multiply and strengthen the adjustment-oriented strands in the policies inherited from his immediate predecessors. Carter set out to narrow the "Lippmann Gap" by reducing U.S. commitments in peripheral areas, sharing burdens more evenly with friends and allies and seeking accommodation with adversaries or rivals where this proved consistent with U.S. interests. The Carter administration believed that a favorable international structure of interests would allow retrenchment to be implemented without serious damage to vital American interests. To achieve its objectives, the U.S. would rely less upon brute power and more upon diplomacy geared toward exploiting the existence of shared interests with other states. Table 3:1 relates specific policies to the administration's overall strategy of adjustment.

TABLE 2.1
Components of Carter's Initial Adjustment Strategy

Reducing Commitments:
- Restrain overall defense spending and shift priorities from strategic and Third World intervention forces to NATO forces.
- Withdraw U.S. troops from South Korea.
- Reduce U.S. arms sales and military aid abroad.
- Restrict CIA covert actions.
- Avoid military entanglements in peripheral regions.

Shifting Burdens:
- Urge NATO allies to spend more on defense.
- Improve relations with Communist China.
- Court regional influentials in the Third World.

Accommodating Rivals:
- Continue détente and arms control with the Soviet Union.
- Normalize relations with radical states (China, Vietnam, Angola, Cuba, etc.).
- Apply preventive diplomacy to solve regional conflicts (Camp David Accords, transition to black rule in Zimbabwe, Panama Canal treaties).

The administrations of the seventies, therefore, attempted to adjust U.S. policies in response to changing configurations in the international distribution of power. As Oye has argued about all three presidents of that decade: "Their rhetoric was attuned to the politics of limits, and their actions were rooted in a strategy of adjustment."[13]

Maintaining a balance between resources and commitments is, of course, a classic realist dictum. In this sense, the Carter administration can be seen as traditionally realist in orientation. This dimension of his presidency has far too often been ignored by those who focus narrowly on Carter's moralistic public image.[14] Oye has correctly observed that much of Carter's idealistic rhetoric was designed to increase "the palatability of a fundamentally realpolitik foreign policy."[15]

This interpretation of the Carter administration's early foreign policies can be supported by examining in detail the philosophy and purposes of the administration as revealed through public statements as well as the ways in which Carter's policies flowed from this world view.

Power and Interests

There is little doubt that Carter and his advisers were aware of the continuing decline in America's relative power and concerned about its implications for American foreign policy. The notion that the U.S. faced new limits on American power abroad spread widely through academic and foreign policy circles during the seventies. America's failure in Vietnam was only partly responsible for these perceptions. The rise of the Soviet Union to military parity with the U.S., the economic revival of Europe and Japan, as well as the growth in the number of newly independent and increasingly nationalistic Third World countries all played a role in reinforcing the belief that the U.S. must adapt its policies to reflect new global circumstances.

These views were frequently expressed, for instance, in the publications of the Trilateral Commission, through which Carter received his initial training in foreign affairs and from which he later drew many of his top appointees. The commission brought together political and economic elites from the United States, Western Europe, and Japan and served as perhaps the most influential forum for the elaboration of liberal internationalism during the seventies. While the membership of the commission reflected a diversity of views and interests, liberal political and academic spokespersons as well as important figures from international business and finance each were heavily represented. The overriding purpose of the organization was to promote cooperation among the advanced industrial democracies in addressing global issues.

The task force reports prepared for the commission often stressed both the ongoing diffusion of international power as well as the increased complexity of the international system. One report, for example, suggested that "the shift from the Manichean bipolar confrontation of East and West of the Cold War to a politically mobile, multipolar world is in full swing."[16] This diffusion of power came about in part because "the revival of Europe and

Japan has profoundly changed the system."[17] Other factors included the proliferation of new Third World states and the erosion of the bloc system, both East and West. As a result of the diminished capacities of the United States, another report concluded that "no country . . . now seems equipped to play a major leadership role alone. The only alternative is collective leadership."[18]

Carter and his aides repeatedly emphasized these themes once in office. In his inaugural address, Carter observed, "We have learned . . . that even our great nation has its recognized limits, and that we can neither answer all questions nor solve all problems. We cannot afford to do everything."[19] In a 1977 speech before the Southern Legislative Conference in Charleston, South Carolina, Carter noted that international change had shifted the context of American foreign policy: "Europe and Japan rose from the rubble of war to become great economic powers. Communist parties and governments have become more widespread and more varied, and I might say more independent from one another. Newly independent nations emerged into what has now become known as the 'Third World.' Their role in world affairs is becoming increasingly significant." As a consequence of these changes, Carter believed "Both the United States and the Soviet Union have learned that our countries and our people, in spite of great resources, are not all-powerful. We've learned that this world, no matter how technology has shrunk distances, is nevertheless too large and too varied to come under the sway of either one or two superpowers."[20]

In an address at Notre Dame in May 1977, Carter stated that "we can no longer expect that the other 150 nations will follow the dictates of the powerful. . . ."[21] Before the United Nations General Assembly in October, Carter proclaimed that "power to solve the world's problems particularly economic and political power no longer lies in the hands of a few nations. Power is now widely shared among many nations with different cultures and different histories and different aspirations."[22] For the United States, this meant that "However wealthy and powerful the United States may be, however capable of leadership, this power is increasingly only relative, the leadership increasingly is in need of being shared."[23] Later in Carter's term, Secretary of State Cyrus Vance echoed a similar view: "[T]he simple notion of a bipolar world has become obsolete. Increasingly there is a profusion of different systems and allegiances and a diffusion of political and military power."[24]

This stress on the declining relative position of the U.S. within the international structure of power was accompanied by a generally optimistic view of the international structure of interests. The negative effects of declining power for U.S. vital interests could be mitigated through a diplomatic strategy attuned to the widespread existence of shared interests between the U.S. and other principal actors. Latent shared interests could be realized through frameworks of cooperation and coordination designed to exploit areas of mutual interdependence. This implied a greater willingness on the part of the U.S. to accommodate change and tolerate compromise in the interests of the long-term stability of the international system.

The existence of shared interests and the necessity of cooperation were believed to flow, in part, from increased interdependence within the international system. In the words of one Trilateral Commission report: "A world which has reached current levels of interdependence and is condemned by technological and economic progress to still more complex relationships in the future, must devise new forms of common management."[25] Similarly, Secretary of State Vance urged that in this new international environment, "each nation must weigh more carefully than ever before its long-term interest in a healthy global community when making decisions about its immediate concerns. . . ."[26]

Carter himself asserted that Americans "cannot overlook the way that our fate is bound to that of other nations. This interdependence stretches from the health of our economy, through war and peace, to the security of our own energy supplies. It's a new world in which we cannot afford to be narrow in our vision, limited in our foresight, or selfish in our purposes."[27]

Although, in the view of the Carter administration, greater interdependence gave rise to shared interests, realizing these mutual aims in a pluralistic and changing world presented difficult problems. Coordinating policy change among independent states required American leadership "to create a wider framework of international cooperation suited to the new and rapidly changing historical circumstances."[28] Cooperation was especially urgent "to resolve conflicts that left unresolved are not likely to be contained."[29]

According to Zbigniew Brzezinski, Carter's national security adviser, this aspiration required a new conception of America's role in the world: "If we are determined to reassert American leadership in world affairs, we conceive of it as shared leadership; no one country today can have a monopoly or even predominance of wisdom, initiative, or responsibility."[30] A genuine commitment to cooperation would require a greater willingness to consult and compromise than in the past.

What were the consequences of decreased power and increased interdependence for the protection of U.S. interests abroad? As Kenneth Oye has astutely pointed out, declining power will lead to disastrous results for a hegemon only if the interests of other states differ radically from its own.[31] Liberal internationalism rested upon the assumption that the intensity of conflicting interests within the international system was not so great as to prevent the U.S. from striking acceptable bargains with other states.

On the basis of these beliefs about the international structures of power and interests, the Carter administration envisioned a selective cutback in American commitments abroad combined with renewed diplomatic activism. These seemingly contradictory strands of policy actually complemented one another. Increased international activism was necessary in order to promote cooperative frameworks that could ease the strains brought about by selective American retrenchment from costly commitments abroad. According to Secretary of State Cyrus Vance, "A world where many must participate in designing the future rather than a few, where progress often requires cooperative effort, demands more not less American leadership. . . . It calls for a new kind of diplomacy."[32]

The cooperative frameworks the Carter administration sought to create and strengthen were designed to render change more manageable and more compatible with American interests. The constraints imposed by an interdependent world, as well as the incentives provided for cooperation by a system of reinvigorated bargaining forums, would help to limit the intensity of the challenges that would flow as a consequence of partial American retrenchment from its hegemonic role.

The Policies of the Carter Administration

This evaluation of the international configuration of power and interests was reflected in virtually all of the major policy positions taken by the Carter administration during early portions of its term. Viewed in this way, the administration's overall international strategy appears much more coherent and intelligible than most observers have acknowledged. Carter's initial policies were preoccupied with closing the gap between resources and commitments that emerged as a byproduct of American decline. A review of the Carter administration's initial policies with respect to U.S.-Soviet relations, U.S.-Third World relations and national defense will illustrate these points.

U.S.-Soviet Relations

The Carter administration's initial stance toward relations with the Soviet Union was characterized by a continued commitment to the policies of détente forged by the Nixon administration. The rise of the Soviet Union to strategic parity with the U.S. was thought to raise the risks of renewed confrontation and to provide an inducement for both superpowers to cooperate in reducing the chances of war and curbing an expensive arms race. While the Carter administration perceived relative growth in Soviet military power, it rejected alarmist interpretations of the U.S.-Soviet balance of power as well as calls for the U.S. to respond to growing Soviet military might with a rapid buildup of its own. The Carter administration, instead, questioned the political utility of large new investments in military power on the part of either superpower, believed that the Soviet Union faced natural obstacles to expansion in the Third World, and preferred to emphasize political and economic means of influence, where the U.S. comparative advantages over the Soviets remained the greatest.

While acknowledging continuing elements of competition and rivalry in the U.S.-Soviet relationship, the Carter administration believed that significant shared interests in the areas of arms control, economic exchange and crisis management provided the basis for increased cooperation between the superpowers and that the Soviet commitments to détente and expanded cooperation were genuine. Finally, and in a departure from the approach of the Nixon administration, Carter's team believed that a less crisis prone U.S.-Soviet relationship would allow the U.S. to reduce its overwhelming preoccupation with East-West problems and begin shifting more attention toward other pressing issues.

The assumption of shared interests formed the crux of the Carter administration's approach to U.S.-Soviet relations. Secretary of State Vance argued that "it is in the interests of both of our nations to search for common ground and to lessen the tensions which divide the nations."[33] The president himself noted that "profound differences" and "elements of competition" between the U.S. and Soviet Union are "real and deeply rooted in the history and the values of our respective societies." As a result, "The basis for complete mutual trust between us does not yet exist." Yet Carter held that "it's also true that our two countries share many important overlapping interests. Our job . . . is to explore those shared interests and use them to enlarge the areas of cooperation between us on a basis of equality and mutual respect." Agreement, Carter suggested, could be reached in areas where "our real interests and those of the Soviets coincide."[34]

These shared interests flowed in part from the mutual stake of each side in slowing "the staggering arms race." This military competition not only constituted a costly burden for both countries, but also, according to Carter, failed to provide greater security for either participant. Instead, Carter argued, "[T]he arms race has only increased the risk of conflict."[35] Carter also believed that the potential benefits of expanded economic ties provided a basis for better U.S.-Soviet relations: "Increased trade between the United States and the Soviet Union would help us both."[36]

The early Carter administration respected Soviet military might and viewed increased Soviet activities in the Third World as challenging. Most officials did not, however, perceive broad geopolitical designs in Soviet behavior or view Soviet capabilities in especially dire or threatening terms. According to Jerel Rosati, the administration, during its first year, viewed the Soviet Union as "occasionally opportunistic," but "generally cooperative in its intentions." Soviet expansionism was thought to be "constrained by the complexity of the international system."[37] Moreover, in the competition for influence in the Third World, the United States possessed strengths that the Soviets did not. Carter's ambassador to the United Nations, Andrew Young, for instance, believed "that newly emerging peoples naturally looked to the United States for help and economic cooperation. . . ."[38] Carter predicted that, given the political and economic strengths of the United States, "in the long run our system will prevail" in the competition for influence in the Third World.[39] In the short run, the U.S. could afford to tolerate and to avoid exaggerated responses to Soviet gains as long as they did not come in areas vital to U.S. interests.

Moreover, the Carter administration was initially reluctant to allow continued U.S.-Soviet competition in the Third World periphery to poison cooperation in areas of shared interest. Thus, the administration rejected an explicit policy of linkage. As Secretary of State Vance explained, the U.S.-Soviet relationship "is not a relationship with a single dimension but with many. . . . [E]ven as we have sharp differences, as we inevitably will, there are many other areas in which we continue to cooperate and to seek useful agreement. . . ."[40]

At the same time that the administration pursued a mixed competitive/cooperative relationship with the Soviet Union, it also sought to expand the foreign policy agenda to allow room for other issues of growing importance. Carter argued that, in the past, "Our national security was often defined almost exclusively in terms of military competition with the Soviet Union. This competition is still critical because it does involve issues which could lead to war. But however important this relationship of military balance, it cannot be our sole preoccupation, to the exclusion of other world issues which also concern us both."[41] Zbigniew Brzezinski explained that the administration's objective was to "assimilate East-West relations into a broader framework of cooperation, rather than to concentrate on East-West relations as the decisive and dominant concern of our times."[42]

U.S.-Third World Relations

The concept of preventive diplomacy played a critical role in the Carter administration's approach to the Third World. Many of Carter's advisers believed that the containment doctrine, as applied to the Third World, had proven too static and reactive. The U.S. had too often treated Third World countries principally as objects in the global struggle between East and West. American policies ignored regional realities and were excessively preoccupied with maintenance of the status quo. Regional conflicts and local problems were allowed to fester until they led to wars, revolutions or political unrest. Attention was shifted to specific countries or regions only after such problems had progressed to the point where local Communists or nationalists, often aided by the Soviet Union, found conditions ripe for radical change. Once the U.S. became engaged, the range of policy options available to U.S. leaders for protecting American interests had often narrowed to those that were excessively costly or accompanied by the risk of confrontation with the Soviet Union.

The concept of preventive diplomacy embodied a number of elements aimed at addressing these problems through changes in U.S. diplomatic practice. Instead of reacting to Soviet moves, the U.S. would identify and seek to resolve emerging conflicts at early stages in their evolution. Diplomacy would take precedence over military intervention, and closer attention would be paid to local and regional factors. The U.S. would seek to avoid becoming too closely attached to unstable and reactionary regimes and would search out and support the forces seeking moderate paths of change in Third World conflicts. No longer would the U.S. automatically intervene on the side opposed to elements backed by the Soviet Union. Where conditions seemed promising, the U.S. might actually compete for the favor of states or movements previously under Soviet influence.

The Carter administration hoped that these orientations would allow the U.S. to help defuse conflicts before they threatened American interests. Moreover, by accepting the inevitability of change, rather than reflexively supporting the status quo, the U.S. would be better able to mold the course of change and, in the process, come to identify more often with the winners rather the losers in Third World conflicts. An approach based upon preventive diplomacy would also lessen the necessity for costly military involvements while allowing the U.S. to better exploit its political, economic and cultural advantages in the competition for influence with the Soviet Union.

These ideas can clearly be seen in both the public statements and the policies of the early Carter administration. Zbigniew Brzezinski, for instance, stressed the need for greater tolerance of change in U.S. policies and attitudes:

> We have sensed that, for far too long, the United States had been seen, often correctly, as opposed to change, committed primarily to stability for the sake of stability, preoccupied with the balance of power for the sake of the preservation of privilege. We deliberately set out to identify the United States with the notion that change is a positive phenomenon; that we believe that change can be channeled in constructive directions. . . .[43]

Carter promised, "We will continue to help shape the forces of change . . . and to use our great strength and influence to settle international conflicts in other parts of the world before they erupt and spread."[44] This required that trouble spots be identified before they exploded into uncontrolled conflict. Vance explained that "when our administration came into office, we decided that we were not merely going to react to situations, but that we were going to shape an agenda of items which we considered to be of the highest priority and would proceed to deal with those issues."[45]

Defusing conflict also required attention to the root social and economic causes of political unrest in the Third World. During his 1976 campaign for president, Carter told a reporter, "We must replace balance of power with world order politics. It is likely in the near future that issues of war and peace will be more a function of economic and social problems than of the military-security problems which have dominated international relations since World War II."[46] Once in office, Carter declared, "We can no longer separate the traditional issues of war and peace from the new global questions of justice, equity, and human rights. It is a new world but America should not fear it. It is a new world and we should help to shape it."[47]

U.S. policies in the Third World, the Carter administration believed, must also be more than simply responses to Soviet moves and must be based upon a deeper appreciation of local and regional factors. In 1977 Vance argued, "The most effective policies toward Africa are affirmative policies. They should not be reactive to what other powers do, nor to crises as they arise. . . . A negative, reactive policy that seeks only to oppose Soviet or Cuban involvement in Africa would be both dangerous and futile. Our best course is to help resolve the problems which create opportunities for external intervention."[48] In a later speech, Vance explained that preventive diplomacy "combines efforts to avoid East-West confrontation and positive regional policies that respond to local realities."[49]

The Carter administration also planned to break with the long-standing assumption that radical or revolutionary change necessarily threatened vital U.S. interests. Carter declared that "we are now free of that inordinate fear of communism which once led us to embrace any dictator who joined us in that fear. . . ."[50]

Part of this new attitude was inspired by the perceived lessons of the Vietnam War. Involvement in Vietnam had been a politically divisive and demoralizing experience for the United States. Carter observed, "The Vietnamese war produced a profound moral crisis sapping worldwide faith in our own policy and our system of life. . . ."[51]

Vietnam also led Carter and many of his advisers to question the costliness and utility of military intervention in non-vital areas of the Third World. Indeed, Carter concluded more generally, "The United States cannot control events within other nations."[52] Previous administrations had often overestimated the capacity of the U.S. to guide the internal social and political evolution of other countries. For the Carter administration, this presumption would be reversed: "We don't have any inclination to be involved in the internal affairs of another country unless our security should be directly threatened. . . . I just think we've learned our lessons the hard way in Vietnam and other instances."[53]

Part of Carter's greater tolerance of radical change stemmed from the belief that the negative consequences of revolutionary outcomes for U.S. interests had often been exaggerated. Even radical governments did not necessarily desire to cut their countries off from economic exchange with the West or to submit themselves to Soviet discipline, although an intransigent attitude on the part of the U.S. toward such governments might leave them with no alternative than to take these paths. If given a choice, the Carter administration believed, radical governments would more often allow interests rather than ideology to dictate their behavior.

In the fullest and most detailed statement of the original orientation toward radical political change in the Third World, Undersecretary of State David Newsom concluded, "We need not fear change. Although we cannot dictate events, we have an unsurpassed capacity to help channel change in constructive directions. Our economy, our technology, our way of life have enormous appeal. If we maintain calm, keep doors open, we are likely, in most cases, to find common interests with new governments. They will find that interest in turning to us as they wrestle with the economic and human needs of their society which lie at the heart of change."[54]

Kenneth Oye has ably summarized the logic underlying the administration's thinking on this issue. Oye states that "the administration's belief in the mutuality of benefits from economic interchange permitted the deduction that *pragmatic* states will continue to be participants in an international economic order irrespective of ideology, simply because it is in their interest to do so." Furthermore, "*Nationalism* was held to reduce the consequences of most internal developments on American national security. If states are interested in preserving national autonomy and avoiding control by the United States and the Soviet Union, their form of government may be immaterial to the balance of Soviet-American military power."[55]

The administration's views on the acceptability of radical regimes were influenced by the example of the MPLA government in Angola. The Marxist MPLA movement emerged victorious from the civil war among various Angolan parties, which broke out after the withdrawal of the Portuguese colonialists. The U.S. had backed a rival party before Congress voted a cutoff of American aid in 1975 and had never recognized the MPLA government. Moreover, continuing to face military threats from other groups and South

Africa, the MPLA depended upon the support of large numbers of Cuban troops stationed in the country. Yet despite its Marxist ideology, its experience of hostility from the U.S., and its dependence on Cuban and Soviet aid, the MPLA government continued to deploy Cuban troops to guard an oil production installation run by the Gulf Oil Company and eagerly sought recognition from the U.S. as well as expanded commercial ties with the West. Countries such as Angola, Carter officials concluded, could be dealt with on a pragmatic basis despite their ideology.[56]

As a practical consequence of these views, the Carter administration initially announced intentions of working toward normal diplomatic relations with a number of unrecognized regimes, including the People's Republic of China, Angola, Vietnam and Cuba. Justifying his policy toward such countries, Carter asked rhetorically: "Should we write them off permanently as enemies and force them to be completely under the control and influence of Communist powers, or should we start the process of giving them an option to be both our friends and the friends of others, hoping that they will come to a more democratic free society and join with us in making a better world?"[57]

The United States would exercise influence in the Third World less through direct intervention and the presence of U.S. military troops than through the cultivation of common interests and improved ties with regionally influential Third World countries. Brzezinski suggested, "It is now increasingly important to widen U.S. relationships of a cooperative type to include those new centers of power and those nations that have assumed newly important regional or international roles."[58] More specifically, according to Carter, "We will cooperate more closely with the newly influential countries in Latin America, Africa, and Asia. We need their friendship in a common effort as the structure of world power changes."[59]

Improved relations with China were perceived as a means of reducing U.S. burdens by alleviating the threat posed to U.S. interests by a former rival power as well as by providing a balance against the expansion of Soviet influence in Asia as the U.S. reduced its presence there. Brzezinski remarked, "We recognize not only that peace in East and Southeast Asia depends upon a constructive Sino-American relationship, but that China can help immensely in maintaining a global equilibrium as well."[60] Nevertheless, the Carter administration did not initially view improved relations with China as an alternative to détente with the Soviet Union but, instead, as a complementary process. While Sino-American ties were seen as a passive instrument of pressure on the Soviet Union, the administration had no intentions of transforming the relationship with China into a military alliance that might prove provocative to the Soviets and threaten détente.

The Carter administration's plan to withdraw U.S. troops from South Korea represented another attempt to reduce costly U.S. commitments abroad. Carter believed that South Korea was then in a position to deter or repel a North Korean attack with less help from the U.S. As noted by Secretary of Defense Harold Brown, South Korea possessed, by the late seventies, twice the population and five times the GNP of North Korea.[61] Moreover, the administration disliked the fact that the presence of large numbers of U.S. troops reduced the flexibility of U.S. options in case of renewed warfare by rendering U.S. involvement virtually automatic. According to Larry Niksch, "The most specific unstated rationale was that withdrawal of ground forces would preclude or make less likely another American involvement in an Asian land war. . . ."[62] The basic strategic document of the Carter administration, PRM 10, "stated that termination of a land-based military presence in Asia would provide the United States with 'flexibility to determine at the time whether it should or should not get involved in a local war.'"[63]

The reduction of U.S. arms sales abroad provided another means by which the U.S. might disentangle itself from intimate involvement with strategically peripheral areas and conflicts. According to Lucy Wilson Benson, Carter's Undersecretary of State for Security Assistance, Science, and Technology, the Carter administration feared that indiscriminate U.S. arms transfers to Third World states harmed U.S. interests by encouraging local arms races and heightening regional tensions, involving the U.S. in conflicts in which it had few compelling interests, compromising U.S. military technological advantages, distorting the allocation of scarce resources in the Third World, and associating the U.S. too closely with repressive and unstable regimes.[64] The Carter administration did not reject arms sales altogether, but believed that they must be screened much more carefully than had been the case in previous years to ascertain just how particular sales might effect U.S. interests.

Defense Policy

The Carter administration's early defense policies were also consistent with its general strategy of adjustment. Carter sought to limit overall defense spending, rejected the pursuit of overall nuclear superiority, adopted a skeptical attitude toward the practical utility of increased military strength and attempted to downplay its priority as compared with diplomatic and economic means of influence, and shifted spending priorities away from Third World intervention forces in favor of forces designed to protect core geographic areas of vital interest.

Some insight into Carter's initial preferences and intentions can be gained by comparing the defense budget projections (as measured by total obligational authority) of the incoming Carter administration for the fiscal years (FY) 1977–83 to similar projections prepared by the outgoing Ford administration.[65]

The Carter administration's projections for the five-year period placed total defense spending at approximately five percent below levels planned by the Ford administration. As measured in constant 1979 dollars, the Ford administration planned increases averaging 3.9 percent per year. Carter proposed increases averaging 2.9 percent per year. The Ford administration projected that defense spending would maintain a constant share of the GNP at roughly 5.4 percent. The Carter administration saw the defense budget's share of the GNP falling from 5.2 percent in 1978 to 4.8 percent in 1983.

Carter's initial budget projections also contemplated important shifts in the composition of military spending as compared with projections prepared by the outgoing Ford administration. Again, these adjustments flowed logically from the administration's overall foreign policy orientation.

Reflecting its hopes for détente and arms control, its desire to slow the arms race, and its intention of reducing overall defense spending, the Carter administration shifted relative emphasis away from strategic modernization and toward conventional forces. Carter rejected alarmist assessments of the U.S.-Soviet nuclear balance and sought equality rather than U.S. superiority in strategic arms. Cyrus Vance warned against the "illusion that we could return to the earlier era" of strategic nuclear superiority. In his view, "Neither side will permit the other to hold an exploitable strategic advantage. . . . That is why essential equivalence has become the only realistic strategy in today's nuclear world."[66]

According to Louis Kraar, Presidential Decision 18, the classified report that outlined the administration's general defense policy objectives, discounted "the practical utility of all those Soviet missiles that so trouble many members of Congress. The Carterites see the threat in what they describe as a more 'measured' way. Soviet strategic weaponry has no overwhelming political significance, they say, provided this country maintains forces that are, and appear to be, essentially equivalent."[67]

In keeping with these views, Carter projected spending at approximately 20 percent less than the Ford administration on strategic systems over FY 1978–83. For the years 1978 and 1979 Carter proposed to spend 36.5 percent more on Cruise Missile development, but planned cuts of 84 percent and 89 percent respectively, for the MX missile and B1 Bomber programs as compared with Ford's projections.

These reductions, along with major cuts in naval shipbuilding (Carter planned to spend 41 percent less on shipbuilding over FY 1978–83 than Ford), also reflected a shift away from new weapons procurement and toward greater emphasis on operations and maintenance. For FY 1978–83, Carter planned to spend 20 percent less on procurement but 8 percent more on operations and maintenance than the Ford administration. Carter eschewed expensive new weapons systems in favor of improving the combat readiness of existing forces.

The administration's final adjustment of priorities involved a redistribution of conventional strength away from East Asia and other Third World areas in favor of Central Europe. This was in keeping with the administration's skepticism regarding the wisdom of military intervention in Third World conflicts as well as its intention of downplaying the priority given geopolitically peripheral regions and its desire to substitute less costly means for exercising influence in such areas. According to Kraar, "In the world described in Decision 18, military power alone, especially nuclear power, isn't as effective as it used to be. The 'new influentials,' such as Saudi Arabia, Nigeria, and Brazil, can't be dictated to by the U.S. but can be counted on as friends provided that our foreign policy is sensitive to their goals."[68]

Military force was still considered to play a vital role in Central Europe where NATO armies helped deter potential Soviet aggression against important U.S. allies. Not surprisingly, given its emphasis on NATO, the Carter administration increased the Army's planned share of the defense budget at the expense of the Navy and the Air Force. Compared with the Ford administration, Carter planned to spend 7.6 percent less on the Navy and 6.9 percent less on the Air Force, but only 1.4 percent less on the Army over a five year period.

Although Carter sought to increase the American contribution to NATO defense, he also pursued greater burden sharing from America's European allies as well as U.S. partners in other parts of the world. Harold Brown declared, "Where our allies have developed the necessary strengths, we will adjust the collective burdens to assure that our long-term security arrangements remain commensurate with the capabilities and stakes of our partners. Otherwise these arrangements cannot endure."[69]

From Adjustment to Resistance

Over time, the Carter administration significantly altered a large number of its initial policies. Many of these changes took place during 1978 or 1979, or well before the Soviet invasion of Afghanistan, which is often viewed as a turning point in the administration's foreign policy orientation. The timing of policy change varied across issues, and not all of the administration's early policies were abandoned or reversed. Nevertheless, policy change was substantial and widespread enough to suggest that the Carter administration eventually abandoned much of its initial strategy of international adjustment. A brief review of patterns of change and continuity in the administration's policies toward the three issue areas surveyed above will illustrate these points.

Changes in the Carter administration's policies toward the Soviet Union began earlier and went further than was true of the other issue areas examined here.[70] In spite of Carter's hopes for détente, U.S.-Soviet relations got off to a rocky start in 1977 when the Soviets rejected the administration's initial strategic arms control proposals and reacted with irritation to Carter's criticisms of the Soviet Union's performance on human rights.

This deteriorating trend continued in 1978. The administration began to criticize the behavior of the Soviet Union and its allies more forcefully during Carter's second year in office, especially with regard to Soviet involvement in regional trouble spots such as Angola, Zaire, the Horn of Africa, the two Yemens, Afghanistan and Southeast Asia.

Also in 1978 the Carter administration began to move toward the full normalization of relations with China, a process that culminated in the restoration of diplomatic ties in January 1979. In accordance with its initial policy objectives, the administration publicly described its moves as part of an evenhanded effort to improve relations with both the Soviet Union and

China simultaneously, despite the rivalry between the two socialist powers. In reality, however, an American "tilt" toward China became increasingly evident as time went on, and Sino-American relations began to take on the appearance of an anti-Soviet alliance.

In 1978 the administration dropped its previous objections to the sale of military arms by U.S. allies to China. In 1979 the U.S. began to share military intelligence with China and reached a mutual trade agreement granting China "most favored nation" status, a privilege still denied to the Soviet Union. By 1980 the Carter administration had decided to step up military consultation with the Chinese and to sell U.S. military equipment to the Chinese armed forces. The Soviet Union reacted with increasing wariness and alarm to these developments.

Although U.S.-Soviet relations improved briefly in early 1979 when the signing of the SALT II agreement took place, they rapidly deteriorated throughout the remainder of the year. The Carter administration began to express increasing concern about the Soviet military threat and, in the midst of the debate over ratification of the SALT II treaty, agreed to accelerated U.S. defense spending. U.S.-Soviet relations also took a turn for the worse in August when the administration raised objections to the presence of Soviet troops in Cuba.

Little remained of the Carter administration's initial policy of détente toward the Soviet Union by the time Soviet troops occupied Afghanistan in December of 1979. Carter's response to the Soviet move decisively confirmed the breakdown in relations when he withdrew the SALT II treaty from Senate consideration, imposed wide-ranging sanctions aimed at the Soviet Union, and suspended virtually all official contacts between the two countries. U.S.-Soviet relations remained in a deep freeze throughout the rest of Carter's term in office.

The pattern of change and continuity was more mixed with respect to the Carter administration's policies toward the Third World. A number of Carter's early Third World initiatives bore fruit. The administration quickly wrapped up negotiations on the Panama Canal treaties and, after a bruising battle, eventually secured their ratification by the Senate. Although the administration failed in its early attempts to convene an international conference on the Israeli-Arab conflict, it recovered quickly by throwing U.S. support behind Egyptian Anwar Sadat's bold moves to break the diplomatic stalemate with Israel. Carter subsequently played a major personal role in moving the two parties toward agreement on the Camp David Accords. Following Great Britain's lead, the U.S. played a supporting part in helping to broker talks culminating in an agreement providing for black majority rule in Zimbabwe. And, finally, as mentioned previously, the administration engineered diplomatic recognition of the People's Republic of China.

Many other initial Third World policies and objectives were, however, reversed or abandoned as time went on. Carter retreated from early pledges to pursue the restoration of U.S. diplomatic relations with Vietnam, Angola and Cuba. U.S. arms sales abroad, rather than decreasing, actually rose substantially from $12.8 billion in 1977 to $17.1 in 1980.[71] After initially removing several thousand U.S. military personnel from South Korea, Carter suspended withdrawals in April 1978 and finally abandoned further withdrawal plans altogether in July 1979.

The administration's early concerns with preventive diplomacy and regionalism increasingly gave way to a preoccupation with the East-West dimensions of Third World conflicts, especially with regard to regional or local disputes in Africa and Southeast Asia. The administration's initial determination to reduce the direct U.S. military role in the Third World and to rely upon regional influentials was belied by its eventual decision to carry forward with the development of Rapid Deployment Forces designed for Third World duties.

The Carter administration's policies on national defense also changed markedly over time. In keeping with its initial priorities, as described earlier, the Carter administration's first two defense budget proposals contemplated modest real increases in spending of 3 percent per year. Emphasis was placed upon readiness and upgrading NATO forces while funding for strategic nuclear systems was cut. In 1977 Carter eliminated the B1 bomber program on the grounds of cost effectiveness, choosing instead to rely upon cruise missiles launched from older B52 bombers. Funding for the proposed MX missile and Trident II nuclear submarine programs was also cut drastically. In 1978 production and deployment of the neutron bomb in Western Europe was deferred after some initial waffling. And, finally, in 1978 the president vetoed a weapons authorization bill over the inclusion of $2.1 billion in funding for construction of a new aircraft carrier.

These patterns, however, did not persist. Carter's last two budgets proposed increases of 5 percent and 6 percent, respectively, in defense spending. Moreover, strategic and Third World intervention forces gained increasing priority. In 1979 Carter decided to go ahead with the production and deployment of MX missiles as well as Trident II submarines. PD 59 accelerated the movement in U.S. strategic targeting doctrine toward the development of flexible response and war fighting options. As already indicated, the development of Rapid Deployment Forces intended for use in the Third World, an idea originally proposed by Zbigniew Brzezinski in 1977, was given greatly increased visibility and priority by the administration in 1979. And in that same year, the U.S. began to seek base agreements and permission to preposition military supplies in friendly countries around the areas of the Persian Gulf and the Horn of Africa, an endeavor given increased impetus in 1980 after the Soviet invasion of Afghanistan.

Conclusion

Previous observers have placed a variety of interpretations on the Carter administration's foreign policies. While some of these explanations aid in understanding various aspects of Carter's approach to foreign affairs, none provides a satisfying overall account of the administration's early world view or its initial core policies toward U.S.-Soviet relations, the Third World and national defense.

This confusion can be alleviated by viewing the early policies of the Carter administration as a relatively coherent set of responses to contemporary changes in the international structures of power and interest. The Carter administration believed that declining relative American power, combined with a relatively favorable structure of international interests, called for adjustments in U.S. foreign policy that emphasized a retrenchment in U.S. commitments in peripheral areas, increased burden sharing with allied states, and new diplomatic approaches to resolving conflicts and protecting U.S. interests abroad. These general views, here labeled liberal internationalism, were evident not only in official statements characterizing the administration's overall philosophy, but were also consistent with many of the administration's early initiatives including the pursuit of détente with the Soviet Union and China, preventive diplomacy in the Third World, and shifts in the both the level and composition of U.S. defense spending. While this interpretation cannot account for each and every policy or for varying viewpoints among Carter's top advisers, it provides indispensable insights into the broad parameters of the Carter administration's initial approach to foreign affairs.

The Carter administration's initial foreign policies, as well as its overall approach, changed substantially over time. These changes emerged gradually over Carter's first two years in office and accelerated during 1979. By 1980 most components of the administration's initial strategy of adjustment had given way to more traditional Cold War policies.

A quantitative study conducted by Jerel Rosati offers further confirmation of the administration's turnabout. Rosati charted Carter's foreign policy priorities by counting the number of times that various issues were mentioned in major foreign policy addresses given by Carter or his aides. Similarly, Rosati used an events data set to establish the number of executive branch actions directed toward various foreign policy issues. In Carter's first year in office, the president directed most of his attention, in both rhetoric and action, toward liberal internationalist issues such as human rights, the normalization of relations with previously unrecognized regimes, arms control and economic relations. Security and defense issues (excluding arms control) ranked at or near the bottom of both scales. By 1980 security and defense issues received overwhelming priority while issues closely related to liberal themes ranked far lower than previously.[72]

Some of the administration's early initiatives were carried through to their conclusion while others survived, in one form or another, this broad shift in orientation. Differences in the timing, speed and degree of change were also evident across those policies that were abandoned, reversed or significantly altered. Nevertheless, the scope of policy change was broad and the overall direction of change varied little. With the appropriate qualifications, it is hardly an exaggeration to suggest that American foreign policy underwent a broad paradigm shift during the Carter years. An initially coherent strategy of adjustment gradually gave way to an almost equally coherent strategy of resistance. The next chapter, and those that follow, turn to the task of explaining this dramatic turnabout in the Carter administration's foreign policies.

CHAPTER THREE

The Sources of Policy Change

TWO THEMES, one major and one minor, emerge from an examination of patterns of variation in the Carter aministration's foreign policies. The dominant theme is that of change and reversal over time. Across a wide variety of issue areas, the Carter administration abandoned, reversed or greatly modified many of its initial policies. Taken together over the four years of Carter's presidency, these changes amounted to a paradigm shift in the administration's foreign policy orientation. Carter's initial strategy of adjustment gave way to a strategy of resistance based upon premises not dissimilar to those that governed U.S. foreign policy during the period of the Cold War and U.S. hegemonic ascendance.

In contrast to this general pattern of policy change, there existed a number of discrete areas where various of Carter's early foreign policy initiatives survived to produce definitive international outcomes. Against the backdrop of Carter's failure to sustain an overall strategy of adjustment, these cases stand out as generally successful applications of the administration's early principles.

These patterns raise some interesting questions. The most obvious of these concerns why the administration abandoned so much of its early foreign policy agenda. This question appears all the more puzzling if viewed in light of the previous chapter's argument that Carter's initial approach appeared consistent with just the sort of adjustment strategy that a Realist perspective would lead one to expect of a declining hegemonic state. The mystery deepens further when it is considered that, where pursued in earnest rather than discarded, a number of Carter's early initiatives led to international successes; suggesting, though not proving, that Carter's early approach may have been internationally viable more generally had it not so quickly been reversed. A convincing interpretation of the Carter experience must explain both why the administration abandoned its initial foreign policy approach across most issue areas as well as why, in contrast, a number of discrete policy areas were characterized by continuity and success.

Competing Perspectives on Policy Change

Broadly speaking, two possible explanations exist for the wide-ranging foreign policy changes that took place during the Carter years. Perhaps the most widely held of the two is the notion that change was forced upon the administration by the incompatibility between its initial policies and the realities of the international environment. According to this argument, the administration belatedly shifted course in response to unanticipated international constraints that exposed its initial assumptions as unfounded and its early policies as unworkable.

A second explanation attributes policy change, by contrast, to inconsistencies between the Carter administration's early policies and the domestic environment of American politics. This line of reasoning suggests that domestic constraints raised the political costs of sustaining Carter's early reforms above tolerable levels and thereby prompted abandonment of the administration's early orientation.

This chapter elaborates upon and compares these alternative explanations for policy change. The first section of the chapter examines the argument that international constraints doomed the Carter administration's program of liberal internationalism. Despite its popularity, this notion has little empirical support. Neither the international developments of the late seventies nor the general configuration of power and interests during the same period were fundamentally incompatible with Carter's initial strategy of adjustment. External compulsion cannot, in any straightforward manner, be treated as the principal source of policy change.

A domestic-centered account of policy change during the Carter years (one grounded in the theoretical model introduced in chapter one) provides a more convincing explanation. Section two below provides the outlines of such an argument. It contains data on trends in public and elite opinion while also characterizing the empirical findings that later chapters present in greater detail.

The final section of this chapter considers the problem of variation in outcomes across cases. Although both the arguments alluded to above predict change and failure for Carter's initial policies, there existed a number of discrete policy areas that were characterized instead by continuity and success. While these cases contradict the general notion that Carter's policies were incapable of success internationally, they can be reconciled with a domestic-centered analysis by fine-tuning the argument to allow for the unevenness of the domestic constraints facing the administration.

Evaluating International-Centered Explanations for Policy Change

Toward the end of Jimmy Carter's term in office, Robert Tucker remarked that "the failure of the Carter administration in foreign policy now elicits a degree of consensus at home and abroad that is . . . without precedent in the post World War II period."[1] Tucker's observation is probably a fair characterization of the perceptions that were popular at the time and remain widely accepted about the Carter administration's foreign policy performance. Carter's failure is commonly thought to consist in his administration's initial inability to comprehend and cope with external forces that proved fundamentally at odds with the world view shared by Carter and his aides. The policy changes that took place in Carter's last years, according to this view, represented a desperate attempt on the part of the administration to discover some firmer foundation upon which to rest its management of the nation's foreign affairs.

Critics of the Carter administration's early foreign policy orientation based their critique upon two fundamental issues: trends in the U.S.-Soviet military balance and U.S.-Soviet competition in the Third World. In both areas, critics argued, the Carter administration mistakenly relied upon Soviet restraint and exaggerated the compatibility of U.S. and Soviet interests. Carter also, according to this argument, overestimated the resource constraints purportedly compelling U.S. retrenchment as well as the effectiveness of displacing military means with diplomatic ones. The Carter administration's retreat from its initial approach, so this argument goes, can be understood as confirmation of this critique and as recognition that its early policies had failed to cope with the realities of the international system.

Although the Carter administration indeed failed to successfully sustain its early approach to U.S. foreign policy, the conventional wisdom is erroneous in attributing the demise of liberal internationalism primarily to external causes. In many instances, Carter's retreat from his early policies can be traced quite specifically to domestic constraints rather than external ones, as later chapters attempt to document. Yet, just as importantly, conventional accounts of the Carter administration's foreign policy experience fail because they provide an unconvincing portrait of the external forces at work during the Carter years. International developments in the late seventies conformed more closely to the administration's early assumptions and expectations than to the views of Carter's critics.

The United States: A Declining Power?

The basis for this claim partly rests upon an analysis of long term trends in relative American power. Those arguing for a return to traditional American foreign policies during the late seventies contended that waning American influence in the world was due not to declining relative power and resources but to a failure of will and assertiveness on the part of American leaders.[2] The Carter administration, by contrast, contended that the U.S. faced genuine constraints arising from declining U.S. power, strategic overextension and a growing gap between resources and commitments. These conditions required adjustments in U.S. foreign policy.

Existing theories about the dynamics of hegemonic orders as well as empirical evidence pertaining to the U.S. case both support the latter perspective over the former. The U.S., during the seventies, faced long-term structural decline rooted in dwindling relative material resources, an increasingly competitive international economic environment and worsening tradeoffs between consumption, investment and defense. Decline was more serious and extensive in economic than in military power. As Posen and Van Evera put it toward the end of the Carter era, "Alarm about the decline of U.S. power may be appropriate, but it is misplaced if it has a military rather than an economic emphasis."[3] No exercise of will was likely to alter the constraints and tradeoffs that the Carter administration correctly identified and, if the Realist dictum regarding the balance between resources and commitments is any guide, some adjustment in policies and priorities might well be considered prudent under such conditions.

Insights drawn from existing theories regarding the rise and decline of hegemonic powers shed considerable light on the long run trends at work in altering the international context of U.S. foreign policy during the seventies. A number of scholars have suggested that hegemony is a cyclical phenomenon and that the eventual decline of hegemonic powers, such as the United States, is dictated by structural factors associated with their role in the international system.[4] Hegemonic powers face the difficult task of inserting order into a system that, because it is composed of independent nation-states, tends toward anarchy. While important interests are served by bringing a degree of organization to a fundamentally anarchic system, the costs of such an undertaking can be high and tend to rise over time.

Robert Gilpin, among others, has argued that hegemonic orders are inherently given to the diffusion of relative power over time, due primarily to growing costs associated with international leadership. In Gilpin's words, "The principal external factor undermining the position of the dominant state is the increasing costs of dominance."[5] In particular, the hegemon tends to lose relative power over time due to its role as the provider of collective goods, the diffusion of technology to rival powers, the hegemon's tendency to overconsume and underinvest, and the burdens of military protection. The effects of each of these processes can be identified in the U.S. case.

The first source of relative American decline has been the U.S. role in providing a variety of important international collective goods during the post World War II period. Among the costs borne by the U.S. in the interests of systemic stability were massive flows of aid to rebuild allied economies after World War II, disproportionate contributions to the budgets of many international organizations, the establishment of the dollar as a reserve currency, the deliberate running of balance of payments deficits designed to provide for growth in global liquidity, and American willingness to tolerate discrimination against U.S. goods on the part of Europe and Japan. While the U.S. benefited, in absolute terms, from the economic cooperation and political stability that resulted from its disproportionate contribution toward these collective goods, the ability of other states to gain a free ride on American efforts helped to undermine America's long run competitive position.[6]

The phenomenon of technological diffusion has also played a role in the erosion of American economic power. The transfer of American technology has been routed through many channels. Some of these include the knowledge acquired by foreign students who return home after schooling at American universities, technical aid to developing countries, direct investment abroad and the signing of foreign licensing agreements by U.S. corporations, the spread of scientific knowledge through international conferences and the distribution of scholarly and technical journals, and foreign imitation of innovations embodied in U.S. products bought and sold around the world.[7] Moreover, the U.S. lead in many technological sectors has been narrowed or erased. Whereas U.S. citizens owned almost 66 percent of U.S. patents in 1970, the same figure had fallen to 54 percent in 1986, reflecting a growing proportion of foreign patent holders.[8]

Besides the costs of providing collective goods and the diffusion of technology, the United States has also suffered from a tendency to overconsume and underinvest as compared with other countries. In 1983, for example, 66 percent of the GDP of the United States went toward private consumption, a rate exceeded only by Spain among the eighteen advanced industrial market economies. Among this group of nations, the U.S. rate of gross domestic savings ranked at the bottom and only Denmark devoted a smaller share of its GDP to gross domestic investment.[9] From 1960 through 1979, the United States devoted an average of 17.6 percent of GDP to fixed capital formation compared to 18.4 percent in Great Britain, 24.1 percent in West Germany, and 32.7 percent in Japan.[10] This pattern of resource allocation has taken its toll on long-term American competitiveness, leaving the United States typically placed at or near the bottom of the list of advanced industrial countries in annual productivity growth.[11]

Another damaging drain on American resources has been the high level of defense spending required by America's global role. Among seven advanced industrial countries, including Great Britain, France, West Germany, Italy, Canada and Japan, the United States spent by far the highest proportion of its GNP on defense between the years 1960 and 1973 (the U.S. spent 8.1 percent of its GNP compared with Great Britain, the next highest country, at 5.6 percent and Japan, the lowest, at .9 percent). During this same period, the United States ranked last among these countries in non-residential fixed investment as a percentage of real output. The same was true for productivity growth in manufacturing. In growth of output, the United States surpassed only Great Britain (which had the second highest level of defense spending). While U.S. defense spending fell to an average of 5.5 percent of GNP during the seventies, when the Nixon, Ford and Carter administrations pursued policies of international adjustment aimed at lowering the defense burden, the relative burden of defense began to rise again during the final years of the Carter administration and continued to climb under the presidency of Ronald Reagan when, from 1981 through 1985, defense spending averaged 6.2 percent of GNP.

While many factors have undoubtedly played a role in determining America's comparatively poor economic performance, there is strong evidence that relatively high military spending can act as a drag on economic growth by attracting resources away from commercial investment. Between 1960 and 1973, there was a strong negative correlation (-.76) between military spending as a percentage of GNP and growth in economic output among the seven advanced industrial states mentioned above.[12] The negative effects of defense spending stem not only from the gross investable resources diverted from the civilian economy but also the considerable scientific and technical resources diverted from civilian industries to often highly specialized military research.[13]

Data pertaining to the period in question, the late seventies and early eighties, suggest that the Carter administration had an adequate basis for concerns about the relative decline in the material basis of U.S. power. In absolute terms, the enormous resources of the United States continued to dwarf those of other states during the seventies. In 1976 the United States accounted for almost one-third (31 percent) of the goods and services produced by all market economies. While still impressive, this proportion represented a considerable decline from the 45 percent share the U.S. commanded in 1960. In 1950 America produced 42 percent of the world's iron ore and 53 percent of its crude petroleum. By 1975 the figures had fallen, respectively, to 10 percent and 14 percent.[14] The United States produced 45 percent of the world's crude steel in 1950 and, in 1960, the United States still accounted for 26 percent of total world production. By 1985 the U.S. share had fallen to 12 percent.[15] While the United States held 43 percent of the world's financial reserves in 1955, it possessed only 8 percent in 1984.[16]

A comparison of the economic performances of the United States, Japan, France, West Germany, Great Britain, Italy and Canada reveals that whether one looks at growth in total GNP or growth in GNP per capita, the American economy outperformed only Great Britain between 1960 and 1981. For the same period, the United States ends up last, behind even Great Britain, if one uses growth in GNP per unit of labor input as the measure of performance. America's relatively laggard growth rate has allowed other industrialized nations to catch up with or surpass America's standard of living despite the once staggering lead held by the United States. In 1960 a group of fourteen advanced industrial countries had an average GNP per capita amounting to only 49.3 percent of that enjoyed by U.S. citizens. By 1979 the average GNP per capita among these same countries had risen to 102.3 percent of that of the United States.[17] Similarly, from a high of 18.4 percent in 1950, the United States share of world trade fell to 13.4 percent by 1977. In the narrower category of manufactured exports, the U.S. portion of the global total dropped from 30 percent in 1953 to roughly 13 percent by the late seventies.[18] One measure suggests that the U.S. share of global leading sector industrial output fell from 64 percent in 1950 to 49 percent in 1980.[19] Between the early seventies and the late eighties, the U.S. share of global high technology exports fell from about 30 percent to around 21 percent.[20]

By the late seventies, a less dramatic, but still significant, decline in U.S. military power had also become evident. America's relative advantage over the Soviet Union had been virtually erased. Immediately after World War II, the United States held a monopoly on nuclear weapons. Three decades later the Soviet Union had clearly achieved nuclear parity. On a global scale, the overall decline in American military power was indicated by the fact that Unites States military spending had fallen from 51 percent of worldwide military expenditures in 1960 to 28 percent by 1980. United States armed forces personnel dropped from 13 percent of the world total in 1960 to 8.3 percent in 1980.[21]

This data belies suggestions that the loss of American influence so remarked upon during the seventies and eighties has been either ephemeral or due simply to a "loss of will." Indeed, existing theory and evidence indicate that the structural sources of U.S. decline have been exacerbated by the failure of U.S. policy makers to adjust America's hegemonic role so as to bring resources and commitments into balance.[22]

The United States-Soviet Military Balance

Though resource constraints suggested the desirability of reducing U.S. commitments, the wisdom of such a course might nevertheless be open to question if, in doing so, vital interests were to be endangered. The Carter administration assumed that the international structure of interests was favorable enough during the seventies to allow limited retrenchment and greater reliance upon diplomatic as opposed to military means without placing U.S.

vital interests at risk. Much of the criticism of the Carter administration's policies was directed toward this very assumption.

As suggested above, Carter's critics focused most intently upon Soviet behavior, arguing that the apparent Soviet commitment to détente hid aggressive designs. The threatening nature of Soviet power and motives was thought to contradict the administration's more optimistic assumptions about its ability to reconcile a strategy of adjustment and retrenchment with the continued protection of critical U.S. interests. According to this argument, the administration was forced to recognize the incompatibility of these objectives by the consistently belligerent military and Third World policies and activities of the Soviet Union. The irreconcilability of Carter's initial views with the external forces confronting the administration prompted his eventual abandonment of liberal internationalism.

The persuasiveness of this argument rests heavily upon the need to demonstrate that Soviet behavior was in fact persistently aggressive, that vital U.S. interests were thereby placed at risk, that Carter's initial policies were inadequate to cope with these purported challenges and, finally, that some alternative set of policies were better suited to protect U.S. interests at acceptable costs.

These assertions are largely unsupported by a close examination of the evidence.[23] While the popularity of these perceptions among elites and the public in the United States surely influenced the Carter administration's policies, this is far different from the suggestion that the international system itself was responsible for liberal internationalism's failure. The inaccuracy of such widely held views suggests instead that they were largely the product of domestic processes that worked autonomously to influence perceptions, selectively amplifying modest international threats into exaggerated fears at home.

A widely held perception, for instance, and one that greatly damaged the credibility of the Carter administration, stemmed from charges that the Carter administration's early defense program endangered U.S. security and vital interests by failing to keep pace with growing Soviet military capabilities.[24] This argument, however, was based upon a series of poorly supported assertions.

First, the often cited Soviet military buildup of the seventies was largely confined to the first half of the decade. Although Soviet military spending grew at rates of 4 to 5 percent per year during the late sixties and early seventies, annual growth dropped to 3 percent in 1974 and further to 2 percent from 1976 onward while, after 1976, new weapons procurement grew not at all.[25]

Second, assertions that total Soviet military spending exceeded American spending levels during the late seventies by as much as half were based upon faulty estimation techniques. More careful studies have shown that U.S. defense spending probably matched or exceeded Soviet levels.[26] Moreover, gross comparisons fail to account for the 25 percent of Soviet spending that was devoted to forces committed along the Chinese border and, therefore, were irrelevant to assessing the European balance. Finally, comparisons of total NATO spending and total Warsaw Pact spending for the Carter period show that NATO spent far more than the Pact, principally due to the larger contributions by U.S. allies as compared with those of Soviet partners.[27]

Third, arguments that the Soviet Union achieved not parity but military superiority during the seventies lack strong support. Careful studies have shown that even before the Reagan defense buildup, NATO forces were fully adequate to defend against a full scale conventional Warsaw Pact attack. Although the Soviet Union developed a rudimentary capacity to intervene militarily in parts of the Third World for the first time during the seventies, Soviet military efforts remained focused overwhelmingly on Europe and Soviet naval and intervention forces remained far inferior to those of the United States. U.S. strategic forces, moreover, remained sufficient to deter a Soviet nuclear attack or to discourage attempts at nuclear blackmail. As the Scowcroft Commission eventually confirmed, the warnings commonly issued during the Carter years about an impending "window of vulnerability" during which the Soviet Union might find it possible to carry out a successful first strike against the United States were greatly exaggerated.[28]

In short, the Carter administration's early analysis of the military balance of power was more accurate than the more alarmist interpretation held by Carter's critics and later embraced by the administration itself. After decades of chipping away at the U.S. military lead, the Soviet Union had achieved rough parity by the early to mid-seventies. Soviet military power fell far short, however, of superiority; the slowdown of Soviet military spending from 1976 onward, combined with the Soviet's willingness to engage in strategic arms control, suggested that the Carter administration was correct in believing that conditions of essential equivalence, along with prudent and restrained levels of American defense spending growth, would induce reciprocal restraint and cooperation from the Soviet Union. Under these conditions, the United States could afford to forego massive increases in military spending without endangering American security or vital interests.

The fact that the Carter administration abandoned an essentially sound interpretation of the U.S. military position in favor of a poorly supported and alarmist viewpoint points to the possibility that domestic, rather than international, incentives played a large role in influencing the administration's evolving views and policies on military affairs.

Soviet Behavior Toward the Third World

As indicated above, those who suggest that the reversal of liberal internationalism must be attributed to external failure base part of their argument upon a series of assertions about Soviet behavior in the Third World during the seventies and its implications for U.S. interests and policies. The thrust of this argument is to suggest that developments in the Third World during the late seventies contradicted the assumptions underlying the Carter administration's policies of détente toward the Soviet Union as well as its preferences for retrenchment and preventive diplomacy in the Third World.[29]

Three propositions are central to this interpretation:

1) During the seventies, the Soviet Union engaged in a calculated strategy designed to outflank Western positions in Europe and the Middle East by sowing and reaping a harvest of unrest along an "arc of crisis" stretching from Southern Africa, through Afghanistan and ending in South East Asia.

2) This strategy brought the Soviets large net gains in the Third World.

3) Excessive American restraint in responding to these moves facilitated Soviet expansion and sacrificed important U.S. interests that could have been secured at acceptable costs through more vigorous American policies.

These arguments, however, have only weak factual support. None of the Third World conflicts commonly cited as evidence of a Soviet grand strategy was in fact initiated by the Soviet Union or, for that matter, its allies. In discussing the regime changes that took place in Afghanistan, South Yemen, Iran, and Nicaragua between June 1978 and July 1979, Samuel Huntington, for instance, observes, "All these developments could be considered, and by many were perceived as, American defeats. Yet all were almost entirely the product of domestic forces within the respective societies, with virtually no known Soviet involvement. With the possible exception of the downfall of Somoza, it is not clear that any U.S. administration could have done anything to prevent them from happening." Yet "they all contributed to the development of the widespread feeling that the Carter administration could not or would not adequately protect American interests in the Third World."[30]

Similarly, in his review of a number of cases of Third World conflict during the seventies, Robert Legvold concludes, "None of the regional events we are discussing was initiated by the Soviet Union nor were more than two, the Angolan and Ogaden wars, decisively influenced by it."[31]

In Angola, for instance, the civil war that accompanied the dismantling of Portuguese colonial rule was initiated not by the Soviet-backed MPLA, which eventually triumphed, but by the FNLA, an American-supported group. The Alvor Accords had provided for power sharing among the MPLA, the FNLA, and a third party, UNITA, prior to the scheduling of elections. But the FNLA, with CIA assistance, ruptured the agreement by undertaking an armed attack against the MPLA. The MPLA invited substantial numbers of Cuban troops to come to its aid only after South African troops intervened to prevent an MPLA victory. In both instances, the Soviet-backed faction reacted defensively to moves initiated by other parties.[32]

In another instance of regional conflict involving Angola, Katangan separatist rebels carried out two separate attacks on Zaire from the shelter of Angolan territory, the first in March 1977 and the second in May 1978. Yet, in both instances, the MPLA's decision to "unleash" the Katangans came in response to Zairean complicity in prior FNLA raids launched into Angola from Zairean territory. Moreover, there is no evidence of Soviet or Cuban involvement with either of the Katangan attacks.[33]

The Ogaden War, involving Ethiopia and Somalia, followed the same pattern of a Soviet ally responding defensively against threats posed by other parties. Although Soviet and Cuban involvement in Ethiopia had been growing after the new Marxist governing regime of that country decided to break long-standing Ethiopian alignment with the West in the mid-seventies, massive numbers of Cuban troops did not enter Ethiopia until invited by the government to help stave off an attack on the Ogaden region of Ethiopia by neighboring Somalia. The Soviets, far from initiating the conflict, attempted to mediate between the parties before siding with Ethiopia when it became apparent that Somalia, a former Soviet client, was bent upon aggression.[34]

The Vietnamese invasion and occupation of Cambodia in December

1978 was also partly prompted by defensive motivations. The Khymer Rouge launched repeated border attacks against Vietnam during 1977 in an attempt to gain control over disputed territory. The Vietnamese finally counterattacked deep into Cambodian territory in late 1977. They soon withdrew, however, and launched a number of diplomatic overtures toward the Khymer Rouge intended to resolve the conflict short of war, including a peace proposal suggesting mutual military withdrawal along the disputed border area. The Khymer Rouge rejected all offers of negotiation and continued to launch border attacks through 1978 until, finally, the Vietnamese decided to invade and overthrow the Khymer Rouge, setting up a Vietnamese supported client government in its place.[35]

Even the 1978 communist coup in Afghanistan was initiated by left leaning army officers only after Prime Minister Douad, with prompting and support from the Shah of Iran, purged and jailed Communist party members who had previously served in his government.[36]

As this brief review suggests, the Soviet role in stirring up Third World unrest and conflict during the seventies has been greatly exaggerated. Indeed, as Robert Legvold pointed out in 1979, "In Africa and elsewhere, there has been an important element of restraint in recent Soviet policy. . . ."[37] This restraint was evident, for instance, in the Ogaden war, where the Soviets persuaded Ethiopian and Cuban leaders to refrain from pursuing Somali troops across the border.[38] The Soviets also did nothing to disrupt the settlement in Zimbabwe, despite the fact that it was engineered by and largely benefited the U.S. and Great Britain.

Moreover, it is erroneous to suggest that the seventies were a period of rapidly expanding Soviet influence in the Third World. Posen and Van Evera point out that Soviet gains were at least matched by Soviet losses: "While in the last decade, the Soviets gained influence in Afghanistan, Vietnam, Laos, Cambodia, Ethiopia, Angola, Mozambique, Grenada, Libya, Cape Verde, and the People's Democratic Republic of Yemen, they lost influence in Egypt, Indonesia, Sudan, Somalia, Iraq, Guinea, and Equatorial Guinea. Moreover, many of their gains are precarious at best and in some cases are a serious drain on Soviet military and economic resources."[39]

Indeed, the only country whose shift in political orientation materially affected the U.S.-Soviet balance of power was the People's Republic of China, which moved from a stance of equal hostility toward both the Soviet Union and the United States during the sixties toward clear alignment with the

West by the close of the seventies.

To a large degree, the extent and permanence of Soviet expansion in the Third World were limited by the same forces that hindered U.S. power and control. Posen and Van Evera point out, "As nationalism increases, more Third World regimes view the two superpowers with suspicion. . . .The emergence of hostile nationalisms in the Third World makes it more difficult for both the United States and the Soviet Union to control events and countries. This enhances U.S. security, even though the United States feels less powerful."[40]

The fact that nationalism served as a natural barrier to permanent Soviet dominance lessened the need for an active policy of U.S. military containment in much of the Third World. Indeed, although Carter's critics often argued that the administration was negligent in not resorting to direct or indirect U.S. military assistance to protect U.S. interests in the Third World, it is difficult to imagine that such alternatives would have been possible or useful in most of the cases discussed above.

In many cases, such as Angola, Iran, Nicaragua, and the 1978 coup in Afghanistan, political turmoil was primarily domestic in origin, and U.S. options were limited by the weakness of the pro-Western factions. Even in cases of international conflict, there existed political barriers to more active military assistance and involvement. In the Ogaden War, for instance, the administration's decision to deny U.S. military assistance to Somali was based upon the fact that Somalia's territorial claims violated a principle, widely accepted among African states, that forcible attempts to alter the borders established by the departing European colonialists were unacceptable.[41] Moreover, Somali aggression prompted the introduction of large numbers of Cuban troops, and continued warfare simply legitimated their presence. In the case of Vietnam's invasion of Cambodia, the Khymer Rouge were already the recipients of Chinese arms, and an outcry, at home and abroad, would likely have accompanied active U.S. efforts to save a regime that was engaged in genocide against its own people.

U.S. policies were most effective where they involved crisis prevention rather than crisis reaction. As suggested below, the Panama Canal treaties, the Camp David Accords, and the settlement in Zimbabwe each eased actual or potential crisis situations and preserved or enhanced U.S. influence in the regions and countries involved.

A review of trends in the U.S.-Soviet military balance and developments in the Third World during the seventies, then, fails to support the argument that Carter's liberal internationalist policies were incompatible with the international environment or that the policy changes that occurred during Carter's term were in some way compelled by external forces. An adequate explanation for Carter's abandonment of his early strategy of adjustment must lie elsewhere.

A Domestic-Centered Explanation for Policy Change

The Carter administration's failure to sustain a strategy of adjustment in American foreign policy stemmed from the shifting currents of domestic politics. Attempts to institutionalize and legitimize the policy reforms embodied in Carter's program of liberal internationalism foundered on the shoals of public skepticism and elite opposition. This interpretation supports the theoretical model introduced earlier in this study, which suggested that the domestic legacies of past policies and strategies of legitimation should serve as barriers to external adjustment in U.S. foreign policy.

Others have pointed to the importance of domestic politics in explaining the changes that took place in the Carter administration's early foreign policies, particularly those toward the Soviet Union. In his massive history of détente, Raymond Garthoff remarks,

> In general, the domestic political influence of both the leadership and the public on détente and the impact on détente of internal developments, are highly important. Indeed . . . ultimately the fate of the efforts to sustain détente between the United States and the Soviet Union in the 1970s foundered on domestic political considerations in the United States as much as on any other factor.[42]

Marshall Shulman, Secretary of State Cyrus Vance's Soviet adviser during the Carter years, has argued that Carter's Soviet policies were "greatly influenced by the vicissitudes of American politics." In Shulman's view, "a resurgence of nationalism in foreign policy" as well as the emergence of a "neo-conservative movement" that returned to "the ideological fundamentalism of the postwar period in its approach to the Soviet Union" undermined the domestic basis for a policy of détente toward the Soviet Union.[43]

Yet, aside from these sorts of passing observations, few studies have examined the domestic obstacles to Carter's reform program in a systematic manner, and fewer still have attempted to explain why policies apparently consistent with international trends met with such serious resistance at home.

To understand the failure of Carter's reforms and the place of domestic politics in explaining this outcome, it is necessary to specify the conditions under which attempted policy paradigm shifts are likely to emerge and prove successful. The far-reaching reform of long-standing and deeply embedded policy patterns requires two critical preconditions: (1) previous policies must be discredited by their failure to cope with emerging anomalies or crises, and (2) the advocates of reform must succeed in fashioning an effective strategy for establishing the legitimacy of policy change.

Neither of these conditions for successful paradigm change in American foreign policy were sufficiently satisfied during the seventies. The international setbacks to which the Cold War paradigm contributed during the late sixties and early seventies led to only a partial decomposition of public support for its central tenets. While the Vietnam War and other international strains did disrupt the old consensus, disillusionment with the established paradigm was far from universal, and crucial remnants of the old coalition survived and even grew in strength through the remainder of the decade. Vietnam thus represented only a partial and limited crisis for the Cold War paradigm.

The incomplete effect of external shocks in weakening the Cold War paradigm ensured that advocates of policy change would meet with stiff resistance from competing elites who held material and ideological interests in the perpetuation of Cold War policies. The fate of policy adjustment would depend to a large extent on the relative domestic strengths of these competing elite coalitions.

The challenge for an adjustment-oriented administration was to limit the domestic political costs of policy change by rallying disaffected elements around a coherent and appealing new foreign policy model. This required the construction of a paradigm that drew strongly upon the larger legitimative themes of American political culture as well as the deliberate employment of appropriate techniques for soliciting legitimacy from the public.

The Carter administration proved incapable of meeting these demands and thereby managing the political costs of change. Carter's failure can be attributed, in part, to the domestic strengths of his opponents. Conservative internationalists drew upon a vast array of political resources in their efforts to stymie policy change. By mobilizing the dense network of interests associated with Cold War policies, Carter's conservative opponents were able to tap into a rich mother lode of political experience, expertise, money, and reputation. These resources were translated into a highly interconnected stable of conservative interest groups whose degree of activism and influence was unique during the post-World War II era; a period when foreign policy interest groups have generally been weak and disorganized. Conservatives also drew upon the continued ideological appeal of Cold War themes and a proven set of techniques for influencing public opinion to reinforce public fears about the Soviet threat and to wrest control of the foreign policy agenda from the Carter administration.

Alongside the domestic strengths of conservative internationalism lay the weaknesses of liberal internationalism. Liberals outside of the Carter administration were not nearly as active or well organized as conservative interest groups. Thus, the pressures placed upon the Carter administration were generated, overwhelmingly, from one side of the political spectrum. Moreover, for reasons detailed in a later chapter, the kinds of policies and rationales inherent to liberal internationalism were not amenable to the traditional means by which policies have been legitimized in the United States. In other words, liberal internationalism was not easily "salable." As a result of these weaknesses, the Carter administration was unable to mount an effective counteroffensive against conservative assaults and increasingly found itself placed on the defensive.

This account of the Carter administration's failure to sustain a strategy of adjustment reinforces the argument that the domestic legacies of hegemony and state weakness served as potent sources of policy rigidity during the seventies, despite international incentives for policy change. The pressures to seek domestic legitimacy and consensus around a hegemonic international role for the U.S. during the Cold War led to the institutionalization of ideological and interest group structures, which later hindered policy adjustment to external decline.

Trends in Public and Elite Opinion

A full empirical defense of the argument that domestic constraints played the greatest role in undermining Carter's early reform strategy must await the succeeding chapters. Nevertheless, it is possible, at this point, to provide some sense of the general political climate surrounding the debate over foreign policy issues during the Carter years by examining the overall movement of elite and public opinion.

Carter's inability to rally domestic opinion around either the individual initiatives or the general purposes of his administration served as one of the more serious liabilities plaguing his efforts to redirect U.S. foreign policy. Indeed, although public support for the liberal internationalist policies and outlook associated with the early Carter administration peaked at about the time of Carter's election, the public's mood turned increasingly conservative during each succeeding year of Carter's presidency.

These trends made it difficult for Carter to isolate elite opponents or to convince potentially sympathetic members of Congress that it was in their political interests to identify themselves strongly with Carter's early reformist aspirations. Carter and his aides were well aware of the political implications of these shifts in public opinion and, after attempts to stymie such unfavorable trends largely failed, the administration gradually moved to align its policies with them.

The deep Cold War period, extending from the late forties through the mid-sixties, was characterized by a broad domestic consensus surrounding the central axioms of U.S. foreign policy. The dominant world view of this period, which Michael Mandelbaum and William Schneider label conservative internationalism,[44] centered around anti-communism, containment of the Soviet Union, and military preparedness. It was not until the later years of America's involvement in the Vietnam War that the Cold War consensus began to crack. The bitter domestic debate over Vietnam led some foreign policy elites to question the basic assumptions of U.S. Cold War strategy and to begin carving out a liberal alternative to conservative internationalism. In 1971 the emergence of a liberal pole in elite foreign policy opinion was symbolized and heralded by the founding of *Foreign Policy*, a journal of foreign policy opinion and analysis intended as a liberal and reformist counterpoint to the more conservative and establishment-oriented *Foreign Affairs*.[45]

Similarly, a significant segment of public opinion began to shift in liberal directions under the stimulus of Vietnam. Mass support for liberal internationalism probably peaked around 1974, shortly after the end of U.S. combat involvement in the war. Sympathy for a liberal version of internationalism, such as that later embraced by the Carter administration, never attracted a public majority.[46] Many remained faithful to conservative internationalism. Others came to reject either version of internationalism, preferring a modern-day version of isolationism. Nevertheless, Vietnam created a space for liberal reform.[47]

Yet this opening proved short-lived. The end of the war removed the key source of the public's anxiety with the status quo. Without the war, calls for foreign policy reform lost some of their urgency and momentum. Indeed, from the mid-seventies onward, a conservative backlash challenged the liberalism of the late sixties and early seventies. Pulled along by these surprisingly powerful political currents, public opinion shifted to the right during the latter half of the decade.

Evidence concerning these trends in foreign policy opinion has been systematically analyzed by a number of scholars.[48] The Chicago Council on Foreign Relations (CCFR) sponsored extensive surveys of opinion on contemporary international affairs in both 1974 and 1978. The CCFR surveys sampled the opinions of both leaders and the general public.[49] Even more comprehensive surveys, commissioned in 1976 and 1980 by the Foreign Policy Leadership Project (FPLP) under the direction of Ole Holsti and James Rosenau, sampled only leadership opinion. The FPLP surveys included a lengthy set of questions designed to tap attitudes toward the Vietnam War as well as contemporary world affairs. These studies, along with data from periodic samplings of opinion carried out by other polling organizations, provide an adequate basis for ascertaining the divisions that characterized public and elite foreign policy opinion during the seventies as well as the shifts which occurred over time.[50]

The data presented in Table 3.1 illustrates the dynamics of opinion described above. While support for liberal internationalist beliefs and opinions grew to substantial proportions in the early seventies, the mood of both elites and the public grew increasingly conservative as the decade wore on. The CCFR surveys reveal that both the public and the leadership sample were greatly more concerned with the problems of national defense and relations with the Soviet Union in 1978 than had been the case four years earlier (although these concerns were more prominent among leaders than among the general public). Among both groups, considerably greater importance was attached to the goals of containing communism and defending American allies against attack later in the decade. Among the general public, support for greater defense spending reached unprecedented highs in the late seventies; attitudes toward the military and the CIA became more favorable; there was a greater willingness to use troops abroad; and support for military aid increased while approval of economic aid decreased (though economic aid was still more popular than military aid). Reflecting these shifts, William Schneider's statistical analysis of the CCFR surveys discovered a significant shift in public opinion toward more conservative positions on foreign policy issues between 1974 and 1978.[51]

TABLE 3.1

Public and Elite Foreign Policy Opinion During the 1970s
(From Chicago Council on Foreign Relations [CCFR]:
Survey Data on Elite and Public Opinion, 1974 and 1978[52])

I. Foreign Policy Goals

A. "What do you feel are the two or three biggest problems facing the country today that you would like to see the government do something about?"

National Defense	1974	1978
Leaders	2%	21%
Public	1%	5%

B. "What are the two or three biggest foreign policy problems facing the U.S. today?"

Relations with Soviets	1974	1978
Leaders	12%	46%
Public	1%	13%

C. Perceptions of importance of foreign policy goals

PUBLIC	very important		not important	
For the Year ...	1974	1978	1974	1978
Containing Communism	54%	60%	13%	10%
Defending Allies' Security	3%	50%	9%	7%
Protecting Weaker Nations	28%	34%	22%	10%

LEADERS	very important		not important	
For the Year ...	1974	1978	1974	1978
Containing Communism	34%	45%	16%	8%
Defending Allies' Security	44%	77%	2%	1%
Protecting Weaker Nations	26%	30%	6%	5%

II. Internationalism

(Public)	Better if we take an active part in world affairs	Better if we stay out
1978	59%	29%
1974	66%	24%
1956	71%	25%
1947	68%	25%

III. Public Support for Defense Spending (%)*

	'60	'69	'71	(Feb.) '73	(Sept.) '73	(CCFR) '74	'74	(CCFR) '76	'77	'78
Too much	18	52	49	42	46	44	32	36	23	16
About right	45	31	31	40	31	32	47	32	40	45
Too little	21	8	11	8	13	12	13	22	27	32

* Gallup Poll; except where indicated as CCFR

IV. Foreign Aid

	Public		Leaders	
% in favor	1974	1978	1974	1978
Military aid	22	29	—	60
Economic aid	52	46	—	90

V. Attitudes toward Military and CIA

A.. "Should the military play a more important role in foreign policy?"

Public	1974	1978
Yes	19%	29%

B. "Should the CIA work inside other countries?"

	Public		Leaders	
	1974	1978	1974	1978
Should	43%	59%	35%	59%
Should not	26%	21%	59%	35%
Don't know	1%	20%	6%	6%

VI. Use of Troops
"Should U.S. commit troops in case of Soviet attack on Western Europe?"

	Public		Leaders	
	1974	1978	1974	1978
Yes	39%	54%	77%	92%

(The following are from Holsti and Rosenau
Foreign Policy Leadership Project, leadership opinion[53])

I. Vital interests of U.S. largely confined to Western Europe, Japan, and the Americas.

	1976	1980	Shift
agreement %	39	25	-14

II. Strengthening countries friendly to us (as a foreign policy goal).

	1976	1980	Shift
very important	23	37	+14

III. Military aid programs will eventually draw U.S. into unnecessary wars.

	1976	1980	Shift
agreement %	41	30	-11

Other Polling Data (Harris Poll[54])

I. "The military defense system of the United States is stronger than that of the Russians, weaker, or about as strong as the Russian military defense system."

	Stronger	Weaker
(Dec.) 1976	21	27
(July) 1978	18	31
(Nov.) 1978	14	40
(Feb.) 1980	16	41

II. "The U.S. should maintain its dominant position as the world's most powerful nation at all costs, even going to the brink of war if necessary."[55]

	1972	1974	1976
agreement %	39	42	52

III. "Who is the chief beneficiary of détente?" (Spring 1977)

USSR	46%
U.S.	5%

The Soviet invasion of Afghanistan in December 1979 accelerated trends that had begun years before, culminating in a militantly anti-Soviet mood. A Gallup poll conducted in February 1980 found that 68 percent of Americans believed that "western countries cannot live peacefully with Russia, sooner or later there is bound to be a major war." A Roper survey carried out during that same month revealed that only 16 percent of the public agreed that "we should do nothing that is likely to provoke a U.S.-Russian military conflict but instead try to negotiate and reason out our differences."[56]

The FPLP study recorded similar shifts in leadership opinion between 1976 and 1980. These trends did not succeed in restoring conservatism to its previous hegemonic position in American foreign policy discourse. But they did tilt the balance against liberal internationalism.[57]

Part of the reason for the more conservative mood prior to the Soviet invasion of Afghanistan is suggested by other items on the foregoing list of survey questions. Harris polls show that in December 1976 27 percent of the public thought that the United States was militarily weaker than the Soviet Union while 43 percent felt that the United States was as strong and 21 percent considered the United States stronger than the Soviets. Less than two years later, 40 percent were convinced that the United States was weaker than the Soviet Union while only 14 percent believed that the United States was stronger. Also revealing is the fact that, in the spring of 1977, 46 percent of the public considered the Soviet Union to be the chief beneficiary of détente versus only 5 percent who thought the United States benefited most from the relationship.

David Moore cites an additional item indicating public skepticism toward détente based upon a CBS-New York Times poll conducted in June of 1978. As Moore describes the results: "A second question probed the public's opinion of what the U.S. posture toward the Soviet Union should be. Just over half felt that the United States 'should get tougher' and only 30 percent indicated that it should 'try harder to relax tensions.'"[58] It is evident from each of these measures that President Carter faced a public increasingly fearful and suspicious of the Soviet Union quite early during his term of office.

Explaining the Rise of Conservatism

What prompted this rightward trend in public opinion that, as will become evident in later chapters, so bedeviled the Carter administration? No definitive answer is possible, of course. Yet it seems likely that changing public perceptions were largely an outgrowth of the domestic debate between the Carter administration and its foreign policy critics. The combination of Carter's inability to find an effective formula for legitimizing his program of reform at home and the unrelenting attacks launched upon his policies by organized interest groups shaped the direction of domestic opinion.[59]

Later chapters provide considerable support for this interpretation. Yet its plausibility can also be strengthened by demonstrating the inadequacy of an alternative hypothesis: namely, that the public embraced conservatism during the late seventies as a direct response to international events. In other words, the shift in opinion merely registered the public's recognition that international trends bore out conservative assumptions while contradicting the premises underlying Carter's liberalism.

This argument fails on a number of grounds. The first of these has to do with the poor correlation between trends in opinion and external events. The survey data presented earlier show that during the latter half of the seventies growing numbers of Americans came to believe that Soviet military spending was accelerating and that the Soviet Union had achieved overall military superiority over the United States. Americans also believed that détente had allowed the Soviet Union to achieve gains far exceeding American ones, especially in the Third World. Finally, Americans believed that the Carter administration's emphasis on diplomacy over military power had brought few gains and contributed to American weakness abroad.

The problem with attributing these beliefs to international trends is that, as suggested earlier in this chapter, they are generally unsupported by the evidence. A close look at these issues reveals that the Soviet military buildup slowed during the same period that Americans perceived it to be accelerating and that Soviet military capabilities fell well short of overall superiority vis-à-vis the Western allies. While the Soviets and their allies were active in a variety of Third World conflicts during this period, they seldom played the role of instigators and their gains were counterbalanced by equally serious losses of influence and corresponding American gains. Finally, the Carter administration's diplomatic efforts brought considerable gains, while few of the cases where American interests suffered provided promising opportunities for the application of U.S. military power. There was, therefore, a significant gap between domestic perceptions and international realities during the seventies.

Moreover, the shifts in opinion described earlier evolved gradually during a period of relative international calm. One might expect shifts of such magnitude to correspond with some highly salient crisis or crises in U.S.-Soviet relations. Yet it would be difficult to identify an event of sufficient magnitude to produce the observed shifts in opinion. The period between the withdrawal of U.S. troops from Vietnam and the Soviet invasion of Afghanistan saw few major crises involving direct confrontations between the U.S. and the Soviet Union. A serious confrontation during the Yom Kippur War occurred fairly early during this period and did promote a degree of public skepticism toward the depth of Soviet-American friendship (especially in light of the exaggerated hopes raised about détente by Nixon during the 1972 presidential campaign). Yet the immediate crisis was overcome and détente survived. It also would be difficult to trace changes in opinion occurring gradually over the next half decade to this single event. Later in the decade, the Iranian Revolution and the taking of the American hostages were traumatic events for Americans, yet they did not directly involve the Soviet Union and the shift in public opinion was well underway before these events transpired.

Generally speaking, the period between Vietnam and Afghanistan, while punctuated by serious disagreements at times, must be viewed as a relatively quiet one in U.S.-Soviet relations when compared with the late forties, the fifties, or the sixties. The leaderships of both sides publicly proclaimed their commitments to a process of détente and improved relations. While the Soviet invasion of Afghanistan, coming at the tail end of this period, altered this climate, it only accelerated a conservative trend in public opinion that began long before the invasion and had already led to substantial shifts before its occurrence. It is difficult, therefore, to attribute shifting perceptions to some watershed international event or events.

If changing public perceptions fit poorly with actual international events during this period, they did closely mirror changes in the domestic balance of power between liberal and conservative elites. Shifts in mass opinion correlate closely with the period of conservative elite mobilization that, as described in chapter five, began during the early seventies and gathered strength through the remainder of the decade. It also appears significant that conservative groups explicitly targeted public opinion in an effort to pressure an administration they believed unsympathetic to their goals and that leaders of these organizations themselves believed that their efforts had a significant impact on public perceptions.

In contrast with a relatively quiet international scene, then, the mid-seventies brought deep domestic contention over the basic directions of American foreign policy. A number of highly charged and visible debates raged over issues such as defense spending, the Panama Canal treaties and arms control. On the issue of the Panama Canal treaties, a massive conservative campaign managed to sustain large public majorities against the treaties in the face of increasingly urgent presidential appeals for support. With respect to SALT II, a similar anti-treaty campaign coincided with a shift from large public majorities in favor of the treaty to a small plurality against it.

Conservative appeals to the public were not uncontested during this period. The Carter administration attempted to sway the public toward beliefs and perceptions consistent with its liberal internationalist paradigm. The public was, for one of the few times during the post-World War II era, presented with a relatively clear choice between two ways of looking at the world, each representing different visions of the national interest and each offering different interpretations of ongoing international events.

Yet, despite Carter's efforts, the growing conservatism of the public provided a measure of the greater success of conservative elites, as compared with liberal opinion makers, in managing public perceptions of the salience and meaning of external events during the period. Conservatives managed to dominate and define the principal foreign policy debates that raged during the Carter years and their success in garnering public support increasingly placed the Carter administration on the defensive. The domestic political dominance of conservatism helps to explain trends in mass opinion that seem puzzling when placed in the context of actual external developments.

Examining Cases of Continuity and Success

While Carter's policies underwent pervasive change and reversal during his term, this tendency was not universal. Indeed, there were a number of cases where liberal internationalist policies were consistently applied and produced results susceptible to evaluation.

The international-centered explanation of policy change would lead one to expect largely negative results in such instances on the assumption that liberal internationalism was inconsistent with the international environment. Yet this was not the case. Where the administration was subject to few domestic constraints, mustered the strength to overcome these constraints or faced domestic obstacles only subsequent to negotiations with other states, its policies generally produced favorable international results.

Consider, for instance, the following five cases. Recognition of the People's Republic of China led to security and economic benefits without imperiling the security of Taiwan. The Camp David Accords, while never fully implemented, did succeed in reducing the risks of another major Israeli-Arab war by removing the most militarily powerful of the Arab states from the coalition confronting Israel. The transition to black rule in Zimbabwe was accomplished without the accompaniment of bloody retribution against the white minority and led to the installation of a moderately pro-Western government. The Panama Canal Treaty removed a troubling irritant from U.S. relations with Latin America while ensuring the continued safety and viable functioning of the canal. And, despite the failure of the ratification process, arms control negotiations with the Soviet Union succeeded in producing a SALT II treaty that included provisions designed to stabilize the arms race without endangering the security of either side.

These cases stand as examples of the considerable success the administration achieved where it proved capable of acting free from or in defiance of domestic constraints. In various ways, as Huntington points out, "These diplomatic achievements significantly reduced the Lippmann gap: consider how different the world would look and what the demands would be on U.S. resources if China were threatening aggression against American interests in Asia, if Egypt were a Soviet ally and military base, and if the Panama Canal were under intermittent attack by guerrilla-terrorists."[60]

Why, in these instances, was the administration able to avoid the constraining effects of domestic politics while the more pervasive tendency was for the administration to retreat from liberal internationalism? The answer appears to lie in the unevenness of the domestic constraints facing the administration. A number of special circumstances worked, either singly or in combination, to provide the administration with relative freedom from domestic constraints in a limited number of cases.

Carter was most constrained with respect to issues requiring extensive congressional involvement or which, due to their high visibility, depended upon general public approval. In cases where congressional input was limited and where public interest was low, Carter experienced fewer constraints. This was often true with respect to largely diplomatic undertakings where the U.S. played the role of international mediator. In such cases, Carter could rely upon his constitutional prerogatives to conduct the nation's diplomacy and the privacy in which negotiations with other countries were often conducted to fend off domestic interference.

Carter was also heavily constrained with respect to issues that tapped heavily into the ideological legacies of the Cold War. He was less constrained in regard to relatively more recent or novel issues that did not involve strong East-West dimensions.

Lastly, while the interest group environment facing the Carter administration was generally an asymmetrical one, tilted in favor of Carter's opponents, there were specific issues that evoked dominant coalitions supportive of the policies favored by Carter. These included rare issues that united liberals and conservatives as well as certain instances where special interest groups found reasons to support particular Carter policies even while opposing or remaining indifferent to the administration's larger agenda.

A closer look at the five cases specified above illustrates these points. With respect to the Panama Canal and SALT II treaties, the administration was able to conclude negotiations with foreign governments because the opportunities for domestic interference were limited during the diplomatic stages of the treaty-making process. Once negotiations were concluded and the administration had to turn to Congress to secure ratification, however, domestic resistance proved stiff. In both of these cases, domestic constraints were considerably tighter than international ones.

While the administration succeeded in negotiating the Canal treaties with Panama, it ran into considerable more difficulty in gaining Senate ratification. Conservatives mounted a massive campaign against the treaties and their passage came with only the narrowest of margins. The victory, however, was somewhat hollow for Carter. Not only did the administration have to expend enormous energies in lobbying for passage, but the entire episode worked to dilute rather than strengthen the president's position with respect to the pursuit of his larger foreign policy agenda. With regard to the treaties themselves, the White House was forced to accept unwelcome amendments and, even after Senate passage, Carter encountered trouble in gaining approval for necessary enabling legislation in the House of Representatives. Moreover, some senators apparently used the leverage provided by their vote to extract promises of higher defense spending in the future in return for treaty support. Others, such as Senator Howard Baker, who considered it an act of political courage to vote for the Panama Canal Treaty, later felt obliged to please conservative constituencies by taking an outspoken stand against SALT II in order to balance their earlier vote.[61]

SALT II itself was another case in which domestic constraints played a more important role than international ones in frustrating the process of international adjustment. The treaty's passage was in great doubt long before the Soviet invasion of Afghanistan, and Carter's efforts to salvage Senate approval prompted him to make a series of important concessions on related policies such as defense spending.[62]

In the other cases cited above, domestic constraints were either weakly negative or actually positive. Moreover, unlike in the cases of the Panama Canal Treaty or SALT II, none of the remaining cases involved treaties requiring Senate ratification.

The recognition of China was opposed by elements of the far right who denounced the diplomatic abandonment of Taiwan and generally questioned the desirability of closer relations with a Communist state. Still, the passions that once existed on the issue were largely diffused by the anti-Soviet thrust of China's foreign policies and the emergence of certain liberalizing trends in Chinese domestic politics. These developments mollified much of the conservative camp, which identified the Soviet Union as the world's principal evil. Thus the feebleness of domestic opposition to the recognition of China did not signal as sharp a break from the attitudes common to the Cold War era as one might suppose. Controversy over the issue generally evaporated only after it was possible to cast recognition in terms of serving the traditional objective of containing Soviet power.[63]

Recognition of China, therefore, constituted a special case because it could be reconciled with the objectives of those who adhered to the old Cold War paradigm as well as those who sought adjustment. While both liberals and conservatives generally supported recognition, however, they did so for different reasons. In fact, these differing perspectives on the relationship with China continued to engender considerable debate over the course of future Sino-American relations both inside and outside the administration even after recognition.[64]

With respect to both the Zimbabwe settlement and the Camp David Accords, the administration played the role of mediator, facilitating agreement among local parties (in the case of Zimbabwe, the British played the lead role in this process). The largely diplomatic nature of these processes limited the intrusion of domestic politics. But insofar as domestic factors played a role, they were largely favorable. Particular constituencies, including blacks in the case of Zimbabwe and Jews in the case of Camp David, largely supported the objectives of the administration.[65] Both were also somewhat novel issues, partially detached from the political dynamics that influence broader, longer standing issues such as those relating to the international economy or East-West relations.

These cases show that liberal internationalism was not necessarily doomed by international factors. Where domestic constraints were, for one reason or another, relatively loose, Carter's program of liberalism internationalism showed considerable potential for success.

The existence of cases of success also shows that domestic constraints were not universally fatal to Carter's policies. In at least two of the cases cited above, the Zimbabwe settlement and the Camp David Accords, the administration possessed relative freedom from domestic hindrances. Recognition of China was possible due to special circumstances surrounding the issue that tentatively reconciled liberal and conservative objectives. The Panama Canal treaties showed that domestic opposition could sometimes be overcome, though at a considerable price. Although these cases were exceptional when viewed in the context of the reversals that took place across a wide spectrum of the administration's initial policies, they reveal that, within the broad set of structural constraints that hindered foreign policy change during the seventies, there remained areas where it was possible to work through the interstices of the system to carry out adjustment-oriented policies.

Conclusion

This chapter has suggested that tight domestic constraints served as the primary sources of sweeping foreign policy change and reversal over the course of the Carter years. More specifically, Carter's attempts to bring about adjustment in U.S. foreign policy were stymied by ideological and institutional legacies of the Cold War years.

There exist two possible objections to the above argument. The first consists of the counter-argument that policy change during the Carter administration was prompted not by domestic constraints but by unfavorable international circumstances that compelled decision makers to reassess the viability of their initial policies and assumptions. This argument revolves around the notion that Soviet behavior, with respect to both military spending and involvement in the Third World, was such as to invalidate the administration's initial beliefs that military restraint, Third World retrenchment, and a more active reliance upon diplomacy could be relied upon to bring U.S. resources and commitments into balance without sacrificing vital American interests.

In fact, however, this alternative explanation for policy change is poorly supported by a close examination of actual international circumstances during the late seventies. The Carter administration's early assumptions appear largely vindicated by such an analysis. Trends in the U.S.-Soviet military balance were not nearly so unfavorable as to necessitate large increases in U.S. defense spending. Moreover, Soviet behavior in the Third World was not as aggressive as critics charged. While it is only possible to speculate on the motives and intentions that Soviet leaders held at the time, the fact remains that the Soviet Union initiated few, if any, of the Third World conflicts that were often attributed to a Soviet grand design. Soviet net gains in the Third World were, in fact, negligible, and the Carter administration's early diplomatic efforts at preventive diplomacy were relatively successful in ways that both protected American interests and reduced the opportunities for the expansion of Soviet influence. In short, objective trends in the international system are inadequate to explain the Carter administration's substantial policy reversals.

This is not to argue that Soviet behavior was always consistent with U.S. interests and preferences. Clearly, it was not. The superpower relationship remained prone to tension and conflict. Nor were the interests of other states in the international system uniformly favorable to the United States. Nevertheless, there is little support for the alarmist view that the United States confronted a largely "hostile world" in the seventies. The Carter administration's belief that it faced a relatively supportive structure of international interests is much more compatible with the available evidence. Even a more cautious and reserved interpretation would suggest that, at worst, the signals emanating from the international system were ambiguous. Yet, when filtered through the American domestic political climate of the late seventies, threat perceptions were systematically amplified into exaggerated fears while alternative interpretations were often dismissed. As noted Soviet expert Dimitri Simes wrote in 1979, this "overreaction to the Soviet challenge" was "more a reflection of American frustrations than of anything the Soviet Union has actually done in recent years."[66]

The second possible objection to the above argument is that it does not allow for a number of important cases of continuity and success in the Carter administration's foreign policies. If domestic politics doomed the administration's initial strategy of adjustment, then how can one account for those instances where Carter's policies were consistently and effectively applied? Why were these policy adjustments not also negated by domestic constraints? A close examination of five major cases of international success show that a number of exceptional circumstances set these cases apart from the normal pattern of domestic constraint that afflicted Carter's broader agenda. This ability to account for success as well as failure strengthens the plausibility of a domestic-centered argument as against international-centered explanations of policy failure and change during the Carter years. The latter have greater difficulty accommodating instances of external success.

The ultimate test of a domestic-centered explanation for policy change during the Carter years lies in the ability to provide a convincing account of how and why domestic constraints compelled the administration to abandon its initial strategy of adjustment. The following two chapters take up this challenge.

CHAPTER FOUR

The Search for Policy Legitimacy

PREVIOUS CHAPTERS have argued that the Carter administration's early foreign policy strategy was principally concerned with the problem of U.S. adjustment to declining relative power. This orientation was eventually abandoned, however, in favor of a strategy of resistance grounded in traditional U.S. Cold War policies. International-centered explanations for this turnabout have been found wanting. As detailed in this chapter and the next, a domestic-centered explanation for policy change and reversal provides a more convincing alternative.

Carter's wholesale retreat from liberal internationalism and the confusion into which his foreign policies eventually descended stemmed principally from his inability to gain domestic legitimacy for the administration's early world view or the policies associated with it. The evolution of Carter's foreign policies was, therefore, driven by contradictory sets of international and domestic pressures. International incentives, arising from the dynamics of U.S. decline, initially pulled the administration toward a strategy of adjustment to external change. Domestic constraints favoring policy rigidity, however, eventually forced Carter to abandon much of his early reformist approach in an effort to salvage his dwindling domestic popularity.

Although Carter's poor leadership skills certainly complicated his task, a more important source of his failure to rally popular support stemmed from structural conflicts between the substantive features of the administration's world view and the imperatives of domestic foreign policy legitimation. The complexity of the administration's liberal internationalist paradigm, as well as the pragmatic flexibility demanded by its strategy of adjustment, rendered

Carter's policies difficult to sell to the American public. The president's failure to rally popular support behind his policies made it impossible for Carter to isolate and overcome the powerful elite opponents who sought to undermine his reform program.

External Adjustment Versus Internal Legitimation

Why was Carter unable to transform his liberal internationalist philosophy into a vehicle for legitimating change in U.S. foreign policy? It is tempting to attribute Carter's troubles to simple political incompetence. The president's early speeches, for instance, were hardly inspirational or visionary. Indeed, Carter's pronouncements often took the form of lists of problems and solutions.[1] In one early foreign policy address, Carter touched upon human rights, allied relations, arms control, the Middle East, nuclear proliferation and arms sales, North-South relations, normalization of relations with China and, finally, South Africa.[2] Although emphasizing the need for policy change and distancing the administration from America's role in Vietnam and the secretiveness and amoralism of the Nixon era, little effort was made to tie together the various elements of policy or the particular rationales offered for them under an overall doctrine.

More than a lack of political savvy, however, is necessary to account for the self-consciously non-ideological political style adopted by Carter and his aides (the exception to this unrelenting pragmatism was Carter's stress on human rights, discussed below). Carter's apparent political ineptitude stemmed most fundamentally from contradictions between the imperatives of external adjustment and the requisites of internal legitimation: adjustment-oriented policies could not easily be legitimated while policies that lent themselves to legitimation were incompatible with adjustment. Thus Carter's vigorous early efforts at external adjustment were accompanied by the lethargic and ineffective pursuit of domestic legitimation. Likewise, as the administration became more concerned about domestic legitimacy later during Carter's term, it began to abandon critical aspects of its early adjustment strategy.

These tensions must be understood, in part, as consequences or legacies of the means by which officials went about bolstering support for U.S. foreign policies during the Cold War period. The relevant literature suggests that policy makers relied upon four primary techniques of legitimation: 1) cast policies into doctrinal form so that specific policy responses appear to flow from the application of generally accepted principles, 2) create simple, declarative explanatory rationales, 3) rely upon symbolic language to link specific policies with consensual ideological values, and 4) overstate threats and oversell solutions.[3] These highly ideological legitimative practices created domestic commitments that tied U.S. policy makers to rigid, categorical foreign policies. The process by which policies were sold at home, in other words, influenced the substance of the policies themselves. Infused with moralism, universalism, and other distinctive ideological traits, U.S. foreign policy became gradually less responsive to international change and increasingly more responsive to the demands of domestic legitimation.

The Carter administration's largely apolitical rhetorical style represented an attempt to avert this trap. Carter's adjustment strategy called for a pragmatic, flexible, case-by-case approach to foreign policy making. Pursuing this course required a conscious departure from the legitimative routines of the past. Because they were tied to past policies and, in any case, promoted policy rigidity, the ideological legitimation strategies of the Cold War period were considered inconsistent with the foreign policy adjustments the administration believed a changing international environment demanded.

Yet in rejecting the tried and true techniques of the Cold War period, the Carter administration left itself without a coherent strategy of legitimation. Carter's emphasis on human rights was a failed attempt to devise an alternative strategy for rallying domestic support. Without an effective means of selling his overall strategy to the American people, Carter's pursuit of reform led to substantial domestic political costs. When these costs eventually became intolerable, Carter fell back upon both the legitimative techniques and the associated policies of the Cold War era in an effort to shore up his political position at home. Once domestic priorities became paramount to the administration, it had little choice but to abandon much of its early foreign policy agenda. The remainder of this chapter pursues this argument by examining four points of contradiction between the imperatives of external adjustment and traditional requisites of internal legitimation.

Doctrine / Flexibility

The first contradiction confronting the Carter team took the form of a trade-off between flexibility and the political imperative of building support for currently favored policies. Carter and his advisers concluded that reliance upon doctrine was dangerous. In the past, U.S. foreign policy officials had resorted to doctrine, in part, as a means of winning public support. A doctrinal foreign policy appeared to rest upon widely accepted principles and appealed to the public's expectations of consistency and simplicity. Yet however useful as a tool for bolstering policy legitimacy, the casting of foreign policy in doctrinal form hampered adjustment to international change. Carter's initial shopping-list approach to presenting policies to the public was designed, by contrast, to maximize flexibility in the pursuit of external adjustment, despite its recognized political costs.

Prominent members of the Carter's team believed that the ideological potency and alluring simplicity of the traditional containment doctrine had blinded policy makers and the public to the growing weaknesses and limitations of the policies associated with it. In a rapidly changing world, they were reluctant to risk repeating this mistake. Leslie Gelb, before joining Carter's State Department, argued that past policy makers had used doctrines as "public relations exercises designed to limit rational and critical discussion of policy." The danger in this practice, Gelb believed, was that doctrines "demand too much consistency" and perpetuate "intellectual rigidity."[4]

The need for policy flexibility as a requirement of external adjustment was rooted in the diffusion of international power and the growth of interdependence. Both conditions served to expand the foreign policy agenda, heighten the potential for conflicts among policy objectives and increase the tension between existing commitments and available resources. While a doctrinal foreign policy may have sufficed to cope with the relatively simple bipolar international structure of the early post-war period, these changes had created an environment that, by the late seventies, was perceived as too fluid and complex to be adequately dealt with by policies rooted in fixed principles, grand schemes, or doctrinal formulations.

In 1977 Gelb, echoing his earlier themes, argued that "the environment we are looking at is far too complex to be reduced to a doctrine in the tradition of post-World War II American foreign policy. Indeed, the Carter approach to foreign policy rests on a belief that not only is the world for too complex to be reduced to a doctrine, but that there is something inherently wrong with having a doctrine at all."[5] Zbigniew Brzezinski, Carter's National Security Adviser, put it similarly: "We did not wish the world to be this complex; but we must deal with it in all of its complexity, even if it means having a foreign policy which cannot be reduced to a single and simplistic slogan."[6]

In maximizing policy flexibility, the Carter administration placed serious constraints upon its ability to make the kind of appeals needed to mobilize domestic political support. A doctrinal foreign policy can inhibit efforts to deal subtly with conflicting objectives or to fashion new and appropriate responses to unexpected international change.[7] Yet, without doctrine and the consensus it helps to mold, policy makers may find themselves immobilized by conflicting bureaucratic and societal pressures.

Simplicity / Complexity

The usefulness of doctrine is rooted not only in its appeal to principle but also in its simplicity as an explanatory device. If the pragmatism that rested at the core of liberal internationalism limited its ability to function as a doctrine in the traditional manner, its complexity did so as well. As George has noted, the "complex objectives and strategy" of détente contrasted sharply with the "stark simplicity of the cold war."[8]

Carter viewed the U.S.-Soviet relationship, for instance, as one founded upon a mixture of shared and conflicting interests: "I remain fully aware that American-Soviet relations will continue to be highly competitive—but I believe that our competition must be balanced by cooperation in preserving peace and thus our mutual survival."[9] Beyond the sphere of superpower relations, liberal internationalists contended that the U.S. role of world policeman was both costly and untenable. The U.S. would have to learn to distinguish among vital and peripheral interests, to tolerate radical change in certain parts of the world, to avoid the temptation to view all Third World conflicts in East-West terms, and to adopt more subtle and sophisticated means for protecting American interests in a world marked by nationalism, turmoil and change.[10]

Given their belief in a complex and differentiated world, Carter officials asked Americans to tolerate a degree of policy inconsistency and to substitute pragmatism for principle. As Anthony Lake, Director of Policy Planning in the State Department, explained, "Our approach is to make constant, pragmatic, case-by-case decisions, seeking the most constructive balance among our interests and adjusting our tactics as circumstances change."[11]

Carter himself pled with the public to understand that "We live in a world that is imperfect and which will always be imperfect—a world that is complex and confused and which will always be complex and confused."[12]

Brzezinski implicitly acknowledged the difficulty of gaining public support for this sort of approach when he noted that

> after World War II our foreign policy, by necessity, was focused primarily on issues connected with the Cold War. This gave it a sharp focus, in some cases making it easier to mobilize public opinion. Today we confront a more difficult task, which calls for support based on reason. We must respond to a wider range of issues . . . stemming from a complex process of global change. A concentrated foreign policy must give way to a complex foreign policy. . . .[13]

Both Carter's break with the universalist tradition in U.S. foreign policy and the domestic difficulties this shift created are well illustrated in remarks by Paul Kreisberg, the Deputy Director of Policy Planning in Carter's State Department. In an interview with Richard Melanson, Kreisberg rejected the notion that "if the Soviets gained influence in, for example, Ethiopia or South Yemen, . . . that this (a) was irreversible and (b) would transform fundamentally the strategic balance. . . ." Kreisberg noted that "the notion that the Soviets were moving again and that we had to draw a line and say 'here, no further' was really, from the State Department's point of view, alien to our basic thinking about the world." The Carter administration's complex view of Soviet activities in the Third World reflected the notion that "the world is a place that is in constant flux, things are never totally black or white, and, on balance, Soviet influence has been diminishing in recent years in a whole series of countries that seemed to be firmly in the Soviet camp." Kreisberg lamented: "The trouble . . . is that it is a very subtle policy, and subtlety is a characteristic that is hard to sell politically."[14]

Kreisberg's complaint reinforces Alexander George's point that the Cold War was "easier to legitimate because it rested on a simple negative stereotype—a devil image of the Soviet leaders. Détente policy, on the other hand, had the more difficult task of getting people to view the Soviets as a limited adversary; but just what that was—neither friend nor foe, something in between—was not easy for many people to understand."[15]

Moralism / Pragmatism

Despite its misgivings about doctrine, the Carter administration did not entirely ignore the necessity of developing an overarching ideological rationale for its new approach to foreign affairs. If anti-communism was the core value around which the containment doctrine revolved, human rights served as the central moral rationale for Carter's liberal internationalism. Unfortunately for Carter, however, human rights did not possess the ideological power, as anti-communism once had, to unite the country around a common vision. Unlike anti-communism, the concept of human rights was often ambiguous, sometimes proved divisive, lacked high salience and held only a tenuous relationship to many of Carter's more pragmatic policies. Due to these weaknesses, human rights failed to provide a consensually accepted core value around which the public could rally.

Anti-communism served the function of uniting broad segments of the public around the central tenets of American foreign policy for more than two decades after World War II. From the standpoint of domestic legitimation, anti-communism held many attractions: it appealed to deeply held liberal values, focused opposition on a particular kind of threat associated with the more concrete interests of containing Soviet power and revolution in the Third World, and could be used to rationalize a broad range of policies.

The Carter administration, however, found anti-communism inconsistent with its new outlook. Moreover, anti-communism, while still powerful, no longer served as a universally accepted basis for American foreign policy. Indeed, U.S. foreign policy, especially during the Nixon era, had come to lack a widely recognized and accepted moral core. The moral skepticism with which the public came to regard U.S. foreign policy in the years after Vietnam threatened America's continuing ability to play a role of global leadership. Carter hoped that the theme of human rights would restore the basis for American activism in the world by convincing onlookers at home and abroad that the U.S. was once again a force for justice and progress in the world.

In 1976 before he joined Carter's White House team, Zbigniew Brzezinski elaborated the rationale that underpinned Carter's later emphasis on human rights. Brzezinski argued that ideological ascendancy can be as potent as other more commonly acknowledged forms of international power and that the ideological appeal of America's liberal values had well served the

U.S. in past decades. Brzezinski believed, however, that recent years had witnessed the deterioration of America's image and ideological influence. Given the rise of egalitarianism and hostile ideologies in much of the world, the United States faced the prospect of "philosophical isolation" in the absence of a concerted effort to reassert the relevance of liberal values.[16]

Perhaps more important than the challenges this presented abroad, the specter of "philosophical isolation" threatened to undermine the domestic basis for a constructive American role in the world. Domestic resentment toward the rejection of American values abroad might give rise to isolationism or policies based upon destructive hostility and intolerance. According to Brzezinski:

> Most Americans have . . . believed that the American-type liberal democracy was a potential model for the rest of the world. Yet implicit in the emergent new mood was the sudden recognition that . . . the American system was no longer the carrier of a universally applicable message . . . the sudden fading of the underlying sources of the system's legitimacy could prove destabilizing and it could prompt many Americans to take refuge in the reassuring simplicity of the notion of the Hostile World as the successor to the Cold War—with both notions substituting political dichotomy for global complexity.[17]

Brzezinski feared that anti-communism was giving way to a jingoistic unilateralism that might lead to an even less appropriate American posture in the world. His answer was to come up with a new central organizing principle appropriate to a liberal and internationally activist set of foreign policies. In his memoirs, Brzezinski recalls that he entered office with the hope that by emphasizing human rights, the administration could "overcome the spreading pessimism, which in the realm of action is particularly dangerous because it can become a self-fulfilling prophesy."[18] Ten months into Carter's presidency, Brzezinski argued that this concern with human rights had "played a significant role in overcoming widespread popular disillusion and cynicism about foreign policy, thus enabling the United States again to play a more constructive role across a broad range of international issues."[19]

Brzezinski was not alone in believing that the pursuit of human rights could play a critical role in the administration's efforts to win domestic legitimacy for its foreign policies. Gaddis Smith asserts that Carter's own motives included not only "his own sincere moral beliefs" but also "the accurate perception that the issue was good politics in the immediate aftermath of the Vietnam war."[20] Convinced of the domestic political utility of a strong human rights stance, Carter's aides downplayed the negative impact that criticism of the Soviet Union's human rights record might have on détente. Indeed, in February 1977 Jody Powell reassured Carter that "surely the Soviets are sophisticated enough to understand that the domestic flexibility we need to make progress in other areas is enhanced by your position on human rights."[21]

Midway through 1977, Leslie Gelb publicly defended Carter's human rights policies as a necessary means of winning back public trust in American foreign policy. Gelb acknowledged, "There are a lot of people who feel uneasy that the United States is taking such a bold and direct position on human rights." To such critics, Gelb replied that it was "absolutely essential to re-establish the confidence of the American people in the Executive Branch of government—in its conduct of foreign policy—to make clear that the administration shares the basic values of most Americans."[22]

The ability of human rights, however, to fill the moral, ideological and political void left by the Carter team's rejection of anti-communism proved limited. Like anti-communism, human rights appealed to widely shared liberal instincts. Unlike anti-communism, however, the standards of human rights could potentially be applied to countries across the political spectrum, friend and foe alike. When applied to Third World allies, Carter was accused of allowing ideals to interfere with self-interest. When not applied to these countries, the administration found itself accused of inconsistency and selectivity by a different set of critics.[23]

While there was thus broad support in principle for the American promotion of human rights abroad, this support eroded considerably when it came to applying such principles to real cases. According to the 1978 CCFR survey, 67 percent of the public and 78 percent of leaders agreed that the U.S. should put pressure on countries that systematically violate human rights. When asked, however, whether the U.S. "should take an active role in opposing the policy of apartheid—that is, racial separation—in South Africa," only 40 percent of the public agreed. One-half of the public and 30 percent of the leaders felt that "how the Soviet Union handles the treatment of the Jews or other minority groups is a matter of internal Soviet politics and none of our business." And 59 percent of the public thought it frequently or sometimes justifiable for governments facing political terrorism to limit civil liberties in order to combat terrorism. Only 25 percent thought it rarely or never justifiable.[24]

Moreover, anti-communism evoked the image of a direct threat to the U.S. and served as justification for the much broader and concrete policies of containment and intervention. Human rights, on the other hand, called for an altruistic response. No direct threat was implied by a failure to deal with the problem. Just as importantly, the salience of the theme of human rights did not expand horizontally to provide justification for other core liberal internationalist policies.

Survey data confirm that the public never thought that human rights deserved to play a central role in U.S. foreign policy. The 1978 CCFR poll asked respondents to indicate whether each of thirteen specified foreign policy goals should be considered very important, somewhat important, or not important. Promoting and defending human rights ranked near the bottom of the list, with only 39 percent of the public and 36 percent of the leaders calling it very important. Securing adequate supplies of energy, by contrast, was considered a very important goal by 78 percent of the public and 88 percent of the leaders. When given the freedom to list the two or three biggest foreign policy problems facing the United States, only 1 percent of the public and 7 percent of the leaders named human rights as a major problem.[25]

Despite the considerable attention Carter devoted to the issue, public support for the promotion of human rights changed little from levels recorded prior to his presidency. In the 1974 CCFR survey, 68 percent of the public favored active support for human rights. Virtually the same percentage (67 percent) was recorded four years later at the mid-point of Carter's term.[26] His efforts had no observable success in broadening the appeal of an issue that already gathered fairly widespread, though tepid, support.

Carter's emphasis on human rights was a failed attempt to invest a fundamentally pragmatic set of foreign policies with some moral core. Human rights was intended to appeal to the moralism of the American public in much the same way anti-communism once had. Human rights, however, proved too far removed from concrete interests to play an effective legitimizing role. The public, while supportive in principle, never perceived the issue as critical and often found reasons to disagree with its application in practice. Moreover, because human rights did not relate in any integral way with Carter's broader strategy of adjustment, it could not easily serve as the bedrock value upon which the remainder of Carter's policies could be justified. The problem with the Carter administration was not, as some have asserted, that it was too moralistic but that its moralism was too peripheral to the main thrust of Carter's policies to invest the latter with some core ideological meaning.

Crisis / Normalcy

The public's growing apathy toward foreign affairs during the first years of Carter's term provided an indication that Carter's message was not getting through. The 1974 CCFR survey indicated that 35 percent of the public were very interested in reading newspaper articles about other countries and 50 percent were very interested in reading about U.S. relations with other countries. By 1978 a second survey showed that the percentages of people very interested in these topics had declined to 26 percent and 44 percent, respectively.[27]

Such apathy is of little consequence during periods of elite consensus and policy stability. For a president trying to institute significant policy changes during a period of elite conflict, public apathy is a serious source of weakness. Public apathy can doom presidential efforts to isolate elite opponents by mobilizing mass opinion. Moreover, apathy means inertia. Public attitudes can undergo significant changes only during periods of heightened attentiveness. Even when events provoke such attention, changes in attitudes can easily melt away with a return to normality unless perceptions are filtered through novel and coherent ideological framework that can transform transitory attitude shifts into relatively permanent belief system changes.

While the Vietnam War produced strong shifts in opinion, many of these changes remained fragile because altered perceptions were not translated into a structured ideological alternative. By the time Carter entered office, few people were paying attention and the international stimuli that could spur renewed attentiveness were missing. As a result, inertia was leading to the restabilization of old patterns of belief. Carter's attempts to stymie this trend were in vain. Apathy played against Carter's efforts to imprint a new set of images on the public psyche.

One traditional means through which public attention is engaged, attitudes are altered and support mobilized is the manipulation of crises, whether real or manufactured. Presidents generally benefit politically, at least in the short run, from the rally around the flag effect that influences the public during periods of external threat. As Lowi has noted, this creates a political incentive for presidents to exaggerate threats and respond with bold rhetoric and actions.[28] Such an approach, however, was antithetical to Carter's philosophy of adjustment, which rested upon the premise that crises could be pre-empted or managed through cooperation and diplomacy. As a result, the early Carter administration shied away from dramatic confrontation and bellicosity. Carter's conservative critics, on the other hand, felt few qualms about using this tactic against the administration.

It is significant that Carter's greatest successes came with respect to issues that could be dealt with through quiet, behind-the-scenes diplomacy such as the Camp David Treaty or the recognition of China. When crises erupted, whether genuine or as a consequence of exaggerated perceptions of threat fostered by Carter's opponents, the administration found it extremely difficult to shape a liberal internationalist response without appearing weak or vacillating. Politically, all the incentives favored abandoning quiet diplomacy in favor of confrontation. Each passing crisis found Carter yielding in growing measure to the rising pressures to stake out a tougher stance. Indeed, Brzezinski, the most hawkish of Carter's advisers, took advantage of such episodes to slowly wrest power from Secretary of State Cyrus Vance and shift policy away from détente.

In a book written along with I.M. Destler, former Carter officials Leslie Gelb and Anthony Lake recall:

> As conservative assaults on his policies began to score more heavily, Carter sought to beat them back by adopting more of their tone, if not their program.... [R]ather than concentrate on what it was accomplishing, the White House (and especially National Security Assistant Zbigniew Brzezinski) went beyond describing the Soviet threat to looking for ways to dramatize it. The result was that the accomplishments, the measures to deal with the threat, constantly paled in comparison, and Carter looked weaker rather than stronger.
>
> [T]he shift in tone was being produced at least in part by political considerations. It was no secret that Carter's White House political advisers wanted him to appear "tough" on East-West issues.[29]

In time, the administration increasingly relied upon oversell to shore up Carter's sinking political fortunes. In the process, Carter moved steadily further from his initial liberal policies, abandoning adjustment for a strategy of resistance. Two events, the Cuban brigade episode and the American response to the Soviet invasion of Afghanistan, reveal how domestic pressures prompted the administration to exaggerate external threats and crises.

The political pressures to resort to oversell to toughen up the administration's image were probably never better illustrated than in 1979 when Carter strenuously objected to the presence of a Soviet military brigade in Cuba. Carter seized upon the issue during the debate over the SALT II treaty as a response to critics who charged the administration with leniency toward Soviet misbehavior. The administration's reaction contrasted sharply with its handling of a similar episode a year earlier, when the Soviets shipped a squadron of MIG-23 fighter-bombers to Cuba. In that instance, Carter played down the significance of the shipment, thereby avoiding an international crisis or prolonged domestic debate over the issue. When the Soviet brigade was discovered, however, the administration decided to dramatize its importance. One aide explained, "This time, with SALT at stake, we felt we had to come out swinging."[30] As it happened, the effort backfired when Carter was forced to concede that the Soviet troops were advisers who had long been stationed in Cuba without American objection and found that the U.S. had no reasonable means for bringing about their withdrawal.[31]

Nevertheless, the brigade incident revealed how insecure the administration had become about the political legitimacy of policies it had earlier embraced. Writing as the episode unfolded, Leslie Gelb, by then a private citizen, argued that what should have been seen as a "little annoyance" was treated with "panic" due to "the climate of near-hysteria about the Soviet Union's military capability and international designs that has been created by right-wingers and abetted and magnified by the news media." The White House, Gelb believed, "latched on to the situation as an opportunity to prove the President's toughness." Gelb advised Carter to resist such pressures by "stak[ing] out a solid middle ground" on relations with the Soviet Union and holding it by "tak[ing] on the right wing frontally." He acknowledged, however, the difficulty of taking such a stand by noting that right-wing threats of electoral retribution against a president who appears soft on the Soviet Union "seem real" because conservatives "have the money and the workers."[32]

Carter did not choose to "take on the right wing" as Gelb advised. Instead, his administration moved to mend fences with conservatives by soft-selling the SALT II treaty, stepping up its criticism of the Soviet Union and promising large increases in defense spending. Indeed, as the White House became increasingly sensitive to outside criticism, power shifted toward the more conservative members of Carter's foreign policy team and a steady stream of liberal foreign policy makers left the administration.

As the SALT II negotiations neared fruition in October 1978, Paul Warnke was replaced as head of the Arms Control and Disarmament Agency by George Siegnious, a retired military general, after Brzezinski convinced Carter that the more conservative Siegnious could provide a better defense of SALT II before the Senate than the liberal Warnke.[33] In mid-1979 Andrew Young, one of the more outspokenly liberal members of the administration, was fired from his post as ambassador to the United Nations after he violated U.S. policy by meeting with a U.N. observer of the Palestinian Liberation Organization.[34]

Perhaps the most telling change in personnel came about when Leslie Gelb, a driving intellectual force behind Carter's early strategy of adjustment, resigned his post as the State Department's Director of Political-Military Affairs after repeated clashes with Brzezinski. The *New York Times* reported, "One aide said the two men exchanged messages that were often 'dripping with venom' in what was viewed as a personal 'struggle of will.'" Gelb's disillusionment may have sprung from the relatively hawkish Brzezinski's increasing dominance in policy making over the more moderate Secretary of State Cyrus Vance. It was perhaps one indication of Brzezinski's ascendance that Gelb was replaced in his former position by Reginald Bartholomew, a Brzezinski staff member with expertise on the Soviet Union.[35]

In this atmosphere, little remained, aside from the seemingly doomed SALT II treaty, of the administration's earlier inclination to seek better relations with the Soviet Union or to pursue innovative policies toward Third World problems. Indeed, Huntington observes that, during the fall of 1979, the domestic climate with respect to U.S.-Soviet relations was such that the "cooperative track of the Carter policy was rapidly disintegrating, and it only remained for the Soviet invasion of Afghanistan to eliminate it entirely."[36]

It is only within this context that the administration's fevered response to the Soviet invasion of Afghanistan can be comprehended. Unlike the Soviet brigade episode, the invasion presented a potentially real, rather than a manufactured, threat to U.S. interests. Nevertheless, as Raymond Garthoff argues, "The vigor of the American reaction cannot be attributed to the Soviet intervention alone."[37] Although the evidence is not conclusive, there are indications that Carter's decision to dramatize the threatening nature of Soviet actions was partially grounded in his desire to rally public support and use the crisis to restore his fractured domestic credibility.

After the Soviet Union sent troops and tanks rumbling across the Afghan border during the last week of December 1979, Carter told Congress in his State of the Union address, "The Soviet Union has taken a radical and an aggressive new step. It's using its great military power against a relatively defenseless nation. The implications of the Soviet invasion of Afghanistan could pose the most serious threat to the peace since the Second World War." Carter adopted a broad and frightening interpretation of Soviet actions: "The Soviet Union is attempting to consolidate a strategic position that poses a grave threat to the free movement of Middle East oil."[38] Consistent with these views, Carter announced what became known as the "Carter Doctrine": "Any attempt by an outside force to gain control of the Persian Gulf region will be regarded as an assault on the vital interests of the United States" and "will be repelled by any means necessary, including military force."[39]

Before Carter's speech, his aides told members of the press to expect an address reminiscent of the Truman Doctrine speech of 1947, which shocked the nation into a Cold War stance. As Leslie Gelb noted after Carter's talk, however, "There was nothing in the Truman speech . . . to compare to the amazing list of Carter responses to the Russians. . . ."[40] Carter initially asked various department heads to prepare lists of possible sanctions against the Soviet Union. The plethora of items emanating from the bureaucracy were to constitute a menu from which selections would be made. Instead, Carter simply added the lists to one another and took each of the suggested steps. Carter's response signaled the shelving of détente for the time being and the severing of almost all official contact between the U.S. and the Soviet Union. Moreover, Carter tied U.S. sanctions to the maximal goal of forcing a Soviet withdrawal from Afghanistan. Even Brzezinski feared that Carter may have gone too far.[41]

It is difficult to attribute Carter's reaction to the Soviet invasion wholly to international considerations. In his study of U.S. and Soviet decision making surrounding the crisis, Raymond Garthoff highlights the disproportionate nature of the administration's response. Garthoff shows that the strategic significance the administration attached to Afghanistan itself was inconsistent with previous U.S. assessments, the interpretation placed upon Soviet motives and aims was in conflict with information available to policy makers at the time, and U.S. policies in the aftermath of the invasion were inconsistent with one another and poorly coordinated with stated U.S. goals. Garthoff's analysis reveals a poor fit between the external stimuli provided by the invasion and the U.S. response.

The administration's behavior appears rather puzzling, for instance, in light of the fact that Afghanistan had never before been considered critical to Western security and had long been subject to Soviet influence. To avoid conflict with its powerful neighbor, Afghanistan had pursued close relations with the Soviets since 1955. An organized Communist party had been active in Afghanistan since 1965. After a 1973 coup against the Afghan monarchy, the new leader, Mohammad Daoud Khan, included members of the Parcham faction of the Communist party in the government. The 1978 coup that brought the Communists to power was instigated by pro-Communist army officers after Daoud first removed Communists from his government and later began to arrest a number of key Communist leaders.[42]

Throughout this period, the U.S. remained aloof from Afghan affairs. Even the 1978 coup aroused no great concern. As Garthoff observes: "The United States . . . reacted to the April 1978 coup and the installation of a Marxist pro-Soviet regime in Afghanistan with equanimity, if disappointment."[43] Indeed, the administration even continued to provide a small amount of aid to Afghanistan after the coup. This behavior contrasted sharply with the administration's expressions of alarm eighteen months later when Carter treated the Soviet occupation as part of a broader pattern of Third World expansionism and a possible prelude to Soviet military moves elsewhere in the region.

Yet, according to Garthoff, this interpretation of Soviet motives was seriously flawed.[44] Contrary to Carter's claims, Soviet intervention flowed from the rapidly decaying political stability of the Communist regime that took power in 1978. The Afghani Communist movement was badly split and the Soviet favored faction was, after a time, purged from the government. The leaders of the dominant Khalq faction, Nur Mohammad Taraki and Hefizullah Amin, pursued, against Soviet advice, rapid and radical social reforms that inspired revolt among the country's traditional, Muslim population.

The worsening divisions within the Communist ranks and the growing popular rebellion worried Soviet leaders greatly during the months prior to the invasion. The Soviets blamed Amin, who had gained effective control over the government from Taraki, for poor leadership. They therefore sponsored a failed attempt by Taraki to have Amin assassinated. Aware of Soviet intrigues against him, Amin began to seek international support from other countries, including Pakistan and the U.S., in an effort to bolster his position.

This series of events convinced the Soviets that they had no alternative but to intervene with military force. Garthoff argues:

> The real Soviet fear was that Amin was neither reliable as a partner nor subject to Soviet guidance, and at the same time was ineffective in controlling the growing resistance. In desperation Amin might turn to the United States as Egyptian President Sadat and Somali General Siad had done. Alternatively, he would likely be swept away by a popular Islamic national movement. In either case the Soviet Union would lose all its cumulative investment in Afghanistan. . . .[45]

Garthoff adds that Soviet leaders intervened militarily because "they saw no other way to ensure that [Afghanistan] would remain a buffer."[46]

Garthoff finds little evidence of opportunism, risk taking, or broader ambitions in Soviet behavior. The Soviets viewed Afghanistan as a vital interest rather than simply another opportunity for expanding their influence. They saw little risk that the invasion might lead to military confrontation with the U.S.; not, as some observers charged, because the Carter administration was considered weak, but because Afghanistan was well within the Soviet sphere of influence while of little apparent strategic concern to the West.[47]

U.S. officials knew of Soviet concerns about the course of events in Afghanistan and had received veiled warnings from the Soviets about possible military action. Nevertheless, American policy makers failed to seriously consider the possibility that the Soviet move was seen by the Soviets not as a steppingstone to further aggression, but as a limited response to local circumstances in Afghanistan itself. The implications of Soviet warnings were never closely analyzed and State Department experts who might have made better sense of what was happening were not consulted by top decision makers.[48]

Due to the U.S. failure to examine Soviet motives carefully, officials neither recognized nor resolved contradictions between the objectives of punishing Soviet aggression and securing Soviet withdrawal. U.S. decision makers neglected to consider, for instance, the possibility that if the Soviet move had arisen from insecurity about instability along their border, a strong U.S. response intended to punish the Soviets might only confirm and heighten Soviet fears and make withdrawal less likely.[49]

In short, a great deal remains unexplained about the administration's behavior if its responses are viewed solely in the context of the actual circumstances presented by the crisis. While entirely plausible, Garthoff's interpretation of Soviet motives cannot be considered conclusive until more information is available. More important to our concerns, however, is that top Carter officials largely ignored evidence available at the time which called into question the alarmist interpretation quickly placed on Soviet actions. It is this rapid closure of debate that remains puzzling.

Carter's response makes more sense, however, if one considers Garthoff's suggestion that "part of the reason for the Carter administration's adamant stand was the president's own concern over the widespread domestic criticism that he had been irresolute on a variety of other issues. . . ."[50] Carter's behavior, in other words, appears less puzzling if it is assumed that he was acting, in part, to save his presidency.

This explanation appears all the more plausible when one considers that the Soviet occupation came at the beginning of a presidential election year and at a low point in Carter's popularity, as he faced skepticism and debate over his handling of the economy as well as a variety of foreign policy issues, including defense spending, arms control, and Soviet/Cuban activities in the Third World. Moreover, as the multiple foreign policy crises of the fall and winter of 1979 raised the domestic salience of foreign policy issues, the stakes attached to Carter's handling of these problems rose accordingly. Whereas in June 1979 only 3 percent of the public named a foreign policy issue when asked to specify the most important problem facing the country, by January 1980 this share had risen to 42 percent.[51]

Indeed, as he no doubt hoped, Carter's tough actions brought him significant gains in public support. Following the president's tough speech of January 4, telephone responses to the White House ran two-to-one in favor of Carter's stand.[52] After his State of the Union address, Carter's foreign policy approval rating rose to 53 percent as against 40 percent who disapproved.[53] According to one polling organization, the percentage of the public that approved of Carter's handling of U.S. relations with the Soviet Union rose from 37 percent in January 1979 to 56 percent one year later.[54]

Still, despite impressive relative gains, Carter's absolute levels of support remained rather modest. Indeed, further survey results revealed considerable public hesitance about embracing a newly assertive Carter and his policies. An image of weakness was so closely identified with Carter in the minds of so many people that even Carter's stern response to the Soviet invasion won him only limited credit. Sixty percent of all respondents to one survey, for instance, wanted the president to get tougher in his dealing with the Soviet Union, while only 3 percent thought that Carter was "too tough." Seventy percent of those who disapproved of Carter's handling of foreign policy thought that he was "not tough enough" with the Soviets. Even among those who approved of Carter's handling of foreign policy, 50 percent nevertheless thought that Carter was "not tough enough," while 45 percent thought Carter's response to the Soviet Union was "about right."[55]

These results left little doubt about in which direction the public wanted Carter to move, although many gave Carter only grudging credit when he did so. The president found himself in an unenviable position: having failed to win popular legitimacy for his strategy of adjustment, Carter's conversion to the politics of resistance came too late to fully rescue his deflated domestic credibility. As Americans went to the polls in November 1980, ten months after Carter approved some of the toughest anti-Soviet measures taken by any post-war president, one survey showed that 70 percent of the public still insisted that "we should take a tougher stand toward the Russians."[56]

Conclusion

Carter's foreign policy difficulties stemmed less from his own inadequacies than from his inability to reconcile structural tensions between the imperatives of external adjustment and the politics of internal legitimation. Carter initially gave priority to external adjustment over domestic legitimacy. Although many of his early initiatives succeeded abroad, Carter's overall strategy proved too complex, too flexible, too pragmatic, and too incompatible with the techniques of oversell to easily sell to the American people. The unpopularity of Carter's foreign policies at home, both among vested interests and the general public, led to unacceptable political costs that eventually prompted Carter to return to traditional policies and legitimation techniques in an effort to bolster his political prospects. The potency of the domestic forces working to prompt Carter's retreat from a strategy of adjustment can best be illustrated by exploring the activities and influence of Carter's elite opponents. The next chapter focuses on the mobilization of conservative foreign policy interest groups during the Carter years. Examinations of the ratification battles over the Panama Canal and SALT II treaties reveal that Carter faced an asymmetrical interest group environment favoring his domestic critics.

CHAPTER FIVE

Interest Group Politics and National Security Policy

TO A SURPRISING DEGREE, students of American foreign policy have largely ignored the impact of organized interests on the policy-making process. The paucity of research on foreign policy interest groups stems from the assumption that such groups are politically marginal. To gauge the persistence of this view, one need only compare Lester Milbrath's mid-sixties conclusion that the "impact [of interest groups] on foreign policy is slight at best" with Joseph Nye's mid-eighties appraisal: "By and large, the influence of such groups [on U.S. Soviet policy] is limited."[1]

While there exists a rich tradition of research on group influence in domestic affairs, foreign policy making has been viewed as a separate realm, standing apart from the messy factional politics of the domestic sphere. In contrast to the "stable structure of interest groups" seeking to influence domestic policy, the foreign policy interest group structure has been described as "weak, unstable, and thin rather than dense."[2] These assumptions are not universally held. Many aspects of foreign economic policy are thought susceptible to group influence, and some ethnic lobbies, it is often acknowledged, carry weight with respect to particular issues. It is safe to say, however, that most scholars consider core national security policies largely beyond the sway of interest group politics.[3]

Such a sharp delineation between the role of interest groups in domestic and foreign affairs is, however, unjustified. This distinction may have held descriptive accuracy during the depths of the Cold War when a broad consensus surrounded U.S. foreign policy. Yet the ideological rifts over America's role in the world that emerged in the wake of the Vietnam war have eroded loyalty to a singular version of the national interest and given rise to occasionally intense group conflict over central features of U.S. national security policy. If this growth in the density and intensity of interest group mobilization and conflict has been overlooked by most scholars, so has the impact of these developments on the making of national security policy. While the influence of such groups should not be exaggerated, the relatively open, democratic nature of the American polity and the growing role of Congress in foreign policy making in recent decades have allowed for greater access and impact on the part of interest groups than one might imagine.

After a brief discussion of the literature on interest groups and national security policy, this chapter focuses on the Panama Canal and SALT II treaty debates. Interest group politics played important roles in each of these ratification battles and indeed served to shift the trajectory of national security policy during the Carter years. In particular, Carter's strategy of foreign policy adjustment met with fierce resistance from groups that shared vested ideological and material interests in defending the policies and institutions of the Cold War era.

The Role of Interest Groups in National Security Policy Making

The notion that national security policy making is exempt from interest group influence rests upon claims about the nature of the issue area as well as the structure of the decision-making arena. Security issues fail to evoke group conflict, it is argued, because they involve national rather than group interests: "The essence of interest group activity is group advantage. But private-group advantage is difficult to calculate in the security-policy arena; we are all more or less advantaged or disadvantaged collectively."[4] Even where particular groups do perceive their special interests at stake and are motivated to influence such policies, they face the problem that they have no presumptive legitimacy to speak on behalf of the national interest.[5]

These issue-related obstacles are magnified by the institutional structure of national security decision making. Important choices are made at the apex of the state, among the president and his close advisers. Congress is routinely deferential on national security issues, while the relevant bureaucracies possess less independence from presidential oversight than their domestic policy equivalents. By design, this structure insulates key decision makers and provides private groups with few avenues of access.[6]

Interest groups may seek to place external pressure on presidents and strengthen their claim to speak for the nation through public persuasion. Yet the relevant literature holds out little hope that such groups can succeed in swaying broad public opinion. Presidents have much readier access to the media, possess a more plausible claim to speak for the national interest, and benefit from the public's presumption that they are more fully informed than their critics.[7]

The institutional claim is the strongest, for it suggests that even if groups do mobilize around national security issues, their chances to exert influence are slim. Yet this depiction of a centralized and insulated decision-making system stands in stark contrast to prevalent descriptions of the American state drawn from the fields of comparative politics and international political economy. From the perspective of writers in these fields, the American state is "weak" in contrast to the "strong" states of countries such as France or Japan.[8] While strong states feature highly centralized authority and a low degree of vulnerability to societal pressures, weak states are characterized by diffused or divided authority and the ready access they allow to societal groups. An important consequence of state weakness is that it forces political authorities to place a premium on coalition building, within both the government and the society at large.[9]

The United States belongs in the weak-state category by virtue of the open, democratic character of its political system, the shared authority among its three branches of government, and its decentralized bureaucratic system. While the institutions created to manage U.S. national security may be less open and more centralized than those responsible for domestic policies, some observers have nevertheless pointed out that the national security apparatus remains relatively fragmented and subject to societal pressures.[10] The growing role of Congress in managing foreign policy during the past two decades has only accentuated these characteristics. These considerations suggest that institutional structure should pose far less an obstacle to interest group influence than many observers have claimed.

This leaves the argument that national security issues, by their very nature, fail to evoke group interest or activity. Stephen Krasner asserts, "A state that is weak in relation to its own society can act effectively in the strategic arena because its preferences are not likely to diverge from those of individual societal groups."[11]

If, indeed, all significant social groups viewed security issues through the prism of a single and apparent national interest, then state strength or weakness would remain untested and, therefore, irrelevant. As is widely recognized, some security-related issues are clearly not viewed in this way by all important groups. Issues such as defense spending or the imposition of economic sanctions involve distributional dimensions or vary in salience across groups. In these cases, the "national interest" and the interests of various groups often fail to coincide.

Yet these exceptions do not generally reach to the core assumptions or the central directions of U.S. national security policy. Does national security in this broader sense evoke societal unity or at least deference to the state? It is widely accepted that something approaching a societal consensus backed U.S. policy during the deep Cold War of the fifties and early sixties. Whether or not the U.S. state was weak, under these conditions, presidents faced few societal constraints on their powers because the politics of consensus did not give rise to group mobilization or opposition.[12]

Yet this condition may have represented more an aberration than the norm. The Cold War consensus rested upon two pillars. International hegemony made it possible for the U.S. to use its abundant resources and global dominance to escape difficult choices and to satisfy the demands of many domestic interests simultaneously. In addition, the ideological chasm dividing East and West was never so wide as during this period. Beginning in the late sixties, however, the relative decline of U.S. power sharpened the trade-offs among groups and across foreign commitments while failure in Vietnam and the loosening of the Cold War bloc system lessened faith at home in the ideological basis of America's Cold War strategy. These changes robbed national security issues of their previously unitary and consensual nature.

As suggested in the chapter 3, data on elite and public opinion indicate that the post–Vietnam era witnessed the emergence of pervasive ideological splits over U.S. national security and foreign policies. It is unsurprising, therefore, that the same period brought an unprecedented explosion in the number of foreign policy interest groups and in the scope and intensity of their activities, as the following case studies will suggest.

No longer able to manage foreign policy on the basis of consensus, political leaders became dependent on the support of partial coalitions. Organized along the liberal/conservative dividing lines that emerged after Vietnam, these alliances became increasingly coherent and well organized as the decade of the seventies progressed (although, as suggested below, asymmetries existed between them). This political environment of contestation exposed the long-hidden structural weaknesses of the American state in the national security realm and rendered presidential management of foreign policy increasingly problematic.

The Structure of Interest Group Competition in the Carter Years

A great deal can be learned about the direction of policy change in the seventies by examining the constraints placed upon presidential choice by the foreign policy interest group environment. This requires attention to both the coalition patterns that joined or divided various groups and the balance of power among them.

The domestic politics of U.S. foreign policy during the seventies was driven by the competition between two opposed coalitions. The first bloc was based upon a loose and rather awkward alliance between internationally oriented business interests and liberal activists, many of whom first entered politics as critics of the Vietnam War. Despite some glaring differences between them, both elements of this coalition supported the reform of America's Cold War policies, détente with the Soviet Union and a broadening of the nation's foreign policy agenda.[13] The high point of liberal mobilization came with the presidential election of Jimmy Carter, who embodied both popular skepticism about the Vietnam War and U.S. interventionism abroad, as well as the interests of internationalist business groupings such as the Trilateral Commission, where Carter received his training in foreign affairs.[14]

Pitted against this liberal coalition was a conservative bloc built around an alliance between the traditional Cold War establishment and the emerging New Right. The former included figures from the military-industrial complex, managers of the national security apparatus and Cold War intellectuals.[15]

The New Right was a popular movement that arose in response to a number of developments many middle-class Americans perceived as profoundly threatening. The social movements of the sixties (e.g., anti-war, civil rights, feminism) challenged traditional middle-class values. The combination of a growing welfare state, higher taxes and economic stagnation squeezed the economic status of middle-income families. Other sources of the New Right included the exhaustion of the New Deal coalition, the weakening of traditional party structures, and population shifts toward the Sunbelt states. All of these factors combined to produce a backlash against the liberalism of the sixties and early seventies. Although primarily domestic in origin and focus, the New Right viewed U.S. withdrawal from Vietnam, détente, and liberal policies toward the Third World as signs of a self-imposed retreat from American global power and leadership. These concerns increasingly pulled the movement toward deeper involvement in foreign policy issues.[16]

Conservative Mobilization

While popular disillusionment with the Vietnam War worked to the advantage of liberals during the early seventies, the conservative coalition proved the stronger and more cohesive of the two as the decade progressed. This conservative mobilization took place in the wake of a series of sudden and unprecedented challenges to the dominance of the Cold War paradigm in American foreign policy. Early in the decade, traditional Cold War policies lacked any coherent organizational sponsor in American politics. George McGovern's presidential nomination signaled the centrality of anti-war critics within the Democratic party, while a Republican president pursued openings toward the world's two largest Communist powers.

The Cold War establishment found itself placed on the defensive by this erosion of popular and elite support for traditional policies. Two events created the political space for a conservative counteroffensive. The end of direct U.S. military involvement in Vietnam reduced the salience of the peace issue and allowed room on the nation's political agenda for criticisms of America's overall security posture. In addition, Watergate first distracted Nixon from the complex game of triangular diplomacy and finally discredited and removed the architect of détente from office altogether. Conservatives responded to these opportunities by mobilizing elements of the old Cold War establishment while simultaneously seeking out new allies.

These efforts first became visible with the revival of conservative activism in Republican and, to a lesser extent, Democratic party politics. Conservative internationalists made the greatest gains within the Republican party. Conservative efforts to jettison Republican support for détente with the Soviet Union picked up steam after Nixon's resignation and the removal of many moderate Republicans from Congress at the 1974 midterm elections. Conservatives argued that a tough stance toward the Soviet Union and radicalism in the Third World made good political sense for the party. By re-embracing the Cold War, Republicans could simultaneously distance themselves from memories of the Nixon years and gain possession of an issue with which they could attack the Democrats.

The conservative wing of the party backed Ronald Reagan over a sitting Republican president in the 1976 Republican primaries. Attacks against détente and Ford's secretary of state, Henry Kissinger, played a prominent role in Reagan's campaign. Although Ford managed a close victory over Reagan, he felt compelled to drop the term *détente* from his vocabulary in the course of the campaign. In addition, the Ford administration was forced to accept a foreign policy plank in the Republican platform that "virtually disassociated itself from the policies it had been following vis-à-vis the Soviets."[17] Finally, Ford stalled negotiations with the Soviet Union on SALT II until after the elections, despite the fact that the two sides appeared close to an agreement, to avoid controversy over a treaty that was sure to come under fire from conservatives.[18]

Nonetheless, partisanship placed limits on how far conservative Republicans could go in attacking détente as long as the policy was the creation of Republican presidents. After Gerald Ford lost the 1976 presidential election, however, conservatives achieved growing hegemony inside the Republican party. The transfer of the responsibility for détente to a Democratic president removed whatever partisan interests might have previously inhibited Republican criticism of policies aimed at improving relations with the Soviet Union.

Cold War activists were less successful within the Democratic party but nevertheless made some inroads. After the nomination of George McGovern in 1972 on an anti-war platform, a group of leading Democrats calling themselves the Coalition for a Democratic Majority (CDM) rose in protest over the liberal foreign policy direction McGovern's nomination signaled for the Democratic party. Calling prominently for a larger defense effort and a more critical attitude toward détente, the CDM was dominated by Southern Democrats and a group of Cold War liberals clustered around Senator Henry Jackson.[19] While unable to prevent the nomination of a liberal internationalist presidential candidate in 1976, Jackson and the CDM nevertheless succeeded in denying Carter the luxury of united support from his own party.

Perhaps more important than party politics, however, was the proliferation of conservative pressure groups that took place during the seventies.

Some grew from the traditional Cold War establishment and were dominated by former military officers, past State or Defense Department appointees, businessmen and union officials tied to large military contractors, and academic foreign policy or defense specialists.

This core constituency augmented its strength through cooperation with the more ideologically oriented and broadly focused groups of the emerging New Right. As the following accounts of the Panama Canal and SALT II treaties debates suggest, this conservative coalition grew in size, sophistication, and resources over time and came to achieve a level of political influence superior to that of its less well organized liberal counterpart.

The Panama Canal Debate

The battle over the Panama Canal treaties emerged as the first major test of strength between these two coalitions. Coming early during the incumbency of liberal President Jimmy Carter, the outcome of the ratification debate was widely anticipated as an indicator of the domestic political viability of Carter's new foreign policy agenda. Both sides, therefore, saw the treaties debate as a pivotal contest and as an excellent opportunity for mobilizing supporters and consolidating organizational networks in anticipation of future battles. Each side had reason to believe that victory could be theirs. Liberals took comfort from the fact that the power of the presidency fell on their side. Conservatives counted upon the high hurdle set by the constitutional requirement that treaty ratification needed the assent of two-thirds of the Senate. Liberals and conservatives alike hoped that a win over the Panama treaties would provide momentum for their future efforts to exert control over U.S. foreign policy.

In the end, the outcome of this important contest proved ambiguous for both sides. Carter and his liberal supporters won the battle with a narrow Senate vote favoring ratification. Yet the Panama debate revealed the weakness and fragility of the liberal interest group network. Victory rested not upon the political and organizational strength of the liberal coalition but rather upon the surprisingly sophisticated political skills of President Carter. Carter's virtuoso performance was, however, hardly the sort of asset that could be relied upon in the long run to fend off an increasingly well-organized and well-endowed conservative opposition.

Conservatives emerged strengthened from the battle despite their immediate defeat. While no doubt disappointed at the results of the Senate vote, conservative leaders could rejoice at the astonishing successes achieved in mobilizing grass-roots opposition to the treaties. The treaties debate provided opportunities for refining the tactics and organizational forms that later proved effective in tapping popular support for a wide-ranging conservative agenda on both foreign and domestic issues.

Setting the Stage for a Showdown

The Panama Canal negotiations resulted in two agreements: one providing for the gradual transfer of the canal's management from the U.S. to Panama by century's end and the other providing for the canal's neutral status and U.S. defense rights after the year 2000. The Carter administration considered these treaties emblematic of its new approach to U.S.–Latin American and, more generally, U.S.–Third World relations. Carter's foreign policies would show greater sensitivity toward the symbolic sources of North-South tension. Before his appointment as U.S. negotiator on the Panama accords under Carter, Sol Linowitz wrote that the long-standing dispute between the United States and Panama over the status of the canal "significantly affects the relationship between this country and the entire Third World, since the nations of the Third World have made common cause on this issue—looking upon our position on the Canal as the last vestige of a colonial past that evokes bitter memories and deep animosities."[20]

Fearing that a continued impasse between the U.S. and Panama over the issue could lead to violent attacks upon the canal, Carter pursued a speedy diplomatic solution. As Secretary of State Vance suggested in 1977, the pacts symbolized the administration's emphasis on preventive diplomacy: "These treaties . . . are, above all, a triumph for the principle of peaceful and constructive settlement of disputes between nations. That is a principle we seek to apply in all aspects of American foreign policy."[21]

Another important purpose in seeking a quick settlement of the Panama Canal dispute sprang from the Carter administration's hopes that a victory on Senate ratification would strengthen its domestic position with respect to other foreign policy issues. As the Senate debate over the treaties neared, Richard Strout of the *New Republic* observed, "Carter would like to make a battleground of the new Panama Canal Treaty, in hopes of . . . using the victory as momentum for tougher tests yet to come."[22] The most important of these, of course, was the SALT II Treaty, still under negotiation at the time.

Indeed, according to the *New York Times*, Carter told aides that "the fate of the treaties [would] set the tone for the remainder of his first term."[23]

Mobilizing the Opposition

The Panama Canal treaties proved among the most contentious pieces of legislation in American history. With the exception of the Versailles Treaty following World War I, no treaty or set of treaties had previously brought forth a comparable level of interest group opposition. The list of groups that mounted substantial campaigns against the canal treaties is a long one, including the American Conservative Union, the Conservative Caucus, the Committee for the Survival of a Free Congress, Citizens for the Republic, the American Security Council, the Young Republicans, the National Conservative Political Action Committee, the Council for National Defense, Young Americans for Freedom, the Council for Inter-American Security, the American Legion, Veterans of Foreign Wars, and the Campus Republican Action Organization.[24]

The coalition mobilized in opposition to the treaties was notable not only for its unusual size and breadth but also for the novelty, sophistication, and effectiveness of the techniques employed by its member groups. Conservatives mounted a highly organized and well-endowed campaign built around a populist, grass-roots strategy for rallying opposition to the treaties. Treaty opponents focused principally on influencing public opinion and only secondarily on direct congressional lobbying. Conservatives saw the anti-treaties campaign as part of a long-term strategy for building popular strength and reasserting control over the nation's foreign policy agenda. In line with these goals, the rationales conservatives used in urging opposition to the treaties often focused less on the canal issue itself than on broader themes relating to America's role in the world. Attacks on the treaties became a vehicle through which conservatives sought to challenge the overall world view epitomized by the Carter administration and its liberal supporters.

One of the striking features of this campaign was the high degree of coordination among the groups involved. Altogether, twenty anti-treaty organizations cooperated through two ad hoc umbrella groups: the Committee to Save the Panama Canal and the Emergency Coalition to Save the Panama Canal. According to Michael Hogan, these umbrella groups played a critical role in coordinating the activities of their member organizations. Through them, "the heads of various organizations planned and coordinated strategy and divided tasks. They taught each other lessons learned in earlier campaigns and they pooled their resources to sponsor projects beyond the means of individual groups."[25] Similar tactics were used in the campaign against the SALT II treaty.

Anti-treaty groups placed secondary emphasis on direct congressional lobbying and rejected the path of bargaining with the administration over specific treaty terms. These traditional sorts of interest group activities were generally eschewed in favor of a grass-roots, populist strategy designed to generate and mobilize public opposition to treaty passage. In contrast to the Carter administration's strategy for gaining treaty approval, which "emphasiz[ed] direct appeals to the Senators and to opinion leaders throughout the country," conservatives focused on gaining "public support directly, with the hope that such support [could] influence the Senators' decisions."[26]

As Richard Viguerie, a conservative political activist, explained: "We're doing some direct lobbying but not as much as the White House. Our strength is not in Washington. Our strength is in Peoria and Oshkosh and White River Falls. And that's where we're going. We want to have the Senators and Congressmen hear from the folks back home, and the closer it gets to Election Day, talking to Ham Jordan and Gen. Brown isn't going to be that effective when the Senator has by that time accumulated 80,000 letters, 20,000 phone calls, 10,000 telegrams against the treaties, or when 80% of his home state press is hollering at him."[27]

Treaty opponents devoted impressive sums of money toward this strategy. Their principal weapons included a massive direct mail campaign supplemented by paid media advertising. To provide some sense of the dimensions of this crusade, it is worth detailing the activities of some of the more prominent groups involved in efforts to defeat the treaties. The American Conservative Union spent $1.4 million, dispatched 2.4 million pieces of mail, broadcast a thirty-minute video on 150 stations in eighteen states (seen by an estimated 10 million viewers), and took out newspaper ads in thirty cities. The American Security Council and the Council on Inter-American Security each sent out 2 million pieces of mail, while the latter group also ran radio spots in thirteen states. The Conservative Caucus spent $850,000, shipped 2 million pieces of mail, mounted a national billboard campaign, held rallies in all fifty states, advertised on five hundred radio stations, and sent a fact-finding mission to Panama. The National Conservative Political Action Committee sent out 500,000 pieces of mail, while the Young Americans for Freedom collected 35,000 names on petitions. Many other groups weighed in with smaller efforts.[28] One estimate suggests that anti-treaty groups outspent treaty supporters by a ratio of 10 to 1.[29]

The most obvious and immediate purpose of all this activity was to place public pressure on the Senate to reject the canal treaties. To this end, many groups targeted their efforts toward undecided senators. The Committee to Save the Panama Canal, for example, dispatched a "Truth Squad" on a seven-city speaking tour through states represented by uncommitted senators. This "Truth Squad" consisted of conservative politicians such as Senator Paul Laxalt and Ronald Reagan as well as retired military officers such as Admiral Thomas Moore, former chairman of the Joint Chiefs of Staff, and General Daniel Graham. As expressed by Graham, the group's principal message was that other nations would consider handing over the canal "an act of weakness" on the part of the United States.[30] One senator targeted by the group was Colorado's Floyd Haskel. At an event in Denver, Paul Weyrick, a political consultant to the "Truth Squad," explained, "We feel a definite show of constituent sentiment might help [Senator Haskel] clarify his thinking."[31]

Yet the principal organizers of the anti-treaties campaign saw its goals in broader terms from the outset. Derailing Senate ratification was only a proximate objective. The fight against the treaties was viewed as a vehicle for building a conservative movement and challenging the legitimacy of the foreign policy world view espoused by the Carter administration.

Gary Jarmin, legislative director of the American Conservative Union considered the Panama Canal dispute "a good issue for the conservative movement. It's not just the issue itself we're fighting for. This is an excellent opportunity to seize control of the Republican party."[32]

Jarmin's hopes were not disappointed. The Republican National Committee officially joined the anti-treaty campaign when it voted overwhelmingly to oppose ratification of the treaties at a meeting in late September of 1977. The committee's resolution included language denouncing the "fragmented, reactive, inconsistent and dangerously weak" foreign policies of the Carter administration. Terrence Smith, in his report on the event for the *New York Times*, commented, "The vote seemed to be an expression of . . . the increasing strength of the conservative elements in the party."[33]

Viguerie, who masterminded the use of direct mail as a means of mobilizing support for conservative causes, shared Jarmin's views on the broader purposes of the anti-treaties fight: "It's an issue the conservatives can't lose on. If we lose the vote in the Senate, we will have had the issue for eight or nine months. We will have rallied many new people to our cause. We will have given our supporters an issue, a cause to work for. The left has had this over the years and the right hasn't. . . . Now conservatives can get excited about the Panama Canal giveaway and they can go to the polls, look for a person's name on the ballot who favored these treaties and vote against him."[34]

Consistent with these objectives, the popular message crafted by treaty opponents stressed the broader ideological symbolism of giving up control over the canal more than any concrete interests that might be damaged by treaty passage. While opponents of the treaties often argued that the Panama Canal was still vital to American military and economic interests and that continued American control was the best way to secure those interests, these aspects of the debate were, as George Moffett suggests, "largely subordinated to popular frustrations over the 'vanished mastery' of the United States."[35]

Conservatives adroitly played upon public uncertainty over America's global role in the wake of Vietnam. Opponents of the new accords treated the "giveaway" of the Panama Canal as symbolic of America's declining power and as proof that this erosion of dominance was due not to long-term trends in world politics, but to mismanagement of the nation's foreign policies and a lack of will on the part of America's leaders generally and Jimmy Carter in particular. Treaty foes also closely linked the canal issue with the East-West conflict and fears of communism by portraying Panama's Omar Torrijos as a "Marxist thug" and raising fears, in Retired Admiral Thomas Moore's words, of a "Torrijos-Castro-Moscow Axis."[36] New Hampshire governor Meldrum Thompson incorporated both these themes in his warning that America must "stand brave and firm for freedom in this real world of spreading Communism" or "crawl into historical obscurity in the face of the hysterical howling of world opinion."[37]

New Right spokesman Phillip Crane presented the case against the treaties in similarly apocalyptic terms in a book distributed widely by anti-treaty forces during the Senate debate. Crane warned that surrendering to Panama on the issue of the canal would be "one more crucial American step in a descent into ignominy—to the end of America's credibility as a world power and deterrent to aggression."[38] According to Howard Phillips, head of the Conservative Caucus, the secret of the opposition's appeal was simple:

"It's patriotism, and that's the issue we do the best with."[39]

The anti-treaty campaign struck a chord with significant segments of the public, resulting in great pressure on many Senators to vote against the treaties. In response to conservative appeals, unprecedented numbers of constituents hammered the Senate with "a barrage of letters" opposing the new canal treaties.[40] Cecil Crabb and Pat Holt report, "Hundreds of thousands of letters and postcards poured in, at one point in ratios as great as 300:1 against the treaties."[41] According to Michael Hogan, "A radio and television blitz promoting the Conservative Caucus' 'pledge card' campaign flooded Senate mailrooms with the prefabricated, yet signed threats to 'never' vote for a treaty supporter."[42] An ad placed by the American Conservative Union in the *Nashville Banner* asking readers to write their senator to oppose the treaties "generated some thirty-six hundred pieces of mail in Senator Howard Baker's office in only a week."[43] By November 1977, well over a year before the treaties came up for a vote in the Senate, Baker "had already received 22,000 letters on the issue, only 500 in support of the treaties."[44] At one point, likewise, Missouri Republican John Danforth's office had received 12,284 anti-treaty letters as compared with only 241 in praise of the treaty.[45] These cases were not atypical. Hogan notes, "A compilation of Senate mail by the American Conservative Union showed that some Senators received as many as four thousand communications in a single week, with opposition to the treaties running from 90 to 100 percent."[46]

Searching for Support

The Carter administration's campaign in support of the treaties took a very different tack from that chosen by treaty opponents. Top officials held little confidence that the public could grasp the complexities of the pro-treaty argument. More significantly, it lacked an extensive grass-roots network of interest groups upon which it could call for help. As a result, the administration relied principally upon appeals to opinion leaders, direct congressional lobbying, and a late television plea for public support by the president himself. When these proved inadequate, Carter found himself forced into difficult concessions on treaty language as well as last-minute arm twisting and log rolling in order to secure the final needed votes.

As its campaign for ratification began in earnest, the administration found it especially worrisome that interest group support for the treaties appeared so weak and disorganized. While liberal, religious, and business groups each offered aid, none seemed capable enough or willing to mount especially vigorous efforts.

The assistance provided by liberal and religious groups proved especially disappointing. In contrast to conservative forces, these organizations failed miserably in their efforts to rally public support. Undoubtedly, this was due in part to the fact that many such groups suffered from poor organization and scarce resources. Just as importantly, liberals found it difficult to craft a message that would resonate with the patriotic and ideological values of most Americans. Both liberal and religious groups often chose to stress moral as opposed to pragmatic themes. These sorts of arguments, which emphasized American guilt for past injustices toward Panama, proved both unpopular with the American people and in large measure contradictory to the themes preferred by the White House.

A recently organized foreign policy lobbying group known as "New Directions" emerged as one of the principal liberal groups to campaign on behalf of the treaties. Calling itself a "citizens lobby," akin to Common Cause, the group hoped not only to help ensure passage of the treaties but also, in the manner of many conservative groups, to use the campaign as a vehicle to build a long-term, mass organization that could institutionalize pressure for a generally liberal set of U.S. foreign policies, such as those pursued by the early Carter administration. Funded by liberal groups such as the AFL-CIO, the Democratic National Committee, the United Auto Workers, the Americans for Democratic Action, and the Washington Office on Latin America, New Directions sent out a 1.1 million piece mailing to liberal supporters asking for support of the Canal treaties. However, New Directions also set up a separate Committee for Ratification of the Panama Canal Treaties that possessed an operating budget of only $19,000.[47] As Michael Hogan points out, the ambitious hopes of New Directions were soon dashed: "The group quickly learned . . . that few Americans would rally to liberal causes out of support for the treaties. Instead of building its support with the Panama campaign, New Directions collapsed under the financial burden of its direct-mail effort."[48]

A variety of religious groups also mounted campaigns in support of the treaties. The National Council of Churches and the United States Catholic Conference publicly backed the treaties and financed the campaigns waged by the Washington Office on Latin America and the Ecumenical Program for Inter-American Communication and Action (EPICA). Organized religious backing, however, proved of dubious value to the administration. Some religious groups based their support for the treaties primarily upon moral grounds and a reading of history that branded U.S. involvement in Panama as "colonial."[49] The Carter administration, however, feared that most Americans would reject a pro-treaty argument that featured the U.S. in the role of the villain and that appealed to American guilt over past sins. The White House not only supported the treaty primarily on pragmatic grounds but believed that these would also sell best with the public and the Senate.

In his televised appeal to the American people, for instance, Carter stressed, "The most important reason—the only reason—to ratify the treaties is that they are in the highest national interest of the United States and will strengthen our position in the world."[50] The Carter administration, while it did raise the issue of "fairness" with respect to the legitimacy of Panamanian claims on the canal, rejected interpretations that charged the U.S. with "colonialism" and joined opponents in pointing with pride to the difficulties Americans overcame in building the canal.[51]

This led to considerable tension between the administration and a number of the religious groups involved in the pro-treaty campaign. The administration found itself uneasy with the support of those whose arguments struck moderates as "un-American" while many religious groups were disappointed that the administration seemed reluctant to base its appeal on the grounds of morality and American guilt. Indeed, one major group, the Ecumenical Program for Inter-American Communication and Action, reversed its support for the treaties in protest over the manner in which the administration decided to sell the treaties as well as concerns that the treaties did not go far enough to right the historical wrongs done Panama.[52]

Business support proved ephemeral as well. Early during the pro-treaties campaign, the State Department helped organize the Business and Professional Committee for a New Panama Canal Treaty, which was backed by two dozen American multinational corporations. The group soon folded, however, after its head had a change of heart about the treaties.[53] Leaders of the Business Roundtable, the National Association of Manufacturers, and the Chamber of Commerce all lobbied personally for the treaties, but because their memberships were divided, none of these organizations took official stances on the issue.[54]

The major business group to campaign on behalf of the canal treaties was the Council of the Americas, a group representing two hundred major corporations accounting for 90 percent of U.S. private investment in Latin American and the Caribbean. The council produced and distributed pro-treaty pamphlets, met with Senators and opinion leaders, and courted broader business support. But the group shied away from grass-roots organizing or a visible public profile. This was because both the White House and the council "feared creating the public perception that the treaties were 'written by Wall Street' for the benefit of big business."[55]

Another semi-private elite organization involved in the campaign for treaty passage was the Committee of Americans for the Canal Treaties (COACT), which consisted of prominent political leaders. While nominally independent, COACT was, to a large extent, actually the creation of and under the direction of the White House. It produced a handbook intended to guide the efforts of local organizers in mounting grass-roots campaigns on behalf of the treaties. This handbook was distributed to opinion leaders from around the country, who were invited to the White House for briefings on the treaties. COACT's ambitions for stimulating local campaigns, however, proved wildly unrealistic. The enormously complex, expensive, and time-consuming plans and methods outlined in its handbook called for heavy commitments on the part of organizers. Yet, not surprisingly, very few of the local notables reached by the White House were so moved that they felt compelled to single-handedly rally the support of their communities behind the treaties. COACT's contribution proved disappointing in other respects as well. It raised and spent only $350,000 compared with initial funding projections of $1 million. It placed some newspaper advertisements and sent out 300,000 pieces of mail, but even its organizers conceded the ineffectiveness of its advocacy efforts on behalf of the treaties.[56]

On top of weak interest group support, Carter also received little help from the Democratic party establishment. In October 1977 Carter, conceding that ratification of the treaties was "in doubt," appealed to the Democratic National Committee to "help him win over Congressional and public support" for treaty passage. Carter soon found the response disappointing, however, when the four-hundred-member committee passed a resolution supporting the "treaty negotiations" and the "ratification process" but neglecting to endorse the Canal treaties themselves.[57]

Pulling Chestnuts from the Fire
With only weak interest group support for the canal treaties, the burden

of the pro-treaties campaign rested heavily upon the administration itself. Contrary to the common image of Carter as politically inept, the president performed brilliantly in guiding the treaties toward Senate passage against long odds.

Carter staffers flew hundreds of locally influential opinion leaders from around the country to the White House for elaborate briefings. It was hoped that, by influencing public opinion in their communities, these allies could offset some of the political pressure to vote against the treaties that the Right's grass-roots campaign had placed on many senators. Carter also sent Cabinet members and aides on extensive speaking tours on behalf of the treaties, carried out intensive lobbying among uncommitted or wavering senators, and made a major network television address on the canal issue shortly before the vote in the Senate.[58]

The Carter administration's public appeals stressed the pragmatic benefits of the treaties to the United States as well as the safeguards contained within them to protect American interests. Carter argued that the United States and Panama shared common interests in keeping the canal open and that the principal threat to the safety and operations of the canal might come from Panamanian resentment and anger were the treaties to be rejected. In his televised address, Carter predicted, "The new treaties will naturally change Panama from a passive and sometimes deeply resentful bystander into an active and interested partner whose vital interest will be served by a well-operated canal. This agreement leads to cooperation and not confrontation between our country and Panama."[59]

Defense Secretary Harold Brown indicated that the U.S. military could not hope to protect the canal from determined saboteurs: "According to the best informed military opinion, we can't defend the canal from a hostile Panama. It is too vulnerable to a sack of dynamite—or to a glove in the gears."[60] Brown, like Carter, argued that the treaties, by giving Panama a greater interest in the canal's continued operation and providing the U.S. with the right to take actions to protect the canal even after it was turned over to Panama, offered the best hope for the canal's future security. Brown's appeal was seconded by the Joint Chiefs of Staff, who also publicly threw their support behind the treaties.[61]

The administration also contended that passage of the treaties would remove a chronic irritant in U.S. relations with Latin America and rob radical nationalists throughout the region of a potent symbol of alleged U.S. colonialism. Finally, Carter maintained that the U.S. image around the world would benefit from its perceived act of fairness toward a small country. The treaties, Carter asserted, would "remove a major source of anti-American feeling" and "provid[e] vivid proof to the people of this hemisphere that a new era of friendship and cooperation is beginning and that what they regard as the last remnant of alleged American colonialism is being removed."[62]

Many senators remained concerned, however, over whether the language of the treaties offered sufficient legal protection of U.S. rights to protect the canal and expedite the passage of U.S. ships through it in the case of war or emergency. These became critical issues in the Senate debate and, although Carter maintained that the treaties provided sufficient guarantees of these rights, the administration was forced to make a series of compromises that were designed to strengthen the treaties' assurances in these regards. Carter and General Torrijos of Panama first issued a clarifying statement affirming the right of the U.S. to defend the neutrality of the canal and to move U.S. ships to the head of the line in an emergency.

On the issue of defending the canal's neutrality, the Carter-Torrijos joint statement declared that

> the correct interpretation [of the principle of U.S. intervention rights] is that each of the two countries shall, in accordance with their respective constitutional processes, defend the Canal against any threat to the regime of neutrality, and consequently shall have the right to act against any aggression or threat directed against the Canal or against peaceful transit of vessels through the Canal. This does not mean, nor shall it be interpreted as, a right of intervention of the United States in the internal affairs of Panama.[63]

The Senate subsequently insisted that the language contained in this statement be amended to the Neutrality Treaty itself. With Carter's tacit acquiescence, these so-called "leadership amendments" passed overwhelmingly.[64]

As the vote on the Neutrality Treaty approached, the White House was still unsure of passage. It was in this atmosphere of uncertainty that Carter was confronted with an unexpected development that almost led to Panamanian rejection of the treaties. Democratic Senator Dennis DeConcini of

Arizona demanded that the Neutrality Treaty be amended with the addition of a new condition designed to strengthen U.S. defense rights toward the canal still further. DeConcini "represented a conservative state where . . . opposition to the new pacts ran high."[65] Hoping to minimize the political damage of voting for the treaties through a highly visible effort to extract additional concessions from the president, DeConcini asked that language be inserted into the treaty guaranteeing that, should the operations of the canal ever be interfered with, the U.S. had the independent right "to take such steps as it deems necessary . . . including the use of military force in Panama, to reopen the Canal. . . ."[66] At least one other senator linked his vote to the DeConcini condition. Fearing that the treaty would fail without these votes, Carter reluctantly endorsed DeConcini's demand despite anticipated protests from Panama.

Only after the passage of the Neutrality Treaty by a one-vote margin did it become apparent just how seriously Panama objected to the DeConcini condition. Panamanians viewed the language of the DeConcini condition as granting to the U.S. the unilateral right to use military force for the purpose of interfering with Panama's internal affairs. Torrijos himself threatened to denounce the treaties over Panamanian television. The situation was salvaged only when Senate leaders helped Carter persuade DeConcini to accept an additional amendment to the second canal treaty, designed to undo the damage caused by the original DeConcini condition. The new amendment stated that any action taken by the U.S. to defend the canal "shall not have as its purpose or be interpreted as a right of intervention in the internal affairs of Panama or interference with its political independence or sovereign integrity."[67] Inserted in the second Panama Canal treaty, which also passed by a vote of 68 to 32, this language served to soothe Panamanian tempers.[68]

Both the leadership amendments as well as the DeConcini condition were important not so much for their substantive effects on the treaties—the rights they asserted were already guaranteed within the treaties to a substantial degree—but for the perception they helped to create that the Senate had forced a reluctant administration to toughen up the protection the treaties offered for U.S. interests. Many senators who felt under enormous pressure to oppose the treaties came around to supporting them once they could take credit for strengthening the treaties. Carter understood these concerns and proved flexible enough to accommodate them.[69]

Another factor that worked in Carter's favor was the widespread acceptance of claims that the administration's efforts to educate the public about the treaties, along with the leadership amendments, had produced a turnabout in public opinion on the issue. In fact, the evidence of such a shift in sentiment is very weak and was based primarily on misleading polling results. Nevertheless, the perception, however erroneous, that the public had finally rallied to the side of the administration played a crucial role in allowing Carter to convert a number of wavering senators to his cause in the days and weeks before the Senate vote.

Survey results on the Panama Canal issue were particularly sensitive to question wording. Some questions provided respondents with only negative information. These tended to produce overwhelming percentages against the treaties. The Opinion Research Corporation, for instance, was commissioned by an anti-treaty organization known as the American Council for World Freedom to ask people, "Do you favor the U.S. continuing its ownership and control of the Panama Canal or do you favor turning over ownership and control of the Panama Canal to the Republic of Panama?" This question contained no reference to the treaties being negotiated, to the transition period through the year 2000 before full control over the canal would be given to Panama, nor to the rights the U.S. would continue to enjoy through the treaties both during and after the transition period. Moreover, by referring to "ownership," the question implied an answer to the controversial question of whether the U.S. held sovereignty over the Canal Zone or merely use rights.

Not surprisingly, when asked in May of 1977, this question produced an overwhelming majority of 78 percent opposed to the transfer of the canal, compared with only 8 percent in favor. Due to the early timing of the poll, these figures became a misleading benchmark against which later polling results were measured. Later surveys, based upon less negatively biased questions, showed less heavy majorities against the treaty and, therefore, allowed Carter to claim progress.[70]

This was especially the case because, as the treaty vote drew closer, some polling organizations began to include more information in their questions, typically containing implied rationales for favoring the treaties. Some questions, for instance, included references to U.S. defense rights or to the leadership amendments. Whenever this sort of additional information was provided, the results tilted in favor of the treaties and, in some cases, actually showed supporters outnumbering opponents. As polling organizations emulated one another in altering their questions over time to include more favorable information, the appearance of a trend was created.

In fact, this appearance was misleading. The most unbiased questions asked respondents their position on the treaties without positive or negative qualifications. These neutral questions consistently produced 5 to 3 majorities against the treaties throughout the treaty debate. Indeed, a survey given in June 1978, several months after the Senate vote, which simply asked respondents, "Do you think the Senate should have approved the Panama Canal treaties or should not have approved them?" once again evoked the familiar 5 to 3 ratio against.[71] Michael Hogan, commenting on trends in public support for the treaties, concludes that "the turnabout was illusory."[72] Carter, nevertheless, encouraged and astutely played upon these illusions to reassure nervous supporters that a vote for the treaties need not be politically damaging.

In addition to Carter's concessions on treaty language and perceptions that the public had become more supportive of the treaties, the other essential ingredient in Carter's recipe for victory involved the wooing of individual senators whose votes were considered crucial. Carter's political courtship of uncommitted senators did not always prove successful. As we indicated earlier, passage of the first treaty remained in doubt even during the final days before the vote. Some senators who privately supported the treaties were too intimidated to take the risk of siding with the White House, when confronted by opinion polls showing large majorities of the citizens in their home states against the treaties.

Senator Edward Zorinsky was a case in point. In his memoirs, Carter recalls that Zorinsky "said he wanted to vote for the treaties" but also that he was concerned about "the lack of support back home."[73] As described by Franck and Weisband, Carter went to comical extremes in his campaign to win over Nebraska's junior senator:

> The Catholic Archbishop of Omaha was called to see what he could do about . . . Zorinsky. . . . Zorinsky, alone, got 250 Nebraskans invited to the White House. Every one of them accepted. Carter talked to the Senator on several occasions. Rosalynn Carter called Mrs. Zorinsky to hope she would urge her husband to do the right thing. Ambassador Sol Linowitz, one of the two top negotiators with Panama, played tennis with Zorinsky and, it is said, let him

win. On the hill, the Senator was visited by Vice-President Mondale, Zbigniew Brzezinski, Cyrus Vance, Defense Secretary Harold Brown, Treasury Secretary Michael Blumenthal, and even Henry Kissinger.[74]

Despite all of this, Carter's ardent pursuit of Zorinsky came to naught when the senator, deferring to home state pressure, cast his vote against the treaties. Other senators proved more open to Carter's entreaties, but often at a steep price. Carter was able to nail down the final votes necessary to bring victory only by "pull[ing] out all the stops in dispensing favors to key senators. For example, the administration switched positions on a government copper purchase, an important public works project, and a costly farm bill.[75] In return for supporting the treaties, Senator S. I. Hayakawa of California demanded and received assurances that Carter would consult with him in setting African policy, where Hayakawa was interested in seeing the U.S. support the white minority regime in Rhodesia, and respond more vigorously to Soviet and Cuban activities on the continent.[76] One high-ranking Carter official remarked, "I hope the Panamanians will get as much out of these treaties as some United States senators."[77]

The Price of Victory
Carter's carefully orchestrated campaign succeeded in nailing down the final votes necessary for treaty passage. While this was a daring political feat, Carter's victory on the Panama Canal treaties nevertheless proved extremely costly. Gaddis Smith observed, "Ordinarily, a President grows stronger by winning a hard political fight. But Carter's narrow triumph, while it prevented possible disaster abroad, gained him no credit at home."[78] George Moffett called the passage of the treaties "a Pyrrhic victory" for Carter and noted that "the administration was not able to generate any discernible sympathy for its guiding world view" from the treaty campaign.[79]

After the passage of the treaties, Hedrick Smith predicted that "this was not the kind of victory that will provide long term political momentum or produce much spillover for the administration in Congress on . . . other key issues," such as arms control. Smith also noted, "Mr. Carter's final bargaining with a few individual Senators is not the kind of tactic that builds bloc support" in the Senate.[80]

Conservatives had vowed during and after the treaty fight that senators voting in favor of the treaties would be punished at the polls. This prediction was partially borne out. When the 1978 mid-term elections arrived, conservatives targeted for defeat, with considerable success, a number of liberal senators who had helped lead the fight for passage of the treaties. As George Moffett notes, "In the elections of 1978 and 1980, 20 of the 68 senators who voted for ratification were defeated in bids for reelections."[81] Only one senator who voted against the treaties, by contrast, was defeated for re-election during the 1978 and 1980 elections.

Another cost to the administration was that, as one contemporary account put it, "The President gave out many IOU's, using up political capital that might be needed later on."[82] Carter's success on the Panama Canal treaties weakened his ability to succeed in future legislative contests. Moderate senators from conservative states, such as Howard Baker, endured considerable criticism over their pro-treaty votes and came under great pressure to balance their vote on the canal treaties by opposing later Carter foreign policy initiatives targeted for opposition from the Right, such as the SALT II treaty.[83]

All in all, Carter won the legislative battle but lost the political and ideological war. Conservatives out-organized Carter and his liberal supporters and clearly won the fight for public support. The struggle for ratification of the Panama Canal treaties proved a costly affair for Carter and helped encourage a growing cautiousness and conservatism in Carter's approach to foreign affairs.

Lessons of the Panama Canal Debate

Perhaps the most important and, for Carter, the most worrisome political fact to emerge from the canal debate was the obvious contrast between the high level of organization among conservatives and the disorganization of Carter's own supporters. Conservatives succeeded in using the canal issue as a rallying point for mobilizing grass-roots support for conservative causes. During the anti-treaties campaign, conservative groups added a total of 400,000 new members to their rolls.[84] Conservatives succeeded in working out a division of labor among the various groups in their coalition and pioneered new political techniques, such as direct mail, which allowed them to raise unprecedented amounts of money and mobilize many thousands of supporters on relatively short notice. The momentum and experience gained from the Panama ratification debate made it easier for conservatives to mobilize similar campaigns on other foreign policy issues in the ensuing years, thus placing Carter perpetually on the defensive.

By contrast with conservatives, the coalition that stood behind Carter's foreign policies was deeply divided. The two distinct groups that supported Carter's policies, multi-national corporate interests and liberal political support groups, found it difficult to work together, each possessing liabilities that limited popular appeal.

Carter's policies appealed first to the most internationally committed sectors of American business. These firms were generally more sensitive to international trends and pressures than firms less heavily engaged in international business. As a result, many of them appreciated the administration's preference for a cooperative rather than confrontational foreign policy approach. These sectors of the business community were heavily represented, for instance, in the Trilateral Commission, which served as Carter's own training ground in foreign affairs and as the source for many of Carter's foreign policy reforms. The same sorts of firms lobbied on behalf of the Panama Canal treaties through the Council of the Americas.

The problem with relying heavily upon this set of allies was that such interests were concentrated in specialized elite circles and possessed little grassroots organization, clout, or appeal. They were weak precisely where conservatives were strong. In fact, close connection with such groups could prove damaging, as when conservatives charged that Carter was pushing the Panama Canal treaties in order to bail out big Eastern banks to whom Panama owed significant amounts of money.[85] Moreover, many of these groups, reticent about taking the spotlight for fear of just these sorts of populist attacks, were happy to let the White House carry the ball alone.

A very different source of support was also available to the Carter administration. Many of Carter's policies appealed to ideological liberals, such as those who had protested the war in Vietnam and who could be found among activists on the left wing of the Democratic party. These individuals were represented by groups such as New Directions and the Coalition for a New Foreign and Military Policy. Liberal church groups could also be included in this category.

Carter, however, generally avoided close ties with these sorts of groups as well. The reasons were several. Liberal groups often possessed too few resources to command much political clout. Moreover, ideological liberals tended to favor more far-reaching reforms than Carter was willing to contemplate. As a result, a significant degree of distrust distanced ideological liberals from the White House. Finally, Carter feared, probably correctly, that explicit association with groups considerably to the left of the general public might hurt more than it would help the administration politically. These divisions within the liberal coalition plagued Carter's efforts to counterbalance conservative strengths throughout his presidency.

Given the asymmetries in the interest group environment Carter faced, it is not surprising that Carter's early victory on the Panama Canal issue did not clear the way for domestic acceptance of other elements of Carter's foreign policy agenda. Indeed, Carter emerged weakened from the struggle and in a poorer position to defend the evolving SALT II treaty.

The SALT II Debate

The debate over the SALT II treaty began long before the actual treaty became available for inspection. Arms control became the focal point of conservative efforts to challenge Carter's larger foreign policy paradigm. The ratification debate represented the climax of an elaborate duel between Carter and his critics over the essential directions of U.S. national security policy. It is instructive, therefore, to examine the early thrusts and parries in this contest before turning to the treaty debate itself.

Among the many groups that formed the organized opposition to Carter's early arms control and security policies, the most formidable was the Committee on the Present Danger. Evolving from a series of discussions among its founders between 1974 and 1976, the committee's membership read like a *Who's Who* list of the traditional foreign affairs establishment. According to Max Kampelman, it was decided that "the principal qualification for membership would be expertise and experience in the areas of foreign and defense policy. . . . [W]e would concentrate on inviting persons who had held top posts in State, Defense, and Treasury, as well as senior figures in appropriate departments at leading universities around the country."[86]

Approximately 150 such notables initially joined the committee. Roughly one-third had previously held government posts, and many, including Paul Nitze, Eugene Rostow, David Packard and Dean Rusk, had long been highly influential members of the Cold War establishment. The committee's name was taken from that of a similar group that had pressed for a posture of global containment and increased defense spending during the early fifties.[87]

While individual members often testified before Congress, the committee eschewed formal legislative lobbying in favor of activities designed to sway public and elite opinion. The CPD cultivated extensive contacts in the press, sent members on speaking tours and prepared a series of statements on contemporary issues concerning defense, arms control, and U.S.-Soviet relations. The first such statement, issued the day following the 1976 presidential election, declared, "The principal threat to our nation, to world peace, and to the cause of human freedom is the Soviet drive for dominance based upon an unparalleled military buildup."[88]

In the coming years, the CPD acted as a foreign policy establishment in exile. The committee enjoyed a coup of sorts very soon after its founding. CPD members had for several years been asserting that the National Intelligence Estimates prepared annually by the CIA greatly understated the Soviet danger. Stung by these criticisms, outgoing President Ford took the extraordinary step of appointing a Team B of conservative defense and foreign affairs experts from outside the government to prepare a report that would parallel the CIA's normal efforts. Dominated by leading CPD members, Team B produced a draft considerably more pessimistic about Soviet capabilities and intentions than that prepared by the CIA's regular Team A. According to one insider account, CIA Director George Bush subsequently intervened in the dispute by ordering Team A to "substantially revise its draft" to produce "an estimate that in all its essential points agreed with Team B's position."[89] By enhancing the intelligence community's sensitivity to conservative criticism, it seems likely that this episode played a role in the increasingly alarmist tenor of intelligence estimates regarding Soviet defense spending as the seventies wore on. A reappraisal conducted by the CIA in 1983 concluded that the agency had previously failed to detect a significant slowing in the rate of growth in Soviet defense spending from 1976 onward and that its estimates tended to overstate the Soviet threat.[90]

Early Skirmishes

The incoming administration soon dampened the CPD's enthusiasm over the success of Team B. Ignoring the CPD's lengthy list of suggested candidates for top foreign and defense posts, Carter appointed a host of liberal foreign policy intellectuals, many relatively young and most critical of previous U.S. involvement in Vietnam.[91] Unable to ignore conservative sentiment altogether, however, Carter crafted a strategy for dealing with his opponents that shifted between confrontation and accommodation, with accommodation playing a more prominent role as time went on.

Conservatives won an early skirmish when their opposition forced Carter to withdraw his nomination of Theodore Sorensen, a former Kennedy adviser and Democratic liberal, for directorship of the Central Intelligence Agency. A more significant debate emerged over Carter's nomination of Paul Warnke for the job of chief SALT II negotiator. Contending that Warnke held overly dovish views, a number of conservative groups formed the Emergency Coalition Against Unilateral Disarmament to oppose his Senate confirmation.[92] By challenging Warnke, conservatives put Carter on notice that the liberal direction of his declared policies would not go unchallenged.

The Senate ultimately confirmed Warnke's appointment after a heated debate. But, as Henry Jackson had predicted,[93] the number of favorable votes for Warnke fell below the two-thirds majority that would be needed to approve any treaty that Warnke might eventually negotiate. This placed pressure on Carter to adopt a tougher negotiating stance and contributed to his ill-fated decision to seek deep, comprehensive nuclear force cuts in SALT negotiations with the Soviet Union during the summer of 1977.

After the close vote on Warnke's nomination, Carter moved "to bring some of his critics into the policy-making process. Henry Jackson, a hardliner generally regarded as the Senate's leading SALT expert, was invited to the White House to advise the president directly and to submit his own SALT proposals in writing."[94] Carter's subsequent proposal incorporated the provisions for deep cuts in Soviet heavy ICBMs favored by Jackson.

The Soviet rejection was swift and harsh when Secretary of State Vance presented Moscow with Carter's "comprehensive proposal" along with a fallback position that contemplated only minor variations on the proposals agreed to in the Vladivostok Accords. The Soviets criticized Carter's new package as too one-sided in favor of the U.S. and a serious departure from the assumptions underlying previous negotiations. The fallback proposals were rejected as well for offering no progress on the agreement reached at Vladivostok.[95]

Jackson's role in shaping Carter's early arms control proposals was accompanied by other White House efforts to appease the powerful senator. Secretary Vance agreed in October 1977 to meet with Jackson's Armed Services Subcommittee on Arms Control every two weeks. Carter also reappointed General Edward Rowney, at Jackson's urging, as the representative of the

Joint Chiefs of Staff to the U.S. SALT delegation.[96] Rowney later resigned from the negotiating team and thereafter denounced the final accord.

Carter narrowly survived yet another early skirmish, this time over his cancellation of the B-1 bomber. In his memoirs, Carter refers to the B-1 lobby as "one of the most formidable ever evolved in the military-industrial community" and recalls that "there was tremendous pressure on Congress to go ahead with plans for an entire fleet" of new bombers.[97] Though Congress narrowly upheld the decision to cancel production (the House vote was 202 to 199), Carter's victory proved neither complete nor lasting. By continuing to fund research and development, Congress allowed the B-1 program to remain alive through 1981, enabling new president Ronald Reagan to revive production.

Arms sales emerged as another arena of struggle over the basic directions of national security policy. Carter moved quickly after taking office to issue new guidelines intended to restrict the size and scope of America's booming arms export business. Presidential Directive 13, announced on May 19, 1977, introduced six new categories of controls on U.S. arms sales and declared that arms transfers would henceforth be considered "an exceptional foreign policy implement" to be utilized only where clearly necessary to further U.S. national security interests. Over subsequent months and years, however, a coalition of arms manufacturers, elements of the bureaucracy, and certain high level officials, including National Security Adviser Zbigniew Brzezinski and Secretary of Defense Harold Brown, moved to dilute or undermine the implementation of Carter's proclaimed policy of restraining arms sales.[98]

Carter's criticisms of burgeoning U.S. arms sales during his presidential campaign in 1976 produced alarm among weapons manufacturers and prompted the formation of the American League for Exports and Security Assistance (ALESA). Consisting of several dozen major defense firms as well as a few unions, ALESA lobbied in favor of new arms sales and against restrictive policy guidelines.[99] ALESA found allies within the Defense Department. Carter pledged to place a ceiling on future U.S. arms sales, using fiscal year 1977 as the relevant base year. During the first months of 1978 (i.e., the final months of fiscal year 1977), officials in the Defense and State Departments rushed through billions of dollars in pending arms sales. This effectively boosted sales totals for 1977 to a high of $12 billion, thus loosening the ceiling placed on future sales. Though reportedly "very angry" when he discovered this bureaucratic maneuver, Carter did nothing to reverse the outcome.[100]

One of the more promising of Carter's efforts to restrict arms sales took the form of Conventional Arms Transfer (CAT) talks with the Soviet Union. These negotiations between the United States and the Soviet Union aimed at setting mutually agreed upon limits on the amounts and kinds of weapons sold to countries around the world. It was hoped that agreement between the two superpowers might pave the way for global restrictions encompassing other arms exporting countries. U.S. representatives from the Arms Control and Disarmament Agency and the State Department met several times with their Soviet counterparts during 1978. Negotiators made considerable progress toward an agreement before November 1978 when Brzezinski, with support from Harold Brown, waged a successful struggle to sabotage the talks. Brzezinski insisted upon saddling U.S. representatives with new negotiating instructions that were sure to be rejected by the Soviet Union at critical talks scheduled for Mexico City in December. As expected, the talks broke down and the possibility of a CAT accord soon faded.[101]

Coping with the Critics: From Accommodation . . .

Despite, or perhaps because of, these early confrontations between the White House and its critics, Carter began to shape an accommodationist track in his dealings with conservatives. The president took pains, for instance, to provide conservatives outside of the government with access to top officials. Though Carter apparently hoped to co-opt some of his critics and thereby alleviate the political pressures on his administration, it seems likely, in retrospect, that this accommodationist strand of Carter's strategy only helped to accelerate the insinuation of conservative influence over policy while doing little to free the administration from outside pressures.

Carter's efforts at accommodation were evident in the preparation of PRM 10, a global strategic review he ordered shortly after taking office. Following the Team B precedent, a group of predominantly conservative outside consultants was asked to join with an interagency team of staff members in preparing the study. Unlike Team B, these outsiders were to work directly with the official task force rather than prepare a separate report. But because this arrangement resulted in repeated conflict, the final report was split into two sections. The first, dealing primarily with political issues, was written in a pessimistic tone by the team of outside experts. The second, focusing on defense requirements, was composed by a more liberal Pentagon team and called for a relatively modest defense program based upon more optimistic assumptions. The result was a confusing and inconsistent statement that did little to add clarity to the direction of Carter's foreign and defense policies.[102]

Carter's sensitivity to conservative opinion was further reflected in an incident that occurred in August of 1977. Stung by criticisms contained in a recently published CPD statement entitled "Where We Stand on SALT II," Carter invited members of the CPD's executive committee to the White House, where he pleaded with them to tone down their attacks on the administration. In return, Carter promised the group greater private access to top administration officials, including Carter's National Security Adviser Zbigniew Brzezinski and Secretary of Defense Harold Brown.[103]

... To Retreat

Conservative criticism nevertheless abated little. The CPD charged Soviet leaders with the aim of "impos[ing] an imperial system dominated by the Soviet will."[104] Complaining of the administration's "unwillingness to compete with the Soviet Union and to hold its drive in check," the CPD warned, "Pursuing a policy built on illusion, we have been adrift and uncertain while the Soviet Union expanded its power and empire on every continent and on all the seas."[105]

Finding a growing echo in Congress and the media, these criticisms appeared to have an impact on public perceptions. Popular approval for Carter's handling of foreign policy sank from 48 percent in July 1977 to only 22 percent in July 1978.[106] A Gallup Poll taken in July 1978 revealed that 43 percent of those surveyed disapproved of the way Carter was handling U.S.-Soviet relations, while 34 percent approved.[107] These trends heightened Carter's desire to toughen up his image as a means of restoring domestic support and accelerated his shift toward more conservative and confrontational policies.

Despite his campaign promise to cut defense spending, Carter proposed a 3 percent increase in his initial State of the Union address and later prodded other NATO countries to go along with similar increases. In addition, 1978 brought tighter restrictions on trade with the Soviet Union involving the transfer of sensitive technologies.[108] Carter suspended the withdrawal of U.S. troops from South Korea in 1978 and dropped such plans altogether the following year. According to Secretary of States Cyrus Vance, the troop reductions in South Korea were doomed by the fact that "Congress continued to hammer home warnings of a political explosion if the withdrawals actually proceeded."[109]

Carter also stepped up his criticism of human rights abuses in the Soviet Union, a move described by Carter aide Hamilton Jordan as an effort to shield the president from right-wing attacks: "One of the first impressions the American people have of their new President is that he's been tough with the Soviets on human rights. . . . And in terms of the SALT talks, it provides a good argument against those who later on might accuse him of being soft on the commies, to be able to point back to an experience when he was really tough on the Soviet Union."[110]

Several days before a March 1978 speech at Wake Forest University, in which Carter took a harsh line toward the Soviet Union, Zbigniew Brzezinski, Carter's National Security Adviser, remarked that Carter's tougher rhetoric was designed to "prove we weren't soft."[111] Samuel Huntington, at the time a Brzezinski aide, later recalled that the "positive response" to Carter's Wake Forest speech "encouraged White House political advisers to believe that a strong defense was good politics."[112] Carter soon found another occasion to lambaste the Soviets in an address at the Naval Academy in June.

In September 1978 Marshall Shulman, Vance's Soviet expert, openly acknowledged in congressional testimony that domestic constraints limited the administration's ability to halt the deterioration in U.S.-Soviet relations: "The blurring of popular understanding of the limitations of 'détente' contributed to a sense of disillusionment and anger. . . . A measured and effective reaction to the military and political competition from the Soviet Union has been made more difficult by the persisting post-Vietnam apprehension that the United States may be seen as lacking sufficient will and resolution."[113]

The Struggle for Ratification

It was in this atmosphere that negotiations over SALT II neared a successful conclusion in early 1979. Mired in controversy over both domestic and foreign issues, Carter's ability to fend off inevitable attacks on the approaching treaty stood in serious doubt. Public approval of Carter's overall job performance fell to 30 percent.[114] An early June survey showed that only

36 percent of the public approved of Carter's handling of foreign policy issues.[115] A survey conducted by Pat Caddell, the president's pollster, in the spring and early summer of 1979 showed that 54 percent of the public thought that the U.S. position in the world was only "fair" or "poor." A small 13 percent felt that the nation's position was "growing stronger" while 62 percent thought that the U.S. was "becoming weaker."[116] Yet dwindling public confidence in the president was only symptomatic of more fundamental ills weakening Carter's ability to guide the nation's foreign policies.

Carter's costly Panama Canal victory hurt rather than helped him with respect to the looming battle over SALT II. Politically moderate senators who had voted with Carter on the canal treaties, such as Republican Howard Baker, were wary of once again defying the right wing. Conservative groups not only proved their ability to mobilize public sentiment in the earlier battle, but also succeeded, during the 1978 midterm elections, in punishing senators who had sided with the administration on the canal treaties. Moreover, the Panama experience taught conservatives that Carter could be forced into concessions in a tough Congressional battle.

SALT II's prospects were also weakened by the widely held belief that the Soviet Union had achieved overall military superiority vis-à-vis the U.S. and that the Soviet drive for military dominance continued unabated in the face of U.S. passivity. The CPD cultivated these perceptions by arguing, "Neither Soviet military power nor its rate of growth can be explained or justified on grounds of self-defense."[117] By mid-1979 a plurality had come to accept the CPD's claim of Soviet military superiority. In a poll taken in early June, 43 percent agreed that the U.S. was "not as strong" as the Soviet Union compared with 11 percent who believed that the U.S. was militarily stronger.[118] These perceptions allowed critics to argue effectively for higher defense spending while attacking SALT II for "ratifying," as Senator Sam Nunn put it, an existing nuclear imbalance.[119]

Partisan Conflict

The final signing of the SALT II treaty thus took place in the context of a weakened presidency, a fearful and insecure public and an active and well-organized conservative opposition. This atmosphere precluded the possibility that debate over the treaty might focus narrowly on its merits. SALT II became a lightning rod, attracting bolts of criticism from those who found themselves at odds with Carter's larger foreign and defense policy agendas.[120]

The growing partisanship of the foreign policy debate provided a measure of Carter's domestic vulnerability. Early 1979 brought an extraordinary meeting of ninety-five top Republican officeholders, including twenty-six senators, at which it was decided that the party should "abandon its traditional bipartisanship in foreign policy and make overall Soviet conduct a key issue in negotiating and considering a new strategic arms treaty." Referring to Republican Senator Arthur Vandenberg, who had championed a bipartisan approach to foreign policy during the post-World War II period, Senator Howard Baker stated that "Vandenberg was right in his time, but I think we're right in our time." With only two dissenting votes, the group passed a resolution "accusing the Carter administration of having let American military power decline and of having ignored 'Soviet aggressiveness.'"[121]

Leading Republicans launched an even harsher attack against the administration less than a month later when the Republican National Committee charged, "The failure of this administration in national security is enormous." The Republicans compared Carter's program with the appeasement policies pursued by British Prime Minister Neville Chamberlain toward Hitler's Germany during the 1930s. Finding an "eerie parallel" between the two situations, the committee stated that "once again we witness a Chamberlain-like government's fervid hopes that a dictatorship's good behavior will compensate for its own inadequacy. Yet these hopes are based more upon an obstinate denial of unpleasant facts than honest and realistic evaluation of the Soviet buildup." According to the *New York Times*, Bill Brock, the Republican National Committee chairman, "made it clear that the Carter administration's defense and foreign policies . . . would serve as key issues in next year's Presidential elections."[122]

The Opposition Mobilizes

This growing polarization between Carter and his critics and the increasingly conservative public mood foreshadowed a bruising ratification battle. Sensing SALT II's vulnerability, conservative interest groups mounted massive direct mail, media, and lobbying campaigns.[123] The Committee on the Present Danger spent $750,000 in its efforts to derail SALT II even before the treaty was announced. CPD executive committee and board members testified on seventeen occasions before Senate committees during consideration of the treaty and participated in 479 television and radio programs, press conferences, public debates, briefings of influential citizens, and major speeches on arms control and defense. The committee distributed more than 200,000 pamphlets and reports.[124] The Committee's key role prompted one government spokesperson to comment, "The interest groups on the right shaped the terms of the SALT II debate. In the community of experts, the Committee on the Present Danger was the most influential. . . ."[125] Similarly, Cyrus Vance, in 1982, remarked, "There is no doubt that the Committee on the Present Danger had a great deal to do with undermining SALT."[126]

Still, as the intellectual wing of the anti-SALT coalition, the CPD's greatest contribution was to issue reports critical of the treaty written by noted arms control and defense experts. The task of mobilizing grass-roots opposition fell to other groups whose activities were coordinated through an ad hoc umbrella organization called the Coalition for Peace through Strength.

Launched under the auspices of the American Security Council in the summer of 1978, the purpose of the coalition, according to its co-chair Paul Laxalt, was to gather "some of the most prestigious names and groups in the defense community to build a formidable organization dedicated to the adoption of a national strategy for peace through strength."[127] The promotion of "peace through strength" translated into a campaign of criticism aimed at the SALT negotiations as well as vigorous calls for higher defense spending.

The coalition was three-pronged. By the time SALT II came before the Senate, it included 191 congressmen among its members, a figure which later swelled to 204. Another arm included well-known conservatives outside of the government, some of whom provided organizational leadership and carried out the coalition's day-to-day activities. Falling under this wing were 2,500 retired generals and admirals. The coalition also helped coordinate the activities of 106 affiliated organizations.[128]

In addition to its coordinating role, the coalition independently spent $2.5 million and organized a 150-member speakers bureau. The coalition's central importance in the anti-SALT II drive was revealed in January 1979 when "a House Armed Services subcommittee used a luncheon given by the organization to release an official report opposing SALT."[129]

In April, the coalition issued its own sixty-two-page report criticizing the treaty, accompanied by a news conference featuring a number of former defense officials and retired military officers. The report argued, "The most important reason for rejecting SALT II is that it is a symbol of defeatist policies which have led to phased surrender by the United States as it retreats around the world in the face of Soviet aggression."[130]

One of the most effective anti-SALT groups was the American Security Council (ASC), a longtime champion of high defense spending with strong ties to leading military contractors. ASC boasted more than 200,000 dues-paying members and an annual budget of $4 million. The council spent $3 million opposing SALT II and sent out 10 million pieces of mail. It produced and distributed three films dealing with defense, nuclear weapons, and arms control prior to and during the SALT II debate. *The SALT Syndrome*, which like the other two included appeals for money and memberships, showed six hundred times on local stations and netted 50,000 new members for ASC. The other two films were shown a total of 1,800 times. The group's speaker program, featuring retired military officials such as Major General George Keegan and Lt. General Daniel O. Graham, reached 800 audiences.[131]

With an enormous roster of 325,000 dues-paying members and an annual budget of $3 million, the American Conservative Union (ACU) also brought considerable resources to bear in its attempt to derail SALT II. The ACU organized a grass roots campaign centered around its forty-two state affiliates. It also sent 1 million pieces of mail and produced as well as distributed two anti-SALT films. One of these showed on three hundred stations and brought contributions of $450,000.[132] Yet another group, the Conservative Caucus, spent $1 million and sent 5 million pieces of mail.[133]

As a direct result of these efforts, many senators found themselves awash with constituent mail expressing opposition to ratification. In a survey of fifty-five Senate staffers, 44 percent reported that mail ran strongly against ratification while 36 percent said mail ran slightly against the treaty. Only 2 percent reported that mail ran strongly in favor of SALT II.[134]

The thrust of opponents' arguments against SALT II had less to do with the treaty's specific terms than with the overall direction of the administration's foreign and defense policies. Senator Jake Garn declared, "I intend to make this a debate on the whole strategic and defense policy of the United States."[135] Treaty foes rejected the symbolism of cooperating with the Soviets on arms control at a time when conservatives viewed the Soviet threat as growing. Senator Henry Jackson darkly suggested that Senate passage of SALT II would be "appeasement in its purest form."[136]

Above all, conservatives feared that by reinvigorating détente, SALT II would lull the public into a sense of complacency and undercut support for a vigorous defense buildup. CPD member Paul Nitze counseled the Foreign Relations Committee that "the Senate must first resolve the question of whether, in times of increasing danger, including military danger, it is wise to let down our guard or whether it is time to pull the country together for the major effort that is required on many fronts." Nitze worried, "To accept the case that is being made for the Vienna terms, with all its fallacies and implausibilities, can only incapacitate our minds and wills for doing the things necessary to redress the strategic imbalance."[137]

The Limits of Interest Group Support for Salt II
Private interest group supporters of SALT II lacked the resources and the high degree of organization possessed by opponents. The principal group to lobby on behalf on the treaty called itself Americans for SALT (AFS). Led by Townscend Hoopes, former Undersecretary of the Air Force, and Charles Yost, former chief delegate to the United Nations, along with other prominent political notables, AFS helped coordinate the efforts of various pro-treaty groups. It functioned, however, only partially autonomously from the White House. The administration played a role in the group's formation and helped direct its activities from behind the scenes.[138] The major purpose of Americans for SALT was "to do the sort of hard political organizing that cannot by done by Government employees."[139] Yet the group's plans included spending only $200,000, far less than any of the major groups working against the treaty.[140] One staffer reported, "It was hard to raise money."[141] AFS suffered from other disabilities as well. Three top-ranking staffers were fired during the first six months after the group's founding, and some in the Senate considered the group lacking in credibility owing to its close ties to the White House.[142]

Business support for SALT II was expressed through the American Committee on East-West Accord, which featured among its 145 founding members many notables such as Donald M. Kendall (president of PepsiCo Inc., a firm active in exporting to the Soviet Union), George Kennan, John Kenneth Galbraith, Jeremy Stone, Fred Warner Neal, Robert Schmidt, Carl Marcy and Jerome Wiesner.[143]

One-third of the committee's funding came from firms actively involved with East-West trade.[144] According to co-director Carl Marcy, the committee was first formed . . . in 1974, because of concern over the Jackson-Vanik amendment to limit U.S.-Soviet trade. Then last year [1976] we shifted our focus to keeping the country from slipping back into the cold war syndrome. Most of the members believe that we can't make headway in arms control unless we have normal business and cultural exchanges and we can't make headway in business unless there's progress on arms control.[145]

The committee's principal contribution to the campaign for SALT II was a half-hour film that showed on more than three hundred local television stations, reaching an estimated 90 million people. Background materials were also mailed to four thousand editors and community leaders.[146]

Liberal activist organizations also worked on behalf of SALT II. The Disarmament Working Group and the Coalition for a New Foreign and Military Policy coordinated the efforts of numerous peace groups.[147] Due to ideological differences, however, coordination between these groups and the elite-centered organizations discussed above was weak.

Despite their work on behalf of SALT II's ratification, the enthusiasm these groups brought to the task was often tempered by philosophical reservations. Many peace activists favored speedy efforts at total nuclear disarmament and considered SALT II a timid and disappointing step in that direction. While negotiations on the pact were still underway, F. Raymond Wilson, chairman of the Disarmament Working Group, predicted, "When the terms of the treaty come out, we will probably be pretty unsatisfied, but it needs to be ratified as a step to SALT III, which, supposedly, will be much more a step to disarmament."[148] Jeremy Stone, a prominent arms control advocate and director of the Federation of American Scientists, drew considerable attention for his criticisms that SALT II did not go far enough.[149]

The effectiveness of most liberal groups was hampered not only by their own qualms about the treaty, but also by shoestring budgets. Bob Brammer, a Disarmament Working Group staff member, conceded, "Letter writing is the bottom line, the bread and butter for every issue, especially because we don't have an awful lot of money to spend."[150]

The fate of one such group is illustrative. Modeled after Common Cause, an organization known as New Directions sprang up in the mid-seventies with the goal of building grass-roots support for a reorientation of U.S. foreign policy. The group drew up ambitious plans for campaigns revolving around a number of issues, including SALT II. The group's founders hoped to use the battle over the Panama Canal treaties as a vehicle for building a mass base of supporters and contributors, much as New Right groups were successfully doing at the time. The hoped-for financial contributions failed to materialize, however, and New Directions' efforts in support of SALT II were hampered by debts incurred due to the failure of its earlier direct mail campaign.[151]

Despite the considerable number of groups involved, interest group support for the SALT II treaty proved relatively inconsequential. Not only did private group foes of SALT II far outspend supporters,[152] but supporters were divided by ideological tensions and their efforts less effectively coordinated than was true of their conservative counterparts.

The White House Campaign

These political realities dictated Carter's strategy for gaining treaty approval. Given the asymmetrical interest group environment that it faced along with precarious levels of popular support for both détente and arms control, the administration chose to soft-sell the SALT II treaty.[153] Hoping to "appeal to skeptics in the Senate," Carter aides began "to publicly maintain that the treaty will neither transform the basic character of Soviet-American relations nor make significant improvements to the country's strategic arsenal unnecessary. Indeed, an important part of the administration's case for the agreement is that it will allow the United States to deploy several new weapons in the 1980's." Carter placed much of the weight of his pitch for SALT II on "the military and political dangers of a failure to impose some constraints on the future growth of the two nations' strategic arsenals."[154]

The cautiousness of the administration's approach was apparent in Secretary of State Vance's testimony on behalf of the treaty before the Senate Foreign Relations Committee: "We do not suggest that SALT II will by itself carry us to a new world of prosperity and peace.... Nor do we suggest that if SALT is not approved, we could not survive." The treaty would, however, make "an important contribution to maintaining a stable strategic balance" and "enable us to broaden the work of arms control." As for détente, SALT would "help us to fashion a balanced relationship with the Soviet Union in which we build on areas of mutual interest, but do not let the benefits of cooperative measures blind us to the reality of our continuing competition."[155]

Vance and Defense Secretary Harold Brown argued that SALT II represented an improvement over SALT I because, unlike the earlier agreement, it provided for equal limits on both sides. The administration defended SALT II's verification provisions as fully adequate and stressed that the treaty "impose[s] on the Soviet Union significant restraints that balance those it imposes on us. . . ."[156] Finally, Carter cited the support of the Joint Chiefs of Staff and America's NATO allies as indications that the treaty adequately served U.S. and Western security interests.

These arguments failed to hold early public support. Momentum clearly favored the treaty's critics. While initial polls showed high public approval for SALT II, a series of surveys taken during 1979 revealed a steady deterioration of popular approbation. The administration's position weakened as the debate over SALT II exposed the public to criticisms of Carter's policies toward U.S.-Soviet relations and the military balance between the two powers.

A Gallup Poll taken in mid-March 1979 showed that those aware of the treaty favored Senate ratification by a ratio of 3 to 1. Yet by late June, public support for the treaty had narrowed to a ratio of 5 to 3. By late September, after months of heated campaigning by both supporters and opponents, public attitudes had completed a remarkable turnaround: a small plurality of informed respondents now expressed opposition to the ratification of SALT II.[157]

Part of the public's skepticism toward SALT II grew from a fundamental distrust of the Soviet Union and lack of faith in the U.S. ability to verify Soviet compliance with the treaty—both themes stressed by anti-treaty groups. In one survey, 47 percent of those polled did not expect the Soviet Union to live up to the treaty terms.[158] Public attitudes toward U.S. defense requirements had also hardened by this time. Whereas a plurality felt that military equality with the Soviet Union was an adequate basis for U.S. security in July 1978, by October 1979, according to an ABC News/Harris survey, 49 percent had come to believe that U.S. military superiority was a necessity, compared with 43 percent who supported equality alone.[159]

These trends provided a measure of the continuing ideological potence of the message carried by anti-treaty groups as well as their success in disseminating their views. Comparing the American Committee for East-West Accord with the Committee on the Present Danger, for instance, one study found that the latter was much more effective than the former in gaining press coverage of its views and activities.[160] David Kurkowski's survey of nineteen Senate staffers found that 63 percent believed anti-treaty groups were more effective than pro-treaty groups in influencing public opinion. Kurkowski concludes that the treaty's failure can be traced in part "to a steady decline in public support for SALT and the creation of a negative political climate. The interest groups opposed to the treaty contributed to this climate. And in this regard, the anti-treaty groups can be said to have won the battle for public opinion."[161]

This dramatic erosion of public support only sharpened the political dilemma faced by moderate senators who privately supported SALT II but feared the political consequences of doing so publicly. For the administration, the negative trend in opinion increased its desire to find ways of defusing charges that it was "soft" on the Soviets.

In this climate, Carter's only hope for treaty passage was to devise some package of concessions that could sway the substantial body of publicly uncommitted senators. Carter resisted significant revision of the treaty's terms for fear that changes might require renegotiation with the Soviets and perhaps doom the treaty altogether.[162] Carter instead sought support by offering concessions on various defense programs and policies. One result, ironically, was that arms control became the lever by which conservatives succeeded in prying greater military spending from the administration.

One of Carter's first moves was to remove Paul Warnke as head of the Arms Control and Disarmament Agency. At Brzezinski's suggestion, Warnke was replaced by the more conservative George Siegnious, a retired military general, who, it was hoped, would provide a better defense of SALT II.[163]

During the campaign for the treaty, Carter came under pressure from a number of senators, whose votes were crucially important, to adopt a tougher U.S. defense posture in return for their support on SALT II. These demands were particularly intense over the issue of strategic force modernization.[164] In June, Carter responded by proposing $40 billion in funding for the deployment of MX missiles and later announcing a new mobile basing plan for the weapons.[165]

Another concession to political realities was Carter's attempt to reassure SALT skeptics that he intended to pursue a hard line in future arms control negotiations. In September Carter issued Presidential Decision (PD) 50, which outlined a new set of arms control guidelines. Prepared by Brzezinski's staff without the knowledge of Arms Control Director George Seignious, PD 50 committed the administration to a more conservative stance toward ongoing and future arms control efforts. Its stringent negotiating guidelines were designed to protect existing and future military programs. The *New York Times* reported that the new directive was intended to "de-emphasize the role of arms negotiations in foreign policy" and give "military considerations greater weight in arms control planning for future talks."[166] This shift was prompted in part by domestic political constraints. According to one aide, the administration hoped that the new guidelines would lead to "less controversial accords."[167]

Carter also came under tremendous pressure to increase military spending faster than the planned rate of 3 percent real growth per year. In late summer, the administration acquiesced when the Senate added $4 billion to the 1980 defense budget. Sam Nunn and other senators also called upon the administration to commit itself to real increases of 5 percent in defense spending for 1981 and 1982. Nunn, whose views on defense were influential among Democrats, linked his SALT II vote to substantial military budget increases.[168] In a September appearance before the Senate Foreign Relations Committee, Harold Brown hinted that the administration might be willing to contemplate future increases in defense spending beyond the 3 percent level. In late November, senior Carter aides engaged in private negotiations with Nunn and Henry Kissinger in hopes of discovering what levels of future defense spending would be sufficient to induce the two to express support for SALT II. Finally, on December 12, Carter announced plans for average real growth in military appropriations of 4.5 percent over the next five years, a rate of increase only slightly lower than the 5 percent level that Nunn had publicly advocated.[169]

Even this, however, left many critics unconverted. Henry Jackson and other senators expressed skepticism about the sincerity of the administration's commitment to higher defense spending. Paul Nitze called Carter's proposal "inadequate in quantity" and "misdirected in quality."[170] Carter's concession neither brought an immediate treaty endorsement from Nunn nor did it stop the Senate Armed Forces Committee from issuing a report critical of SALT II one week after the announcement.[171]

In the wake of the Soviet invasion of Afghanistan, Carter requested that the SALT II treaty be withdrawn from consideration by the Senate. This reflected his recognition that Soviet actions had spoiled whatever chances the treaty had for passage. Yet its prospects were quite doubtful in any case. Prior to the invasion, the Foreign Relations Committee recommended ratification of the treaty by a lukewarm 9 to 6 vote. The committee report included, however, a call for increased defense spending to make up for the treaty's inadequacies. Led by Henry Jackson, the Armed Services Committee voted out a report recommending against ratification that concluded that the SALT II treaty "is not in the national security interests of the United States."[172] Howard Baker, with presidential aspirations, was expected to lead the fight against ratification. None of this boded well for the treaty. Senate head counts by Americans for SALT, by the Conservative Caucus, and by Senator Alan Cranston each indicated that SALT II was headed for defeat even prior to the invasion of Afghanistan.[173] It is probable that the Soviet action, by forcing Carter to withdraw the treaty, spared him a humiliating personal defeat.

The battle over ratification of the SALT II treaty revealed the stunning degree to which conservatives managed to parlay their organizational and ideological strengths into control over the terms of debate on national security issues. Throughout 1979 the Carter administration was placed on the defensive by conservative attacks on the treaty and its overall foreign and defense policies. As public polls and readings of congressional opinion revealed the growing momentum behind conservative perspectives, the administration spent most of the year backpedaling in an attempt to regain domestic legitimacy. Instead of defending détente and arms control in positive terms, Carter adopted a defensive posture: stressing that things would be worse without SALT II, promising to speed up strategic modernization and increase defense spending, and attempting to cultivate an image of toughness toward the Soviet Union. Many liberal appointees left the administration during 1979 and 1980, culminating in the resignation of Cyrus Vance. During the same period, domestic considerations led the administration to dramatize, or oversell, external threats, as, for instance, during the incident of the Soviet brigade in Cuba and the Soviet invasion of Afghanistan. Though it won him little political credit, Carter's responses to an asymmetrical environment of interest groups considerably narrowed the distance between him and his critics.

The Asymmetries of Interest Group Conflict

Some have argued, convincingly, that Carter or his aides mishandled various aspects of the administration's campaign to sell the SALT II treaty.[174] How critical these mistakes may have been to the ultimate outcome is difficult to ascertain. Yet attention to Carter's tactical political errors should not blind one to broader structural characteristics of the domestic political landscape in which debates over arms control and national security took place during the late seventies.

Especially important were the ways in which broad and enduring interest group coalitions dominated the environment in which Carter was forced to maneuver. A potent alliance of conservative interest groups stiffened congressional resistance to SALT II, contributed to an erosion of public support for the treaty, and created a climate in which Carter felt compelled to steer his national security policies to the right in an attempt to appease conservative critics. A weaker liberal coalition proved ineffective as a counterbalance to these pressures on the administration.

These conclusions are consistent with the argument that national security issues can indeed serve to evoke group mobilization and conflict. They also demonstrate that institutional arrangements in the national security realm do not serve as insuperable obstacles to interest group influence. The decentralized, open, and democratic nature of the American political system and its shared authority between the legislative and executive branches—in short, the "weakness" of the American state—provide interest groups with routes of access and means for influencing policy that might not be available in a more centralized system.

Conclusion

Scholars have generally assigned interest groups little weight in the study of U.S. national security policy. This neglect stems from the common assumption that the political environment surrounding national security policy differs dramatically from that associated with domestic policy. The former fails to evoke group activity due to the existence of a shared national interest with regard to such issues. Moreover, the institutional structure of national security policy making denies access to even mobilized interest groups.

These pervasive assumptions bear reexamination. Only under circumstances of extreme threat does the international environment impose a singular version of the national interest upon a society. Instead, conceptions of the national interest are socially constructed and vary with the interests and values of the society's participants. The degree to which a specific version of the national interest is widely shared will also vary over time. A peculiar set of international and domestic conditions made possible the cultivation of a relative consensus around a particular conception of U.S. national interest during the Cold War. Yet as historical circumstances changed, consensus gave way to division during the seventies. In the post–Vietnam era, national security issues once again became available for interest group mobilization and contestation, much in the same way that domestic issues had always been.

The institutional structure of the American state never posed quite the obstacle to interest group influence on national security issues that many analysts claimed. It is more accurate to say that the U.S. has had a "weak" state all along, making it potentially accessible to interest group influence. State strength and autonomy were not seriously put to the test, however, for much of the Cold War due to the near consensus surrounding national security issues. Once exposed to social divisions and interest group pressure during the seventies, however, it quickly became apparent that national security policy makers were not as insulated from society as observers had commonly believed. Moreover, institutional structure does not remain static, as evidenced by the growing role of Congress in foreign policy and national security issues during this period.

While it is important to note that growing availability of national security issues for interest group influence during the seventies, it is just as significant to stress the asymmetries that characterized group competition during this period. The political advantages that conservative groups possessed over their liberal rivals stemmed from the domestic legacies of America's Cold War strategy. A set of vested interests were created, organized, and empowered by the policies and institutions of the Cold War era. It is not surprising that these groups would mobilize in opposition to the policy reforms of the early Carter administration. Nor is it unexpected that the loose coalition that organized around Carter's strategy of international adjustment would lack the cohesion and resources of its more well established counterpart.

CHAPTER SIX

American Foreign Policy under Reagan, Bush, and Clinton

During the seventies and eighties, U.S. foreign policy became trapped within a structurally determined cycle of instability and vacillation. Policy makers faced the difficult task of devising a foreign policy strategy capable of reconciling contradictory international and domestic constraints. Not surprisingly, neither Jimmy Carter nor Ronald Reagan succeeded in accomplishing such a feat. Over time, each found himself compelled to abandon or compromise critical elements of his initial foreign policy strategy. Carter's early foreign policy reforms were molded in response to declining U.S. power. Carter's adjustment strategy, designed to narrow the gap between U.S. resources and commitments, was frustrated by domestic obstacles stemming from ideological, material, and institutional legacies of the Cold War. Reagan's strategy of resistance was premised upon the view that what the U.S. lacked was will, not power. As we discuss below, however, Reagan instead discovered that the limits on American power were more severe than initially anticipated. Indeed, the mounting costs of Reagan's assertive unilateralism eventually compelled the administration to retreat from many of its initial ambitions.

The contradictions that enveloped U.S. foreign policy during these two decades could neither be finessed nor wished away. The dilemmas plaguing both the Carter and Reagan administrations were structural, not intellectual. Policy makers do not have the luxury of ignoring domestic political imperatives, even when these imperatives work against otherwise sound policies. Neither is it possible for a nation to long sustain a strategy of resurgence, no matter how popular at home, if it lacks the power to support such ambitions or if the result is to widen the gap between the nation's resources and its commitments.

If structural contradictions of this sort cannot be easily reconciled through strategic choice, how are policy makers to be delivered from the dilemmas they pose? Under such circumstances, history itself sometimes intervenes by providing an exogenous shock that removes, or at least eases, the contradictions bedeviling policy makers. The historically pivotal events of 1989–1991, including the collapse of communism, the disintegration of the Soviet Union, and the end of the Cold War, have played such a role by dramatically changing both the international and domestic contexts of U.S. foreign policy. The end of the Cold War has disorganized, though not entirely eliminated, the constellation of political interests that previously worked to block or slow efforts toward foreign policy adjustment and reform. Likewise, communism's retreat has undermined the ideological rationale that long served to legitimize an activist U.S. foreign policy, while the decline of the Soviet threat has eased public fears about U.S. security and lessened support for high levels of defense spending. Internationally, the diminished strength and altered political orientation of America's major military rival has eased the external demands on U.S. resources.

These events have thus significantly reworked the structural context of U.S. foreign policy. The international setting now offers a more favorable climate for reducing U.S. commitments abroad than at any time since World War II. Moreover, the domestic constraints that previously mitigated against a coherent strategy of adjustment have been greatly relieved as well. The opportunities for fashioning a successful and sustainable strategy of foreign policy adjustment are far more favorable today than during the Carter era.

If this analysis is correct, then U.S. foreign policy may, during the nineties, finally exit the debilitating cycle of instability and vacillation that so characterized the foreign policy strategies of the seventies and eighties. Before accepting this optimistic conclusion, however, a number of significant qualifications must be considered. Contemporary domestic and international conditions are not uniformly favorable to a successful and sustained strategy of adjustment. Indeed, the Clinton administration's efforts to forge a post-Cold War strategy of adjustment in U.S. foreign and domestic policy have so far met with only uneven success.[1]

This chapter analyzes U.S. foreign policy during the Reagan and Bush presidencies and examines the opportunities and constraints currently facing the Clinton administration. As suggested above, the Reagan administration's initial strategy of resistance encountered serious international constraints, stemming from unaccounted for limitations on American power, and led to growing U.S. overextension abroad. During Reagan's second term, U.S. policy makers gradually adjusted to these realities and abandoned or modified important aspects of Reagan's initial foreign policy strategy. The Bush administration adopted a pragmatic approach that carried this process further. Yet the steps toward adjustment during the last years of Reagan's term and the four years of Bush's presidency remained halting and incomplete. The gap between U.S. resources and commitments persisted, the sources of America's declining economic competitiveness remained largely unaddressed, and no coherent and forward-looking strategy emerged for adjusting U.S. foreign policy to the fundamental changes of the post-Cold War era. Newly elected President Bill Clinton inherited much unfinished business from his predecessors.

Resistance and Reality: The Reagan Experience

The evolution of the Reagan administration's foreign policies provided a mirror image of the previous administration's experience. Carter initially pursued a strategy of international adjustment. While reasonably successful abroad, Carter's policies provoked intense domestic opposition that eventually compelled the president to abandon critical components of his adjustment strategy in favor of policies of resistance. Contrarily, Ronald Reagan came to office intent upon carrying out a straightforward strategy of resistance and resurgence. While reasonably popular at home, Reagan's strategy met with serious international obstacles and had to be altered to reintroduce elements of adjustment. Both leaders were frustrated in their efforts to carry through a consistent, coordinated strategy in American foreign policy, although the sources of constraint in each case differed.

Ronald Reagan's presidency brought to power Cold War interests that had been relegated to the status of outsiders, albeit influential ones, through much of the seventies. Reagan and his conservative appointees, thirty-three of whom were drawn from the ranks of the Committee on the Present Danger,[2] rejected not only the policies of the early Carter administration but also the assumptions that underlay them.

The Reagan administration discarded the notion, for instance, that declining American power was attributable to irreversible structural forces as well as the assertion that a gap existed between U.S. resources and commitments. Instead, waning U.S. influence was believed to flow from the unwillingness of leaders during the seventies to marshal U.S. resources or exercise the full range of potential American power. Power, to a much greater degree than before, was equated with military strength; a resource that, according to Reagan, had been dangerously neglected by previous administrations over the previous decade. U.S. interests were conceived in wide-ranging terms. The Reagan administration embraced an encompassing globalism and declined to draw distinctions between vital and peripheral areas of the world or to weigh costs closely against the value of new and existing commitments.

Reagan's foreign policy team viewed the international structure of interests as basically hostile. The Soviet Union was considered irredeemably untrustworthy and expansionist. Radical Third World movements and regimes were pictured in threatening terms. The new administration rejected the propositions that compromise or accommodation with these sorts of states could sometimes serve U.S. interests, or that limited U.S. power required a degree of tolerance toward unwelcome changes as long as vital interests were not at stake. Even U.S. allies were treated with a certain amount of suspicion when they persisted in the pursuit of détente or treated radicalism in the Third World with equanimity. The Reagan administration refused to allow the qualms of differently minded friends to constrain its global strategy of resurgence and resistance. Indeed, it sometimes brought pressure to bear on allied countries when their cooperation was deemed necessary but insufficiently forthcoming.

In sum, the Reagan administration's favorable view of the structure of world power led to the conclusion that a strategy of adjustment was unnecessary, while its negative outlook on the structure of interests convinced its leading members that the retrenchment implied by a strategy of adjustment was downright dangerous to U.S. interests. Instead, under Reagan, the U.S. would rebuild the foundations of American power while once again marshaling the will to put that power to vigorous use.[3]

While Reagan's vision of an America once again "standing tall" on the international scene proved popular at home, at least initially, his administration's foreign policies suffered from a yawning gap between promise and performance. Reagan's strategy of resistance often ran up against international complexities and ultimately served to widen the gap between U.S. resources and commitments. Indeed, faced with serious external obstacles, the administration eventually altered or abandoned important elements of its original strategy. Its most widely acknowledged foreign policy successes came in those areas where the administration finally reverted, at least tentatively, to a strategy of adjustment. A close look at the administration's experience in a number of key policy areas reinforces the argument that declining American power and growing interdependence ruled out a successful strategy of resistance and provided powerful and continuing international incentives for policy adjustment.[4]

The Reagan administration believed that renewed American military strength and more assertive policies would allow it to gird existing alliances against the Soviet Union and states friendly to it as well as to forge new ones. This view assumed that local and regional complexities could be subordinated to the logic of global containment and that the states involved would welcome more forceful American leadership. Yet actions that the administration viewed as vigorous leadership were often seen by U.S. allies as unwelcome attempts to dictate behavior and limit their own autonomy. Moreover, other states often considered the globalist perspective of the U.S. insensitive to regional realities.

The U.S. experienced failure in the Middle East, for instance, when it tried to join Israel and the conservative Arab states in an anti-Soviet alliance. Even in Central America, where the Reagan administration sought to hold together an anti-Nicaraguan alliance among the handful of states in the region, the U.S. found it difficult to ensure the full cooperation of its generally conservative and highly dependent allies. Each of the states in the region opposed outright U.S. military intervention, several were skeptical about the U.S. supported anti-Sandinista Contras, and all remained involved in independent diplomatic efforts to forge a solution to the region's conflicts through negotiations among Central and Latin American countries. Although the original Contadora peace talks failed, in no small part due to obstructionism from Washington, the Arias Plan, sponsored by Costa Rica's president, bore fruit in the form of an agreement among the countries of Central America, including Nicaragua, despite open skepticism and displeasure on the part of the Reagan administration.

Among America's closest allies in Western Europe, Reagan's military buildup and tough anti-Soviet stance led to serious differences.[5] The administration's bold talk about winning a nuclear war with the Soviets, its early antipathy toward arms control, and its eagerness to place new intermediate nuclear weapons in Western Europe alarmed rather than reassured large segments of European opinion. Reagan's Cold War rhetoric and policies were in no small part responsible for the emergence of a massive peace movement, much of whose wrath was directed against the United States. The Soviet Union, with some success, took advantage of this situation by launching a peace offensive designed to appeal to West Europeans by speaking to them with a voice of reason at a time when the U.S. seemed bent on confrontation.

These sorts of tensions extended to intergovernmental relations among the allies as well when the Reagan administration attempted to nix allied cooperation with a gas pipeline project designed to funnel Soviet natural gas to Western Europe. The U.S. was ultimately forced to soften its objections when Western European governments balked at scrapping the project.

The Reagan administration also believed that heightened U.S. military strength was the key to restoring American influence in the world. It therefore sought and obtained congressional approval for large increases in defense spending. Between 1981 and 1985, the defense budget increased 32 percent in real dollars. Among the priorities of the administration were a substantial commitment to strategic modernization, including development and deployment of the MX missile, the Trident D-5 missile, and the B-1 Bomber; increased funding for forces designed for intervention in the Third World; the construction of a six-hundred-ship Navy along with a reorientation of naval doctrine toward offensive operations; and, beginning in 1982, development of the Strategic Defense Initiative designed to shield American missile sites and population centers against incoming Soviet ballistic missiles. Along with this military buildup came substantial increases in U.S. foreign aid, especially security assistance, during Reagan's first term.

Although this ambitious defense program undoubtedly increased the gross military resources available to the U.S., the payoff on this enormous investment in terms of enhanced U.S. power and influence proved doubtful while the economic costs were high. The administration assumed, for instance, that renewed economic growth would allow these expensive programs to be funded without substantially diverting resources from the civilian economy. Yet among the immediate consequences of the Reagan defense program was a worsening of the tradeoff between protection, consumption, and investment, and a broadening in the gap between U.S. resources and commitments. The shares of national income going to defense and consumption both grew during the Reagan years at the expense of savings and investment. Combined with the large tax cuts of 1982, rising defense spending contributed to enormous budget deficits. From levels of 2 percent of GDP in the seventies, federal budget deficits rose to 4.5 percent of GDP in the mid-eighties. In 1987, deficit financing alone absorbed two-thirds of net private savings.[6] A tight monetary policy and high real interest rates, designed to attract the foreign funds needed to finance these large deficits, led to an overvalued dollar and a growing trade gap.[7] The U.S. net savings rate declined from close to 8 percent in 1979 to only 2 percent in 1987.[8]

Moreover, the Reagan administration's allocation of defense funds as well as its relative indifference toward the issue of allied burden-sharing both reflected priorities that might be considered inappropriate from the standpoint of a declining hegemon. The Carter administration sought to concentrate scarce resources on the defense of core U.S. interests in Western Europe. To strengthen European defenses without rapid increases in overall spending, the administration shifted resources from strategic and Third World intervention forces toward NATO. To ensure that increases in NATO funding would not come solely at U.S. expense, Carter obtained commitments from West European allies for matching increases in spending.

The Reagan administration, by contrast, shifted U.S. spending priorities away from a geographical focus on Western Europe, where vital U.S. interests were engaged, and toward the Third World, where U.S. interests were often marginal. Spending on Third World intervention forces, as well as strategic nuclear systems, grew much more rapidly than funding for NATO forces. In addition, spending on such basics as readiness, operations, and maintenance, each priorities during the Carter administration, took a back seat to the funding of expensive new weapons systems under Reagan.[9]

This shift in emphasis away from NATO was unaccompanied by larger contributions on the part of U.S. allies in Western Europe, whose defense budgets grew only modestly. Ironically, therefore, while the large military spending increases of the Reagan years significantly increased the gap between the relative defense burden borne by the U.S. as compared with its principal economic competitors, they only marginally improved the East-West military balance in the critical European theater.[10]

Other difficulties surrounding the Reagan administration's defense program stemmed from its doctrinal underpinnings. The two most important departures in U.S. military strategy and policy during the Reagan era were the administration's embrace of strategic defense and the development of a new maritime strategy. Both initiatives suffered from similar flaws. Each was based upon unrealistic strategic and technical assumptions. And each contemplated enormous and continuing budgetary expenditures at a time of fiscal scarcity.

The initial planning for Reagan's Strategic Defense Initiative, reflected a faith that the combination of enhanced American willpower and high technology could allow the U.S. to free itself from the ever-present threat of nuclear annihilation. This ambitious goal quickly drew scathing criticisms from independent defense and scientific experts who argued that even the most sophisticated strategic defense system would almost certainly fall far short of providing a perfect shield against nuclear attack and that an imperfect defense could even prove strategically destabilizing.[11] Over the ensuing years, the goals of SDI were repeatedly reformulated and scaled back while the Congress consistently resisted full scale funding. Aside from a few continuing spinoffs, SDI was eventually abandoned by the Congress in the early nineties.

Like SDI, the Reagan administration's new maritime strategy was based upon optimistic assumptions about the practical utility of a more assertive defense posture and vastly augmented military hardware.[12] Previously, the U.S. Navy's principal assignment in a conventional European war was limited to "defensive sea control" in the North Atlantic, which involved ferrying troops and supplies to the European theater. Under Reagan, Naval Secretary John Lehman championed a new offensive role for the Navy focused around three principal tasks: bottling up Soviet attack submarines in their home ports before they could threaten allied shipping, "horizontal expansion" of the war through attacks on Soviet proxy states in the Third World as well as amphibious landings on the Soviet mainland, and the destruction of the Soviet ballistic missile submarine fleet. To facilitate this new offensive orientation, the Reagan defense program called for an expansion of the U.S. Naval fleet from 460 ships in 1977 to 600 ships by 1989. The Navy's ship-building budget, consequently, grew from $7.5 billion in 1979 to $12.1 billion in 1985 with the bulk of new funding going toward the construction of new aircraft carrier groups.[13]

Critics raised serious questions about the expense, feasibility, and wisdom of this new maritime strategy. Plans to contain the Soviet fleet contemplated, among other things, a headlong attack on the massive Soviet naval complexes located on the Kola Peninsula. In attempting such a bold strike, U.S. fleet would find itself under heavy assault by Soviet air, sea, and ground-based defenses long before it sailed within striking range of its targets.[14] Moreover, planned amphibious landings on the Soviet mainland could not hope to gain the element of surprise, would require unattainable local air and sea superiority, and could not succeed without forces far larger than those the Navy contemplated devoting to the task. Critics also argued that similar attacks planned against Soviet allies in the Third World would only use up scarce resources without materially affecting the main battle raging in Central Europe. Finally, plans to destroy the Soviet ballistic missile submarine force raised the risk that a conventional war might quickly escalate to a nuclear one. Given the potential vulnerability of Soviet land-based missiles to a combination of highly accurate U.S. missiles and strategic defenses, it was argued that the Soviets would likely have viewed conventional attacks on their missile bearing submarines as a prelude to an American first strike. Facing the neutralization of their retaliatory nuclear capabilities, the Soviets could only have been tempted to launch a preemptive strike of their own. The combination of such criticisms, a declining perception of Soviet threat in the late eighties, and budgetary considerations forced a scaling back of the Reagan administration's initial plans for a new maritime strategy and a six-hundred-ship fleet.

Besides SDI and the development of a new naval strategy against the Soviet Union, the other major component of the Reagan administration defense plans involved the more active use of U.S. military might in the Third World. The administration came to office with the firm belief that the U.S. must overcome the "Vietnam Syndrome," or, in other words, a reluctance to commit U.S. forces abroad. Yet the experience of the Reagan years provided only uncertain confirmation for its initially optimistic views on the utility of military force.

The administration itself found reasons, for instance, to reject the use of force in situations of great risk or uncertainty. In 1981, the U.S. found itself powerless to prevent the Polish generals from crushing Solidarity, the independent trade union movement in Poland. And the administration's tough talk about terrorism and hostage taking in the Middle East was seldom matched by actions.[15] Finally, as we suggested above, opposition in Latin America, as well as at home, foreclosed the use of U.S. troops against

Nicaragua despite mounting evidence that the Contras lacked sufficient military and political strength to achieve the administration's ultimate goal of dislodging the Sandinistas from power through force.[16] Later, the Bush administration likewise dismissed the utility of U.S. military force as a response to the complexities of the civil war that engulfed the former Yugoslavia.

The record on the actual use of force was mixed. The invasion of Grenada, a tiny country defended by a handful of Cuban troops, succeeded in its objectives despite later evidence that the operation was poorly run. Yet the disastrous deployment of U.S. troops to Lebanon led to failure; culminating in a car bomb attack that resulted in the death of 241 U.S. marines and a thinly disguised American retreat.

Other instances where the administration turned to the use of force were less clear-cut. The huge U.S. naval buildup in the Persian Gulf was designed to protect shipping through the Gulf. Initially, the U.S. Navy experienced considerable frustration in coping with Iranian mining operations and attacks by small speedboats. Moreover, tragedy struck when a U.S. Navy destroyer mistakenly shot down a civilian Iranian airbus. On the other hand, Iranian attacks on Gulf shipping eventually waned and Iran accepted a ceasefire in its war with Iraq, although the contribution of U.S. actions to these decisions is difficult to judge.

The U.S. bombing raid on Tripoli failed in one of its apparent, though unstated, objectives: to kill Libyan leader Muammar Khadafy. Although Libya's enthusiasm for the sponsorship of international terrorism appeared to wane for a time, fears of renewed terrorism rose once again in late 1988 when suspicions grew that Libya was constructing a chemical weapons plant.[17] Overall, the Reagan administration found rather few opportunities for the actual use of force and its effectiveness in practice varied greatly.

If the Reagan administration's sometimes militant rhetoric was belied by its relatively cautious behavior with respect to the use of force, the Bush administration's rhetorical pragmatism and prudence masked a more activist approach to the employment of American military might. The invasion of Panama and the offensive against Iraqi forces in Kuwait were each far more ambitious than any American military endeavors since the Vietnam War.

The Panama invasion succeeded in toppling Panamanian leader Manuel Noriega and bringing him to trial in the U.S. on charges of narcotics trafficking. Yet the larger objectives of the Panamanian operation have proven more elusive. According to many accounts, for instance, Noriega's removal had little apparent effect on the flow of drugs and drug money through Panama into the United States.

The Persian Gulf War was among the most lopsided in history. A largely American force easily reversed the Iraqi invasion and occupation of Kuwait after a brief but bloody ground campaign while the use of air power rained destruction on strategic targets throughout Iraq. Yet even this ferocious and largely successful application of U.S. military might provided lessons about the limits of American power. That the use of force was necessary at all resulted from the failure of a five month campaign of coercive diplomacy. A stringent set of economic sanctions, an orchestrated crescendo of diplomatic pressures, and the looming threat of force proved insufficient, even in combination, to compel Saddam Hussein to pull back his forces short of military defeat.[18] After the war, Hussein survived politically despite his country's thrashing and managed to maintain a grasp on power through the remaining two years of Bush's term in the face of vigorous American efforts to encourage his removal.

It is also significant to note that America's victory in the Gulf War was not a unilateral one. Success depended heavily upon the cooperation of other states, whether in the form of votes in the United Nations Security Council, participation in the economic blockade, the contribution of troops and diplomatic support, the willingness of Saudi Arabia to allow the use of its territory and air bases, or the financial pledges from allied states that largely underwrote the war's expenses. That the United States proved capable of organizing such a broad coalition of forces is only partly a testament to continuing American influence. Iraq's bid for hegemony over the world's most critical oil-bearing region invested this conflict with unique stakes. This, as much as U.S. leadership per se, explains the unified response of the international community.

Where the use of American military forces was deemed too risky or expensive, the Reagan administration often turned to proxy forces.[19] The Reagan Doctrine called for the U.S. to go beyond containing communism and Soviet power to actually rolling back Soviet gains in Third World states where recently installed pro-Soviet governments held somewhat tenuously to power against internal foes. Among the countries targeted by the administration were Nicaragua, Angola, Afghanistan, and Cambodia.

In some respects, the Reagan Doctrine worked. The provision of aid to rebel groups did not give way to more intrusive and costly forms of U.S. involvement as some critics feared. The stubbornness of U.S.-supported resistance groups imposed considerable costs on the Soviet Union and its clients. The Soviet-supported government of Afghanistan was finally toppled from power by Islamic rebel groups two years after the Soviet Union removed its troops from that country. Vietnam has withdrawn its troops from Cambodia and the Vietnamese-installed government left behind has cooperated with a United Nations-sponsored peace process. Cuban troops exited Angola after the left wing government there reached an agreement with South Africa providing that South Africa withdraw support for the rebel group, UNITA. Subsequent peace talks brokered by the United States led to a cease-fire and a temporary end to the civil war in that strife-torn country. The Sandinista government in Nicaragua first took steps to assuage the security concerns of its neighbors before holding elections that led to the victory of a coalition of opposition parties.

Yet a closer look at each case reveals important limitations on the U.S. ability to control events. Moreover, it is not apparent that the Reagan Doctrine has served U.S. interests better than alternative strategies might have. In none of these cases were U.S. objectives fully met. Only in Afghanistan did U.S.-supported rebel groups succeed in gaining power through military means. Yet various Muslim clans quickly fell into fighting among themselves after ousting the previous government. Despite past American aid, none of these factions is clearly pro-Western. Indeed, the potential consolidation of another fundamentalist Islamic state in this region may well complicate the task of gaining Western influence among the largely Muslim republics along the Southern tier of the former Soviet Union, an area also eagerly being courted by the Iranian government.

The electoral victory of opposition leader Violetta Chammaro in Nicaragua did not end Sandinista influence or foreclose the possibility of a future return to power by the Sandinistas. The Chammaro government remains weak and divided and has often been forced into concessions to the Sandinistas, who retain considerable clout over the army, the police, the bureaucracy, and the unions.

At the close of the Bush administration, the MPLA remained in power in Angola. The United Nations–sponsored peace settlement with UNITA had, however, unraveled. After losing national elections in late 1992, UNITA and its leader Jonas Savimbi once again took up arms in a renewed attempt to gain power by force. The nation braced for another round in a seemingly unending civil war. Ironically, the new Clinton administration blamed UNITA, America's longtime ally, for the renewed warfare and was rumored to be considering a restoration of diplomatic relations with Angola's MPLA-led government. Similarly, in Cambodia, the Khymer Rouge, formerly the recipient of indirect U.S. aid, served as the principal obstacle to implementation of a United Nations-sponsored peace settlement.

The Reagan Doctrine succeeded in imposing costs upon both the Soviet Union and its client states and, in some cases, securing desired political concessions. It proved less successful in toppling Third World radical regimes and ensuring their replacement with pro-Western governments. Indeed, one unintended effect of the Reagan Doctrine was to cement, at least for a time, alliances between the USSR and radical Third World states that may have otherwise been difficult to maintain. Throughout the eighties, Nicaragua, Angola, and even Vietnam each repeatedly provided indications that they would prefer better political relations with the U.S. and other Western powers, aid and economic ties to the West, and less dependence on the Soviet Union. The Reagan Doctrine foreclosed the possibility of exploiting the pragmatic interests such states held in greater independence and economic development by confronting them with only sticks rather than carrots. The limited successes of the Reagan Doctrine must therefore be measured against the possibilities that an alternative set of policies may have produced results at least as acceptable in terms of U.S. interests at lower costs.[20] In addition, an alternative course might have averted, or at least limited, the enormous havoc, destruction, and loss of life visited upon those countries that found themselves targets of the Reagan Doctrine.

The administration's efforts to support conservative, pro-American dictators in the Third World were scarcely more successful. During the Reagan years, the United States poured an estimated $3 billion in military and economic aid into the tiny country of El Salvador in an effort to help a military dominated government fend off a violent, left wing insurgency. U.S. aid, however, allowed the government in San Salvador to achieve no better than a costly stalemate that ultimately ended in a compromise peace settlement embodying significant concessions to the rebels.

In at least two other cases, fast moving events forced the Reagan administration to modify its initially staunch support for right wing dictators and to accommodate change in the Third World. In the Philippines, popular opposition forced Ferdinand Marcos from office to be replaced by a leader of the democratic opposition.[21] "Baby Doc" Duvalier met a similar fate in Haiti. In both of these cases, which were largely viewed as successes for the president, the administration responded by improvising a strategy of adjustment after circumstances undermined its initial strategy of resistance.

This became an increasingly common pattern during the last years of Reagan's term. When faced with the failure of policies that neglected to take into account ongoing international change and the constraints imposed on U.S. freedom by declining power, the administration modified some of its original goals and methods.

In its last years, for instance, the administration showed a renewed interest in arms control, leading to an INF treaty, and superpower summitry. Budgetary pressures slowed the growth of defense spending. And the administration rediscovered the art of diplomacy with respect to regional conflicts such as those in the Middle East and Southern Africa.

The unilateralist foreign economic policies of the first Reagan term also gave way under growing pressures for the United States to address international economic problems in a cooperative manner. After years of neglect, the administration finally crafted a modestly interventionist approach to the Third World debt crisis beginning in 1985. The administration's early economic policies produced a rising dollar and a growing trade deficit. The protectionist pressures these circumstances produced at home finally compelled Reagan officials to engage in a coordinated effort with other major economic partners to drive down the dollar in hopes of narrowing the trade gap. Reagan also initiated new GATT trade talks in his second term, designed to bring down global trade barriers in services and agriculture.

Nevertheless, the administration's transition from a strategy of resistance to adjustment remained far from complete. Negotiations with the Soviet Union on strategic arms reduction remained stalled over the Reagan administration's refusal to bargain away SDI. Defense spending, while no longer rising, remained at levels far exceeding those of the seventies. And some elements of the Reagan Doctrine remained in place. Most importantly, the administration neither repudiated its previous policies nor articulated a new vision of America's role in the world.

The primary factors driving the Reagan administration's modification of its original strategy of resistance were external in nature. As our review of Reagan's initial policies has demonstrated, international constraints on U.S. power and its ability to control events abroad were much tighter than the administration originally believed. The partial and limited adjustments in the administration's international strategy represented grudging accommodations to reality.

Domestic constraints, although they tightened over time, were much looser than international ones and had less to do with changes in policy. During Reagan's first term Congress gave the president much of what he asked for in the way of increased defense spending, higher military aid, growing arms sales, increased funding for the CIA and covert operations, tighter restrictions on technology transfer to the Soviet Union, and funding support for implementation of the Reagan Doctrine. Reagan faced less severe interest group opposition than had Carter. Groups organizing in support of the nuclear freeze or in opposition to the administration's policies in Central America operated with some degree of success. Overall, however, the groups opposing Reagan's policies possessed only modest cohesion, resources, and influence.

Despite what may be considered a lackluster record of achievement in foreign affairs, Ronald Reagan built a positive popular image of strength and resoluteness in sharp contrast to the negative image of weakness and vacillation that the public came to associate with Carter.[22] Especially during Reagan's first term, the public largely supported a get tough policy toward the Soviet Union and agreed with key tenets of Reagan's world view. A survey taken in March of 1981 revealed that 81 percent of the public agreed that "[a]ll the tough talk to the Russians will not be effective unless we back it up with a stronger military" while 73 percent believed that "[b]y sending military aid to countries threatened by communism and being tough with the Russians, Reagan will rebuild respect for the U.S. in the Kremlin." In May of 1984, another survey showed that 56 percent of the public agreed that "The Soviet Union is like Hitler's Germany—an evil empire trying to rule the world," a characterization often endorsed by Reagan himself.[23] Although foreign policy issues were not decisive in the 1984 campaign, Reagan's appeal to American patriotism and nationalism and his rhetoric of restoration probably contributed to the size of his landslide re-election victory over Walter Mondale.

Domestic opposition to Reagan's policies centered on issues where the actual or potential effects of those policies threatened to expose the public to heightened risks or costs. Reagan's policies toward Central America created fears of a costly, Vietnam-style American military intervention. Loose talk by administration officials about the winnability of nuclear war brought charges of recklessness and contributed to the growth of the nuclear freeze movement. Public support for increased defense spending, initially high, declined as worries about U.S. inferiority were calmed by the administration's rapid military buildup and as growing budget deficits sharpened perceived trade-offs between defense and domestic programs.[24]

Domestic support for Reagan's policies eroded during Reagan's second term, particularly from 1986 onward. Congress more regularly challenged the president on defense spending, arms control, and Central America. The Iran-Contra scandal damaged Reagan's image of competence. And support for Cold War policies declined in response to news of internal and external reforms taking place in the Soviet Union. Nevertheless, domestic resistance to Reagan's foreign policies never reached the level of breadth or intensity as that faced by Jimmy Carter during his presidency.

A Time of Transition: The Bush Experience

Although too little time has passed for rendering firm judgments, the Bush presidency may well come to be regarded as a transitional period in U.S. foreign policy. Preceded by an era of failed resistance to international change, the Bush years could be followed, if initial indications are correct, by a period of vigorous adjustment. Although the events that made this transition possible (i.e., the collapse of communism and the end of the Cold War) occurred on George Bush's watch, his administration responded to these revolutionary developments with an approach that one observer has aptly labeled "competent drift."[25] The Bush administration choose to react to events rather than to shape them. The virtue of Bush's prudent pragmatism was that the U.S. avoided major missteps. Indeed, the Bush team brought an admirable degree of professionalism to the day-to-day management of U.S. foreign policy and guided the nation safely through a turbulent era. Yet Bush's cautious incremental approach failed to provide strategic direction for U.S. foreign policy in the post-Cold War period and left unattended the serious domestic weaknesses that plagued the U.S. position both at home and abroad.

In many ways, the Bush years brought the United States a measure of respite from its international burdens. After some initial hesitation, the Bush administration threw its support behind Mikhail Gorbachev and his efforts to bring reform to the Soviet Union. Bringing the Cold War to an effective close, the United States entered into a virtual partnership with Soviet and, later, Russian leaders after the failed coup organized by Soviet hardliners. Indeed, the United States helped organize a multilateral program of aid to Russia and the other successor states of the disbanded Soviet Union. During this period, the Bush administration negotiated two far-reaching strategic arms control agreements with Soviet and Russian leaders that provided for deep cuts in the nuclear arsenals of both sides.

The collapse of communism in Eastern Europe, the dissolution of the Warsaw Pact, the withdrawal of Soviet troops from Eastern Europe, and the reunification of Germany all paved the way for a substantial reduction in the number of U.S. troops stationed in Central Europe. Overall defense spending underwent a modest decline during the Bush years. A combination of increased U.S. diplomatic flexibility, Soviet retrenchment, and changing local circumstances allowed the U.S. to reduce its engagement in many Third World regional conflicts, including those in Nicaragua, El Salvador, Angola, Afghanistan, and Cambodia.

Yet the Bush administration's movement to restrain U.S. commitments abroad was not universal. The U.S. committed forces to two major military engagements in Panama and Kuwait. Bush dispatched over 20,000 U.S. troops to restore order and deliver food aid to famine stricken Somalia. Prior to the Persian Gulf War, Bush's vague rhetoric about the need to secure a "new world order" raised the prospect of an open-ended U.S. commitment to global orderkeeping. In other cases, the movement toward adjustment was exceedingly cautious despite the revolutionary changes taking place in the international environment. The Bush administration adopted a slow and gradual approach to cutting the defense budget and made plans to maintain over 100,000 U.S. troops in Central Europe despite the receding Soviet threat. The administration also clung to NATO, discouraging the Europeans from exploring alternative arrangements for providing European security. In general, the administration failed to spell out a new vision of U.S. interests or the requirements for securing them in the post-Cold War world.

Most significantly, the Bush administration did little to address the domestic sources of U.S. economic decline. The federal budget deficit soared to record levels, economic growth slowed to a standstill, and, after falling briefly due largely to the recession at home, the U.S. trade deficit once again swelled during Bush's last year in office. On the whole, Bush rejected activist government intervention to increase savings and investment, enhance the nation's technological dynamism, or address growing social problems. This inattention to the country's domestic ills ultimately cost George Bush a second term in office.

Beyond the Cycle of Instability in U.S. Foreign Policy? The Clinton Era

For the past two decades, the U.S. has postponed, at great cost, the foreign and domestic policy adjustments necessary to compensate for hegemonic decline and strategic overextension. Jimmy Carter's efforts to carry out a strategy of adjustment were frustrated by domestic obstacles. Ronald Reagan, eschewing the need for adjustment, attempted a strategy of resistance, only to find that the U.S. lacked the power to sustain such ambitions and that the attempt to do so worsened the gap between resources and commitments. George Bush choose a middle path, curbing the excesses of the Reagan era while nevertheless rejecting the sort of bold reforms needed to provide strategic direction in the post-Cold War world or to tackle growing domestic weaknesses.

Bill Clinton's election as president in 1992 offered the possibility that this structural cycle of strategic indecision might finally be brought to a close. In contrast to Ronald Reagan and, to a lesser extent, George Bush, Clinton demonstrated an awareness of the sources and nature of America's decline and strategic overextension. His campaign message and early moves in office suggested a commitment to reform and adjustment. Unlike Jimmy Carter, Clinton faces fewer domestic obstacles to foreign policy adjustment. Not only has the end of the Cold War, the collapse of communism, and the disintegration of the Soviet Union eased the international demands on U.S. resources, but these events have also provided the sort of external shock needed to weaken the constellation of interest groups and ideological forces that have to date stood in the way of policy adjustment.

Yet if the challenges facing Bill Clinton are in some ways more manageable than those that confronted Jimmy Carter, they remain formidable in other respects. By postponing adjustment, previous presidents have provided Clinton with a dwindling inheritance. America's relative economic decline has continued apace during the intervening years, accelerated by foreign and domestic policies that have created yawning budget and trade deficits. Compared with the sixties and seventies, America's rates of savings and investment have fallen. Productivity growth has slowed and U.S. industry has lost technological leadership in many areas. America's educational system has faltered, social ills have worsened, and popular faith in government has declined. The U.S. faces growing competition from Japan, the newly industrializing countries of East Asia, and an increasingly unified European Community.[26]

A successful strategy of adjustment for the nineties must cope with these new realities. No longer, as during the Carter era, can adjustment focus exclusively on restraining commitments abroad or searching for less costly ways of meeting them. While such steps remain necessary, they are no longer sufficient. Curtailing commitments cannot serve alone to close the gap between resources and commitments if the country's resources are themselves declining as well. A contemporary strategy of adjustment must thus seek ways of enhancing resource growth by stimulating economic competitiveness. A healthy economy is a prerequisite for both domestic well-being as well as international power. Strategic adjustment must be two-pronged, encompassing both domestic and foreign policy reforms.

A detailed discussion of the domestic and foreign policy adjustments that might be necessary to slow U.S. decline and close the gap between resources and commitments is beyond the scope of this study.[27] Nevertheless, some comments on the general outlines of such an adjustment strategy are appropriate.

Although the circumstances of the post-Cold War period clearly differ significantly from those of the late seventies, there is much that the Clinton administration could learn from a close examination of the Carter administration's early foreign policy approach. The principles underlying Carter's initial strategy of adjustment continue to serve as useful prescriptive guidelines for contemporary U.S. foreign policy. Foremost among these are the following:

PREVENTIVE DIPLOMACY: Where important U.S. interests are engaged, the U.S. should respond quickly to emerging regional and domestic conflicts before these disturbances escalate to crisis proportions. Early diplomatic intervention can obviate the need for more costly forms of involvement later on.

MULTILATERALISM: In many circumstances, the U.S. no longer has the power or resources to dictate international outcomes through unilateral action. Acting in concert with like-minded states, however, the U.S. can still help to craft the international agenda and organize collective responses to international problems in a constructive manner. Multilateralism requires that the U.S. give greater weight to the sometimes differing interests and preferences of potential partners. While this may, in some instances, restrict U.S. options, multilateralism enhances the international legitimacy of the nation's diplomatic efforts and averts the costs and inefficiencies that result when the U.S. and its allies work at cross-purposes. Whenever possible, multilateralism should be implemented through strengthened international or regional institutions.

BURDEN-SHARING: In a post-hegemonic world, the U.S. must organize regularized methods for distributing the burdens and costs of international leadership rather than continue to carry them alone. This principle applies to military intervention, peace-keeping activities, foreign assistance, environmental safeguards, and support for international institutions. Burden-sharing need not imply proportionality in each area of endeavor. Rather, various nations may specialize in different tasks according to their resources, interests and areas of comparative advantage.

DISTINGUISH BETWEEN VITAL AND PERIPHERAL INTERESTS: During the Cold War, fears of bandwagoning, falling dominoes, and harm to U.S. credibility led American policy makers to invest distant regions with strategic significance, even where U.S. interests were marginal. If this impulse was exaggerated in the past, it possesses even less justification in the post-Cold War period. A narrower definition of vital U.S. interests as well as a more skeptical attitude toward the utility of military force are both in order. In particular, U.S. stakes in the Third World are often overstated by many observers.[28]

CASE-BY-CASE: In an era of rapid international change and diminished resources, the U.S. must avoid sweeping foreign policy doctrines that commit the country to grand global objectives. A flexible, case-by-case approach that carefully measures new and existing commitments against U.S. interests and resources is more appropriate to contemporary circumstances. While there may be many occasions when the U.S. can and should promote democracy abroad, for instance, it makes little sense to lock the U.S. into a pattern of costly and, very often, futile intervention for such purposes by promulgating a universal doctrinal commitment to such an objective. Similarly, the selective use of U.S. influence to promote order and discourage aggression in various regions should not give way to crusading visions of a U.S.-sponsored "new world order."

Clinton's first months in office provided hope that his administration might heed many of these lessons. Indeed, a number of Clinton's top foreign policy appointees, including Secretary of State Warren Christopher and National Security Adviser Anthony Lake, served in important posts during under the Carter administration.[29]

Indications of Clinton's initial commitment to a strategy of adjustment were many. During his presidential campaign, Clinton often criticized the Bush administration for its failure to undertake the domestic reforms needed to keep America strong at home and abroad. Clinton promised to place international economic competitiveness at the top of his foreign and domestic agendas. Clinton spoke of the need to increase American savings and investment rates, both public and private. Clinton's recipe for spurring economic competitiveness included deficit reduction, lower interest rates, public-private partnerships to promote technological innovation, and a more active trade policy. Clinton's longer-term plans included new initiatives in the areas of health, education, crime, and welfare in an effort to attack the social ills that weaken the United States from within.

These interventionist programs would be partly financed by way of the peace dividend the United States could be expected to enjoy with the end of the Cold War. Clinton promised to accelerate cuts in military spending. Like Carter, physical retrenchment would be accompanied by an activist diplomacy. Clinton administration officials promised to aggressively pursue preventive diplomacy as a means of heading off potential conflicts abroad. Also consistent with a strategy of adjustment were Clinton's promises to embrace multilateralism, greater allied burden-sharing, and a strengthened set of global and regional security institutions (e.g., the United Nations).[30]

Like Jimmy Carter during his term of office, however, Clinton has found it difficult to adhere consistently to his initial strategy of adjustment. This is evident, for instance, with respect to military spending.[31] While defense spending declined by one-third between 1985 and 1994, as measured in inflation-adjusted dollars, U.S. military spending in 1994 remained 10 percent higher in real terms than the 1975 defense budget.[32] Indeed, the United States continues to spend almost as much on its military forces as the rest of the world combined. Most of the additional savings over the Bush administration's final five-year defense budget plan rest upon hopeful projections of lowered inflation and ill-defined pay and management reductions or efficiencies. Base closings have in some cases been circumvented through sleight of hand. The Pentagon has threatened to axe several major weapons systems favored by the Congress unless additional funding is forthcoming, a tactic that has worked in the past.

Moreover, the doctrinal underpinnings of the Clinton administration's avowed defense strategy are in conflict with existing budget projections. The Defense Department's current goal is to retain the ability to successfully fight two major Desert Storm-size wars simultaneously at opposite ends of the globe without help from U.S. allies. Meeting this demanding but improbable requirement would necessitate spending between $20 and $150 billion beyond planned funding levels between 1994 and the end of the century.[33] This gap between doctrine and budgetary projections is already being cited by the Pentagon and influential members of Congress as a rationale for increasing planned military spending in the years ahead.

The Clinton administration's plans for bringing about conversion of military industries to civilian purposes are proceeding slowly. Indeed, the administration has often chosen instead to keep weapons plants open by aggressively pursuing U.S. arms sales abroad. Such sales more than doubled between Bush's last year in office and Clinton's first year.[34] This continued proliferation of advanced weaponry only increases the potential costs of U.S. military engagement overseas if these weapons are one day used against American forces, as has indeed occurred in the past.

Similarly, the Clinton administration has had an uneven record in restraining U.S. commitments abroad. Having inherited a humanitarian relief operation from the Bush administration, Clinton expanded the aims of U.S. military involvement in Somalia to include a large nation-building role. This futile effort led to bloodshed for American troops, failed to curb conflict among Somalia's warring factions, and ended in a thinly veiled retreat. By contrast, Clinton wisely chose to avoid the insertion of U.S. ground troops in the midst of the violent civil war among Muslims, Croats, and Serbs in the former Yugoslavia. Yet Clinton was also unable to convince Western European states or Russia to support a lifting of arms embargo on the Muslims so as to allow their forces to fight on equal terms with the aggressive and superior Serb army. The U.S. military occupation of Haiti succeeded in restoring democratically elected Jean-Bertrand Aristide to power with little bloodshed. Yet much of Haiti's traditional power structure remained intact and the obstacles to democratization and economic revival in such an impoverished and class-divided society remain formidable.[35]

A central component of Clinton's foreign policy agenda has been the commitment of U.S. resources toward the "enlargement" of the community of democratic nations. While this is a laudable goal, Clinton's apparent willingness to use military coercion to implant democracy abroad, as in Haiti, could lead to a costly and open-ended pattern of intervention in the complex domestic politics of societies where the prospects of lasting democratization are poor.

Clinton's "Partnership for Peace" sought to stake out a middle ground between leaving the states of Eastern Europe to fend for their own security and allowing such countries immediate entry into NATO. The Partnership for Peace nevertheless represents a gradual expansion of U.S. commitments in a dangerous and unstable part of the world. While ties between NATO and the countries of Eastern European countries are presently limited, Clinton has held out the promise of eventual membership in the future. All in all, the Clinton administration has taken few steps to substantially narrow U.S. security commitments abroad, despite the end of the Cold War, and has actually broadened them in some areas.

The administration has been somewhat more steadfast in its commitment to preventive diplomacy. The U.S. helped broker an agreement between Russia and the Ukraine that called upon the Ukraine to give up the nuclear arsenal it inherited from the former Soviet Union. Under Clinton's watch, progress has been made toward peace in the Middle East and Northern Ireland, though the administration played a relatively minor supporting role in each case. After months of escalating tensions, the Clinton administration managed to strike an acceptable deal with North Korea that would halt that country's drive toward acquiring nuclear weapons. Finally, last minute negotiations succeeded in persuading Haitian military leaders to step aside and averted armed resistance to U.S. occupying forces.[36]

Increasingly over time, however, Clinton has retreated from his early commitment to multilateralism. As in the case of Haiti, the U.S. has curtailed consultation with other states and the use of international institutions in favor of a largely unilateral approach. While sometimes necessary, this growing reliance upon unilateralism does little to build the institutional basis for a functioning system of collective security that might provide an effective departure from the power struggles that have dominated international politics in the past.

The task of adjustment appears more daunting in light of the results of the 1994 congressional elections. New Republican majorities in both the House and the Senate have once again led to divided government. With different parties in control of the executive and legislative branches, the prospects for policy stalemate and paralysis can only rise. While the Republican party appears to favor some forms of international retrenchment, the philosophy of its leadership veers more toward unilateralism than adjustment. While attacking foreign aid and U.S. involvement with the United Nations, Republicans have also called for increased defense spending, a more confrontational approach to relations with Russia, and the rapid expansion of NATO to include Eastern Europe.

Clinton's success in pursuing his domestic agenda for strengthening the United States has been similarly inconsistent. Clinton's successful deficit reduction package helped to spur lower interest rates and contributed to economic recovery. Largely eliminated from Clinton's budget bill, however, were provisions for taxing energy more heavily and boosting public investment on infrastructure, technology, and resources, both measures that might have strengthened the basis for long-term economic growth and adjustment. Congress failed to pass Clinton's ambitious health care package, which was designed to correct the inefficiencies and inequities that plague a sector accounting for one-seventh of the U.S. economy. Less tangibly, survey data reveal that Clinton has made little progress toward restoring a greater sense of community and common purpose to American society or in reviving American's confidence and faith in government. Time and time again, Clinton's plans for adjustment and reform in both domestic and foreign policy have been frustrated by the resistance of vested interests and more diffuse ideological rigidity.

Conclusion

While the years since the end of the Cold War have witnessed modest progress in narrowing the gap between U.S. resources and commitments, the tasks of reforming America's institutions at home and adjusting to the role of a normal power in a multipolar world abroad largely remain to be accomplished. Despite widespread dissatisfaction with the status quo, there exists no consensus about the appropriate cure, and divisions remain over how the burdens should be distributed. Ideological, partisan, regional, class, sectoral, and ethnic cleavages complicate the task of building a consensus for change, or even, less ambitiously, a working majority. Moreover, the weakness and permeability of the American state provides ample opportunities for vested interests to form effective blocking coalitions.

Perhaps the most promising means for overcoming these obstacles and selling reform is to spread the costs of adjustment widely and fairly while creating mechanisms designed to encourage the winners from change to compensate the losers through side payments. Such a strategy can help to ease the intensity of opposition to change and divide obstructionist coalitions. Above all, as the Carter experience suggests, the Clinton administration must pay close attention to the domestic viability of its strategy for domestic and foreign adjustment.

CHAPTER SEVEN

A Structural Approach to Foreign Policy Analysis

SOCIETIES, LIKE INDIVIDUALS, succeed only to the degree that they adapt to changes in their environment. This common sense maxim applies with special force in today's world. The pace of international change has accelerated in recent years. The familiar features of the half-century following World War II have melted away. Communism has largely collapsed, the Soviet Union lies splintered into so many fragments, and the Cold War, so long the stuff of newspaper headlines, is now fodder for historical debate. Economic interdependence has grown rapidly, producing complex patterns of cooperation and rivalry among the major industrialized states and a handful of newly industrializing countries. New global issues, such as human rights, environmental sustainability, and immigration, have crowded their way onto the international agenda. Some of these developments have worked in favor of U.S. interests. Others have brought less welcome consequences. All have contributed to a more dynamic, complex, and confusing international scene.

Periods of turbulence and change in world politics do not give rise to uniform effects on all nations. States differ in their willingness and ability to adjust old policies and institutions in response to new problems and circumstances. Those states that prove best able to adapt gain power at the expense of those that are less flexible.

During the seventies and eighties, the U.S. faced the challenge of responding to declining relative power. From the perspective of American policy makers, the problem of decline manifested itself in a widening gap between resources and commitments. This challenge, never fully addressed, remains with us. Alongside quantitative calculations about power and resources is an added set of qualitative concerns associated with the altered power structure and ideological climate of the post–Cold War era. The need for flexible, adaptive, and creative policy responses to these new environmental conditions is greater than before.

As argued in previous chapters, however, the U.S. has done poorly at confronting the need for policy adjustment over the past two decades. From the perspective of realist theory, this is surprising. Microeconomic theory treats firms as if they were rational, profit-sensitive entities, constantly adjusting prices, production, and other parameters in response to changing market conditions. Similarly, realism assumes that states respond in a rapid and calculating manner to changes in the structures of international power and wealth.

Yet these assumptions are not universally valid and can produce erroneous and misleading predictions if applied without sensitivity to the underlying structural conditions that influence state policy making. This study has argued that state responsiveness to international change is dependent upon two variables: international power and domestic state strength. In particular, a state that possesses hegemonic power abroad combined with state weakness at home will fail to adjust readily to international change. Instead, policy rigidity is likely.

Policy change is less automatic and more difficult to accomplish than realists acknowledge. Change produces uncertainty. The psychological and intellectual obstacles to coping with this uncertainty are considerable. Vested interests, located both in the bureaucracy and the society at large, spring up around existing policies and resist their alteration. Old policies are associated with institutional sunk costs that are expensive to abandon or reform. The public itself may fail to perceive the need for policy change, making it difficult for political leaders to rally popular support for adjustment.

Given these obstacles to policy change, successful adjustment depends upon the right combination of international and domestic conditions. States are more likely to carry out policy adjustment if the international pressures to do so are strong and immediate and if decision-making authority at home is relatively centralized and insulated from domestic pressures.

A hegemonic power is not immune to deleterious trends in the international system. But, due to its surplus power, a hegemon will experience these international pressures in the form of gradual erosion rather than acute crisis. The international incentives for policy adjustment will be felt less strongly, at least in the short run—the relevant time horizon for most politicians. If hegemony is accompanied by state weakness at home, then adjustment becomes even less plausible. State officials will lack the autonomy and authority needed to manage the domestic politics of policy change. Efforts to carry out external adjustment will be deflected by vested interests and institutional resistance.

This argument explains why American foreign (and domestic) policies have so often appeared frustratingly unresponsive to international change over the past two decades. Owing to a combination of international hegemony and domestic state weakness, U.S. presidents have either failed to acknowledge the need for adjustment (e.g., Reagan's first term) or have found their attempts to do so blocked by domestic obstacles (e.g., Carter). As a result, U.S. foreign policy has failed to keep pace with ongoing international change. The consequences of this failure, as outlined in the previous chapter, have been serious.

Comparing Approaches to Foreign Policy Analysis

The central purpose of this study has been diagnostic rather than prescriptive. Relatively little has been said about (1) the precise policy changes needed to cope with specific international problems and trends, (2) the institutional reforms that could possibly allow policy adjustment to proceed more smoothly, or (3) the political strategy that might best succeed in accomplishing either of the first two tasks.

The theoretical tools that social science can bring to bear on such problems are simply too crude to offer much practical assistance to policy makers. At best, a study of this sort can help to outline the big picture and to offer retrospective analysis and appraisal of past policies.

Still, the contributions of theory to foreign policy analysis should not be dismissed. The remainder of this chapter offers, therefore, a number of observations suggesting how the craft of foreign policy analysis might be improved. In particular, the discussion that follows compares the structural approach adopted in this study with other analytic models.

This study has outlined a model that seeks to explain otherwise confusing patterns of policy change and stability. American foreign policy is seen as a product of the dual sets of constraints and incentives arising from the international and domestic structures that enclose the decision-making arena. In particular, American policy makers have been driven by the sometimes contradictory imperatives of balancing resources with commitments abroad while maintaining popular legitimacy for American policies at home.

A tenuous reconciliation between these imperatives was fashioned during the Cold War period. American policy makers, fearful of the constraints imposed by state weakness at home yet eager to take advantage of new opportunities for influence abroad, succeeded in forging an elite and popular consensus around an activist and highly ideological style of foreign policy. This proved viable as long as America's hegemonic status assured it of surplus resources with which to pursue a uniquely ambitious foreign policy strategy. But expanding commitments combined with declining power eventually led to an external imbalance between resources and commitments.

Although presidents during the seventies, Jimmy Carter in particular, attempted to bring about policy adjustments designed to close this gap between resources and commitments, they faced opposition from those with material and ideological interests in maintaining previous policies. The ensuing battle between the advocates of adjustment and resistance revolved around basic issues of foreign policy legitimacy. Both sides sought to control the public agenda and build popular support. Conservative defenders of the status quo forced Carter to abandon his strategy of adjustment chiefly because conservatives controlled important institutional assets and managed to craft a more effective ideological appeal for gathering public support. While conservatives did not succeed in restoring the old foreign policy consensus around their preferred policies, they did manage to acquire veto power over attempts to carry out broad adjustments in American foreign policy. This stalemate left unresolved for another decade or more the continuing overextension of American power and commitments abroad.

Behind these substantive conclusions is a broadly gauged approach to the study of American foreign policy that focuses our attention on the underlying structural determinants of policy change and stability. It is worth highlighting a number of ways in which the analytic assumptions undergirding this approach differ from those of either realism or decision-making theories.

Decision-making theories are principally concerned with evaluating the procedural rationality of foreign policy. In other words, decision-making theorists focus on the formal characteristics of the process by which decisions are made. Analysts in this tradition have concentrated on understanding the ways in which psychological and bureaucratic factors impede the attainment of full rationality in decision making.[1]

The approach adopted here instead describes variance in foreign policy according to its substantive rationality. In other words, a structural approach to the study of foreign policy measures rationality with respect to a theoretically derived set of criteria that, in turn, are based upon assumptions about the relationship between the state and its environment. The ways in which states define their interests will, of course, vary across cases and over time. Yet some interests are so basic to the nature of statehood and so widely pursued that they may be taken as given. One may then evaluate the substantive rationality of actual policies according to whether or not they further or retard the attainment of these assumed interests.

Foreign policy decision makers have an interest in maintaining a rough equilibrium between external resources and commitments. Declining power may, however, lead to the emergence of a gap between resources and commitments in the absence of appropriate policy changes. A situation of declining power, then, can be said to present a state with incentives to close this gap through a strategy of adjustment. Beginning with certain reasonable assumptions about interests and empirical knowledge about how environmental change affects the imputed interests, one can compare actual policies with ideal or "rational" policies.

While this approach differs substantially from that of decision-making theory, it does resemble realist approaches in certain key respects. Realists also measure rationality according to externally imposed criteria. Yet realist attempts to predict behavior are based solely upon international incentives. This study assumes that policy makers pay attention to domestic incentives as well. In particular, policy makers are concerned with maintaining domestic legitimacy for their policies. Adding this additional set of structural constraints to the analysis of foreign policy change makes it possible to understand why decision makers sometimes depart from behavior that realists would consider rational in terms of external incentives.[2] Thus, as in the case of the final stages of the Carter administration, one can explain the adoption of strategies of resistance that exacerbate declining power as a consequence of domestic constraints. Realist theories are powerless to do so.

In short, decision-making theories that focus on procedural rationality, while they may help account for discrete decisions, are not well suited to explaining broad patterns of policy change. Realism is more promising for this purpose because it focuses on substantive rationality, i.e., the degree to which presumed state interests are served by a state's general foreign policy strategy.

The rationality of broad patterns of policy change is measured by the degree to which these changes appear to be responsive to external constraints and incentives. Yet realism ultimately proves inadequate as well due to its assumption that state interests are one-dimensional. It is more plausible to assume that states are Janus-faced creatures with important interests in internal as well as external order.[3] Both sets of interests are better served to the extent that the policies of the state are accorded domestic legitimacy. This is as true of foreign policies as it is of domestic policies. Attention to the constraints imposed by both domestic and international structures allows for a richer and more realistic account of state behavior than the practice of treating each in isolation from the other. Considering both together allows us to become sensitive to the possibility, for instance, that domestic and international structures may interact or, even more interestingly, that domestic and international incentives may conflict.[4]

Another important difference between a structural approach to the study of foreign policy and either decision making or realist theories lies in the treatment of history. If it is true that the foreign policy strategy a state chooses is often a product of constraints imposed by both domestic and international structures, it is also true that the resulting policies can, in some measure, alter the future evolution of these structures. This is most plausibly the case with respect to domestic structures. The vested interests that form around current policies as well as the strategy chosen for building legitimacy around these policies can alter domestic structures in such a way as to constrain future policy choices.

Neither decision-making theories nor realist theories account very well for the constraining influences of past policies on present decisions. Realism presumes that decision makers respond to contemporaneous evaluations of the international distribution of power and interests. What matters is not what previous policies looked like but which policies, among the available alternatives, appear most likely to maximize present benefits.

Decision-making theories sometimes address the effects of past policies in a limited and indirect manner. Psychological theories, for instance, posit the notion that decision makers may be influenced by lessons of the past.[5] Although some decision-making theories assume that policies are often shaped by certain bureaucratic arrangements that are, in themselves, institutional legacies of past decisions, decision-making theorists do often think about them in these terms. Decision-making theories are limited, however, in their ability to address the broader domestic consequences of past decisions by their focus on the immediate arena of decision rather than the society as a whole.

In contrast to these approaches, Stephen Krasner's notion of "punctuated equilibrium" takes into direct account the constraining influence of past policies. Krasner's institutionalist argument suggests that policy change is likely to be erratic rather than incremental. Policies selected during certain generative periods when fluid international and domestic structures have begun to harden again become enmeshed in evolving domestic structures and will remain rigid despite ongoing environmental change. They take on, as it were, a life of their own. Even if international change creates incentives for policy reform, adjustment to external trends may be stymied if decision makers find the domestic political costs of policy change too high.[6] As Krasner suggests, there exist cases where "prior institutional choices limit available future options."[7]

By allowing for the interaction of domestic and international variables, a structural approach to the study of foreign policy helps us to better specify the conditions under which Krasner's model is likely to apply. In particular, states enjoying hegemonic power abroad combined with state weakness at home seem rather more vulnerable to the pattern of policy rigidity specified by Krasner than other sorts of states.

This sort of perspective aids in understanding the otherwise puzzling failure of the Carter administration's efforts to bring resources in line with commitments. The tragedy of the Carter administration was one of historical timing. Carter's belief that domestic conditions were ripe for reform proved incorrect. Efforts to foster lasting policy change collapsed under the weight of longstanding institutions and interests. In his memoirs, Carter captured this reality in his plaintive observation, "Americans were not accustomed to limits—on natural resources or on the power of our country to influence others or to control international events."[8]

The arguments around which this book is organized also shed light on the experience of the Reagan administration which, like that of Carter, failed to sustain a consistent strategy in U.S. foreign policy. The failure of both presidents can be traced, along differing routes, to structural contradictions between the conflicting international and domestic constraints impinging on U.S. foreign policy. A structural approach is thus helpful not only in unraveling the mysteries of policy change under Carter but also in specifying the underlying sources of policy vacillation over much of the past two decades.

Structures do not, however, persist forever. External shocks can serve to break up or loosen existing structures and to initiate periods of rapid change and flux. The policy choices made during such times of great uncertainty gradually become institutionalized and thus give rise to new structures that establish the basic parameters and ground rules of political life in the ensuing era. The collapse of communism and the end of the Cold War may have provided the blow necessary to break up long-standing domestic and international arrangements. After the frustrating policy stalemates of the seventies and eighties, it is possible, though far from certain, that the United States may once again have the freedom of strategic choice and a new opportunity as a world power to adjust to a changing international environment.

NOTES

INTRODUCTION

1. Gaddis Smith, *Morality, Reason and Power: American Diplomacy in the Carter Years* (New York: Hill and Wang, 1986), p. 8.

2. I will use the term "liberal internationalism" to label the set of beliefs and policy preferences adopted by the early Carter administration and its supporters. The term "conservative internationalism" will refer to the strongly anti-communist beliefs and policies that dominated U.S. foreign policy during the deep Cold War years and once again during the early Reagan administration. My use of these terms is consistent with that found in Ole Holsti and James Rosenau, *American Leadership in World Affairs: Vietnam and the Breakdown in Consensus* (Boston: Allen & Unwin, 1984).

3. The literature on Carter's foreign policies is reviewed in chapter 3. For a general review of the literature on Carter's presidency as a whole, see Gary Reichard, "Early Returns: Assessing Jimmy Carter," *Presidential Studies Quarterly* 20 (summer 1990): 603–20.

4. For a useful discussion of these points, see Douglas Van Belle, "Domestic Imperatives and Rational Models of Foreign Policy Decision-Making," in *The Limits of State Autonomy: Societal Groups and Foreign Policy Formulation*, ed. David Skidmore and Valerie M. Hudson (Boulder, Colo.: Westview, 1993).

5. On the weakness of the American state, see, for instance, J. P. Nettl, "The State as a Conceptual Variable," *World Politics* 20 (July 1968): 559–92, and Stephen Krasner, "United States Commercial and Monetary Policy: Unraveling the Paradox of External Strength and Internal Weakness," in *Between Power and Plenty: Foreign Economic Policies of Advanced Industrial States*, ed. Peter Katzenstein (Madison: University of Wisconsin Press), 1978.

6. While the existence of a consensus around the central tenets of U.S. foreign policy during the Cold War years is generally supposed among scholars, the evidence on behalf of this proposition is not conclusive due to limited survey data. Ole Holsti and James Rosenau muster what data is available to support the notion that a consensus did in fact exist in *American Leadership in World: Vietnam and the Breakdown of Consensus* (Boston: Allen & Unwin, 1984), pp. 216–23. Much of the remainder of the Holsti and Rosenau volume discusses the breakdown of that consensus during the seventies, especially pp. 83–216. For additional sources on the breakdown in the post–World War II consensus and its consequences, see James Chace, "Is a Foreign Policy Consensus Possible?" *Foreign Affairs* 57 (fall 1978): 1–16;

Thomas Hughes, "The Crack Up: The Price of Collective Irresponsibility, " *Foreign Policy*, no. 40 (fall 1980): 33–60; and George Quester, "Consensus Lost," *Foreign Policy*, no. 40 (fall 1980): 18–32.

7. The need for approaches that recognize the interaction of domestic and international variables in producing foreign policy behavior was pointed out in the late seventies by Peter Gourevitch. Gourevitch particularly stressed that "in using domestic structure as a variable in explaining foreign policy, we must explore the extent to which that structure itself derives from the exigencies of the international system." Peter Gourevitch, "The Second Image Reversed: The International Sources of Domestic Politics," *International Organization* 32 (autumn 1978): 882. This study takes Gourevitch's advice to heart by treating hegemony as a source of policy rigidity. Works which attempt to trace linkages between domestic and international factors in explaining foreign policy behavior have proliferated in recent years. See, for instance, Miles Kahler, *Decolonization in Britain and France: Domestic Consequences of International Relations* (Princeton, N.J.: Princeton University Press, 1984; Michael Mastanduno, David Lake and G. John Ikenberry, "Toward a Realist Theory of State Action," *International Studies Quarterly* 33 (December 1989): 457–74; Charles Kupchan, *The Vulnerability of Empire* (Ithaca: Cornell University Press, 1994); Robert Putnam, "Diplomacy and Domestic Politics: The Logic of Two Level Games," *International Organization* 42 (summer 1988): 427–60; Harold Mueller and Thomas Risse-Kappen, "From the Outside In and From the Inside Out: International Relations, Domestic Politics and Foreign Policy," in *The Limits of State Autonomy: Societal Groups and Foreign Policy Formulation*, ed. David Skidmore and Valerie Hudson (Boulder, Colo.: Westview, 1993); Mark Brawley, *Liberal Leadership: Great Powers and Their Challengers in Peace and War* (Ithaca: Cornell University Press, 1993); and Jack Snyder, *Myths of Empire: Domestic Politics and International Ambition* (Ithaca: Cornell University Press, 1991).

8. This discussion of hegemonic decline largely follows that of Robert Gilpin, *War and Change in World Politics* (Cambridge: Cambridge University Press, 1981).

9. See Kenneth Oye, "Constrained Confidence and the Evolution of Reagan Administration Foreign Policy," in *Eagle Resurgent? The Reagan Era in American Foreign Policy*, ed. Kenneth Oye, Donald Rothchild, and Robert Lieber (Boston: Little, Brown, 1987).

CHAPTER ONE

1. Although the specific terminology varies, the following pieces each discuss, in some fashion or another, the choice between adjustment and resistance: G. John Ikenberry, "The State and Strategies of International Adjustment," *World Politics* 39 (October 1986): 53–77; James Rosenau, *The Study of Political Adaptation: Essays on the Analysis of World Politics* (New York: Nichols, 1981); Kenneth Oye, "Constrained Confidence and the Evolution of Reagan Foreign Policy," in *Eagle Resurgent? The Reagan Era in American Foreign Policy*, ed. Kenneth Oye, Robert Lieber, and Donald Rothschild (Boston: Little, Brown, 1987); Samuel Huntington, "Coping with the Lippmann Gap," *Foreign Affairs: America and the World 1987–88* 66, no. 3: 453–77. On foreign policy change more generally, see Charles Hermann, "Change Course: When Governments Choose to Redirect Foreign Policy," *International Studies Quarterly*, 34 (March 1990): 3–21 and various essays in *Foreign Policy Restructuring: How Governments Respond to Global Change*, ed. Jerel A. Rosati, Joe D. Hagan, and Martin W. Sampson

III (Columbia: University of South Carolina Press, 1994).

2. The bulk of the literature on the concept of international hegemony is devoted to two problems: (1) attempts to explain the cyclical rise and decline of hegemonic powers; (2) discussion of the consequences of hegemony, or its absence, for international order, particularly the openness and stability of the international economy. Scholars have recently turned to the task of understanding how hegemonic powers respond to decline. Resolving this third problem, however, is obviously critical to addressing the first two: the strategic responses of the hegemon may alter the pace of its own decline as well as the prospects for international stability. For the principal sources on hegemony in general and the American experience as a hegemon in particular, see Robert Gilpin, *War and Change in World Politics* (Princeton, N.J.: Princeton University Press, 1981); Paul Kennedy, *The Rise and Fall of the Great Powers: Economic Change and Military Conflict from 1500 to 2000* (New York: Random House, 1987); George Modelski, "The Long Cycles of Global Politics and the Nation-State," *Comparative Studies in Society and History* 20 (April 1978): 214–35; Christopher Chase-Dunn, "International Economic Policy in a Declining Core State," in *America in a Changing World Political Economy*, ed. William Avery and David Rapkin (New York: Longman, 1982); David Calleo, *Beyond American Hegemony: The Future of the Western Alliance* (New York: Basic Books, 1987); *The Economic Decline of Empires*, ed. Carlos Cipolla (London: Methuen, 1970); Mancur Olson, *The Rise and Decline of Nations: Economic Growth. Stagflation. and Social Rigidities* (New Haven: Yale University Press, 1982); Arthur Stein, "The Hegemon's Dilemma: Great Britain, the United States, and the International Economic Order," *International Organization* 38 (spring 1984): 355–86; Duncan Snidal, "The Limits of Hegemonic Stability Theory," *International Organization* 39 (autumn 1985): 579–614; Robert Keohane, *After Hegemony: Cooperation and Discord in the World Political Economy* (Princeton, N.J.: Princeton University Press, 1984); *International Regimes*, ed. Stephen Krasner (Ithaca, N.Y.: Cornell University Press, 1983); Aaron Friedberg, "The Strategic Implications of Relative Economic Decline," *Political Science Quarterly* 104 (fall 1989): 401–32; Mark Brawley, *Liberal Leadership: Great Powers and Their Challengers in Peace and War* (Ithaca, N.Y.: Cornell University Press, 1993); and the essays found in *World Leadership and Hegemony*, ed. David Rapkin (Boulder, Colo.: Lynne Rienner Publishers, 1990). A literature review is provided in David Lake, "Leadership, Hegemony, and the International Economy: Naked Emperor or Tattered Monarch with Potential?" *International Studies Quarterly* 37 (December 1993): 459–89.

3. Gilpin, *War and Change*.

4. It is important to note the existence of tensions between the analytic structure of realism, as described above, and the normative dimensions of realist thought. Analytically, realism purports to explain state behavior as a function of externally imposed constraints. This assumption lies behind much of the systemic theorizing about international relations. States are depicted as functionally similar units driven by the pursuit of national interests in an anarchic world. Variance in both behavior and outcomes is explained in terms of varying national power capabilities across states and over time. Yet this analytic structure of realist theory is incompatible with the normative dimensions of realist thought. Normative realism holds that statesmen, because they are agents rather than principals, have a moral duty to maximize the power, security, and well-being of the nation they represent. The critical function of this school of thought has been to question actions, policies, and behavior that fail to maximize

the national interest. The analytic and normative strands of realism stand in tension because the former asserts that nations pursue their own national interests as a function of their participation in an anarchic international system, while the latter implicitly acknowledges that important deviations from realist standards of behavior are common. These tensions are evident not only among different realist thinkers but often in the work of single authors. See, for instance, Hans Morgenthau and Kenneth Thomson, *Politics Among Nations: The Struggle for Power and Peace*, 6th ed. (New York: Knopf, 1985), pp. 4, 7, 10, and passim. I do not attempt to resolve this contradiction in realist thought. Instead, my purpose is limited to the demonstration that analytic realism is inadequate to explain the response of hegemonic states to the experience of decline.

5. Robert Keohane, "Theory of World Politics: Structural Realism and Beyond," in *Neo-Realism and Its Critics*, ed. Robert Keohane (New York: Columbia University Press, 1986), p. 165.

6. Ibid., p. 167.

7. Ibid.

8. Morgenthau and Thomson, *Politics Among Nations*, p. 5.

9. Keohane, "Theory of World Politics," p. 163. For an example of how this approach has been applied in practice to one aspect of American foreign policy, see David Lake, "International Economic Structures and American Foreign Economic Policy, 1887–1934," *World Politics* 35 (July 1983): 517–43.

10. See, for instance, Robert Nisbet, *Social Change and History: Aspects of the Western Theory of Development* (New York: Oxford University Press, 1969), pp. 272–304; Olson, *Rise and Decline*; Thomas Kuhn, *The Structure of Scientific Revolutions* (Chicago: University of Chicago Press, 1962); Stephen Skowronek, *Building a New American State: The Expansion of National Administrative Capacities* (New York: Cambridge University Press, 1982), p. 10; and Jerel Rosati, "Human Needs and the Evolution of U.S. Foreign Policy," in *The Power of Human Needs in World Society*, ed. Roger A. Coate and Jerel A. Rosati (Boulder, Colo.: Lynne Rienner Publishers, 1988).

11. See Stephen Jay Gould and Niles Eldredge, "Punctuated Equilibria: The Tempo and Mode of Evolution Reconsidered," *Paleobiology* 3 (spring 1977): 115–51.

12. Stephen Krasner, "Approaches to the State: Alternative Conceptions and Historical Dynamics," *Comparative Politics*, 16 (January 1984): 240–44. Also see Stephen Krasner, "Sovereignty: An Institutional Perspective," in *The Elusive State: International and Comparative Perspectives*, ed. James Caporaso (Newbury Park, Calif.: Sage, 1989), pp. 80–88.

13. Stephen Krasner, "State Power and the Structure of Foreign Trade," *World Politics* 28 (April 1976): 317–47.

14. For a similar argument that attributes imperial overexpansion to log-rolling among vested interest groups, see Jack Snyder, *Myths of Empire: Domestic Politics and International Ambition* (Ithaca, N.Y.: Cornell University Press, 1991). Another important source is Peter Gourevitch, *Politics in Hard Times: Comparative Response to International Economic Crises* (Ithaca, N.Y.: Cornell University Press, 1986), which offers a crisis-driven model of policy change mediated by periodic realignments in domestic coalitions.

15. Krasner, "State Power," p. 341.

16. Kenneth Waltz, *Theory of International Politics* (Reading, Mass.: Addison-Wesley,

1979), p. 106.

17. Robert Keohane, "Hegemonic Leadership and U.S. Foreign Economic Policy in the 'Long Decade' of the 1950's," in *America in a Changing World Political Economy*, ed. William Avery and David Rapkin (New York: Longman, 1982), p. 70.

18. Peter Katzenstein, for instance, has emphasized the adaptability of the small, democratic corporatist states of Europe in coping with international economic change. See Peter Katzenstein, *Small States in World Markets: Industrial Policy in Europe* (Ithaca: Cornell University Press, 1985).

19. Keohane, "Hegemonic Leadership," p. 70. Also see James Rosenau and Ole Holsti, "The United States In (and Out of) Vietnam: An Adaptive Transformation?" in James Rosenau, *The Study of Political Adaptation: Essays on the Analysis of World Politics* (New York: Nichols, 1981), p. 174.

20. Stephen Krasner, *Defending the National Interest: Raw Materials Investments and U.S. Foreign Policy* (Princeton, N.J.: Princeton University Press, 1978), pp. 340–42.

21. Olson, *Rise and Decline*.

22. On strong and weak states, see J. P. Nettl, "The State as a Conceptual Variable," *World Politics* 20 (July 1968): 559–92; as well as Peter Katzenstein, "Domestic Structures and Strategies of Foreign Economic Policy," and Stephen Krasner, "United States Commercial and Monetary Policy: Unraveling the Paradox of External Strength and Internal Weakness," in *Between Power and Plenty: Foreign Economic Policy of Advanced Industrial States*, ed. Peter Katzenstein (Madison: University of Wisconsin Press, 1978).

23. I say "loosely" because, given the serious psychological and organizational complexities of making decisions with reference to an often uncertain and complex international environment, no state, whether strong or weak, perfectly emulates a rational, unitary actor.

24. Alexander George, "Domestic Constraints on Regime Change in U.S. Foreign Policy: The Need for Policy Legitimacy," in *Change in the International System*, ed. Ole Holsti, Randolph Siverson, and Alexander George (Boulder, Colo.: Westview, 1980), p. 236.

25. On the linkage between ideology and legitimation, see B. Thomas Trout, "Rhetoric Revisited: Political Legitimation and the Cold War," *International Studies Quarterly* 19 (September 1975): 251–84.

26. On the role of doctrine, see Katarina Brodin, "Belief Systems, Doctrines and Foreign Policy," *Cooperation and Conflict* 7, no. 2 (1972): 97–112.

27. Theodore Lowi, *The End of Liberalism: The Second Republic of the United States*, 2d. ed. (New York: Norton, 1979), pp. 128–48. Lowi links the frequent resort to oversell to state weakness and the pressures of legitimation.

28. See Charles Kupchan, *The Vulnerability of Empire*, (Ithaca: Cornell University Press, 1994). Kupchan also suggests that efforts to legitimate existing policies at home can serve to tie the hands of policy makers at a future point in time. Kupchan applies this argument to early U.S. Cold War policy as well as other cases.

29. Brodin, "Belief Systems," pp. 106 and 108.

30. Lowi, *The End of Liberalism*, p. 148.

31. Trout, "Rhetoric Revisited," pp. 280–81.

32. I am not arguing, it is important to note, that the leaders of states combining modest power abroad and strength at home will never wrap their foreign policies in ideological

rhetoric. They will often engage in such practices, for a variety of reasons. What I instead contend is that the pressures to do so are more systemic and persistent for weak states, due to the greater dependence of weak state leaders on gaining broad societal su3pport. Also, strong state leaders, because they are more insulated from societal constraints, will find it easier to abandon previous ideological rationalizations once they decide it expedient to do so. Ideological routines therefore serve as greater obstacles to future policy adjustment for weak states than for strong states.

33. George, "Domestic Constraints," pp. 249–50.

34. The above discussion of the Truman Doctrine is based upon Stephen Ambrose, *Rise to Globalism: American Foreign Police. 1938–1976*, rev. ed. (New York: Penguin, 1976), pp. 146–52; John Lewis Gaddis, *The United States and the Origins of the Cold War. 1941–1947* (New York: Columbia University Press, 1972), pp. 350–51 and Marshal Shulman, "Four Decades of Irrationality: U.S.-Soviet Relations," in *World Politics 88/89*, ed. Suzanne P. Ogden (Guilford, Conn.: Dushkin, 1988), p. 23.

35. Ernest May, "The Cold War," in *The Making of America's Soviet Policy*, ed. Joseph Nye (New Haven: Yale University Press, 1984), p. 226.

36. Philip Wander, "The Rhetoric of American Foreign Policy," *The Quarterly Journal of Speech* 70 (November 1984): 344.

37. Charles Hermann, "New Foreign Policy Problems and Old Bureaucratic Organizations," in *The Domestic Sources of American Foreign Policy: Insights and Evidence*, ed. Charles Kegley and Eugene Wittkopf (New York: St. Martin's, 1988), p. 262.

38. Ibid., p. 258.

39. For an original interpretation of U.S. foreign policy that also depicts state weakness as a source of policy rigidity, see Ira Katznelson and Kenneth Prewitt, "Constitutionalism, Class, and the Limits of Choice in U.S. Foreign Policy," in *Capitalism and the State in U.S.–Latin American Relations*, ed. Richard Fagen (Stanford, Calif.: Stanford University Press, 1979).

40. On this point, see Miles Kahler, *Decolonization in Britain and France: The Domestic Consequences of International Relations* (Princeton, N.J.: Princeton University Press, 1984).

41. The newly industrializing countries of East Asia (e.g., South Korea and Taiwan) are often cited as examples of how even very small countries can sometimes maneuver around the serious international constraints they face if led by a strong, autonomous state. This theme is explored in David Yoffie, *Power and Protectionism* (New York: Columbia University Press), 1983 and Stephan Haggard, *Pathways from the Periphery* (Ithaca, N.J.: Cornell University Press, 1990).

42. Gilpin, *War and Change*, pp. 173–74. For dissenting views on the notion that U.S. power has undergone significant erosion, see Bruce Russett, "The Mysterious Case of Vanishing Hegemony; or Is Mark Twain Really Dead?," *International Organization* 39 (spring 1985): 207–32; Susan Strange, "The Persistent Myth of Lost Hegemony," *International Organization* 41 (autumn 1987): 551–74; Joseph Nye, "Short-Term Folly, Not Long Term Decline," *New Perspectives Quarterly* 5 (summer 1988): 33–35; and Stephen Gill, "American Hegemony: Its Limits and Prospects in the Reagan Era," *Millennium: Journal of International Studies* 15 (1986).

43. Keohane, "Hegemonic Leadership," p. 70.

44. Paul Kennedy, "The (Relative) Decline of America," *The Atlantic Monthly* 260 (Au-

gust 1987): 36.

45. Aaron Friedberg, *The Weary Titan: Britain and the Experience of Relative Decline, 1895–1905* (Princeton, N.J.: Princeton University Press, 1988), pp. 290, 294.

46. Friedberg, *The Weary Titan*, p. 295.

47. Stephen Krasner makes a similar argument, suggesting that institutional rigidity and vested interests accounted for Great Britain's continued attachment to policies of free trade even after Britain's declining world economic position rendered such policies increasingly costly. According to Krasner, "Institutions created during periods of rising ascendancy remained in operation when they were no longer appropriate." In this particular case, the Bank of London and the powerful British financial community resisted more mercantalist policies due to their heavy dependence on international financial flows and open trade. Stephen Krasner, "State Power," p. 342.

48. Friedberg, *The Weary Titan*, p. 290–91.

CHAPTER TWO

1. The most persistent advocate of the view that Carter's foreign policy management was plagued by incoherence and a lack of strategic thought has been Stanley Hoffmann. His arguments were developed in a series of articles appearing in the late seventies and early eighties. Among them are "The Hell of Good Intentions," *Foreign Policy*, no.25 (winter 1977): 97–140; "A View from Home: The Perils of Incoherence," *Foreign Affairs: American and the World. 1978* 57, no. 3: 463–91; "Requiem," *Foreign Policy*, no. 42 (spring 1981): 3–26; "Carter's Soviet Problem," *New Republic*, July 29, 1978; "Reflections on the Present Danger," *The New York Review of Books*, March 6, 1980. For similar interpretations of Carter's foreign policies, see Richard Barnet, "Carter's Patchwork Doctrine," *Harper's*, August, 1977; Kenneth Adelman, "The Runner Stumbles: Carter's Foreign Policy in the Year One," *Policy Review*, no. 3 (winter 1978): 89–115; Arthur Schlesinger, "The Great Carter Mystery," *New Republic*, April 12, 1980; Vincent Davis, "Carter Tries on the World for Size," in *The Post Imperial Presidency*, ed. Vincent Davis (New York: Praeger, 1980); Walter LaFeber, "From Confusion to Cold War: The Memoirs of the Carter Administration," *Diplomatic History* 8 (winter 1984): 7–12; Donald Spencer, *The Carter Implosion: Jimmy Carter and the Amateur Style of Diplomacy* (New York: Praeger), 1988, and Richard Thornton, *The Carter Years: Toward a New Global Order* (New York: Paragon House, 1991).

2. For examples, see Robert Osgood, "Carter Policy in Perspective," *SAIS Review* 25 (Winter 1981); Gaddis Smith, *Morality. Reason and Power: American Diplomacy in the Carter Years* (New York: Hill and Wang, 1986); Coral Bell, "Virtue Unrewarded: Carter's Foreign Policy at Mid-Term," *International Affairs*, October, 1978; Linda Miller, "Morality in Foreign Policy: A Failed Consensus," *Daedalus* 109 (Summer 1980): 143–58; and Brian Klunk, *Consensus and the American Mission* Lanham, Md.: University Press of America, 1986), pp. 115–68.

3. See Robert Tucker, "America in Decline: A Foreign Policy of 'Maturity,'" *Foreign Affairs: American and the World* 58, no. 3: 449–84; and Robert Tucker, "Reagan Without Tears: His 'Simple' World View is Truer than Carter's 'Complex' One," *New Republic*, May 17, 1980. Tucker's criticisms of Carter are sometimes echoed in the more polemical writings of conservative authors. Yet, while Tucker, a realist, is generally suspicious of attempts to anchor U.S. foreign policy in sweeping moral principles (as opposed to material interests), many of

Carter's conservative critics offered their own kind of moralism, one based upon anti-communism, in place of Carter's variety. For a sampling of conservative responses to Carter's foreign policy performance, see Norman Podhoretz, "The Culture of Appeasement," *Harper's*, October, 1977; Norman Podhoretz, *The Present Danger* (New York: Simon and Schuster, 1980); Jeane Kirkpatrick, "Dictatorships and Double Standards," *Commentary* 68 (November 1979): 34–45; and Carl Gershman, "The Rise and Fall of the New Foreign Policy Establishment," *Commentary* 70 (July 1980): 13–24.

4. Jeff Frieden, "The Trilateral Commission: Economics and Politics in the 1970's," in *Trilateralism: The Trilateral Commission and Elite Planning for World Management*, ed. Holly Sklar (Boston: South End Press, 1980), p. 69. For additional interpretations in this vein, see Marcus Raskin, "The National Security State (Carter Style)," *Inquiry*, April 3, 1978; Holly Sklar, "Trilateralism and the Management of Contradictions," in *Trilateralism*; Alan Wolfe, "Trilateralism and the Carter Administration: Changed Realities and Vested Interests," in *Trilateralism*; Kai Bird, "Coopting the Third World Elites: Trilateralism and Saudi Arabia," in *Trilateralism*; Fred Block, "Trilateralism and Inter-Capitalist Conflict," in *Trilateralism*; James Petras, "U.S. Foreign Policy: The Revival of Interventionism," *Monthly Review*, February 1980; Stephen Shalom, "Remembering the Carter Administration," *Zeta Magazine*, October 1988; and Lawrence Shoup, *The Carter Presidency and Beyond: Power and Politics in the 1980's* (Palo Alto, Calif.: Ramparts, 1980).

5. See LaFeber, "From Confusion to Cold War"; Osgood, "Carter Policy in Perspective"; Tucker, "America in Decline" and "Reagan Without Tears"; and Podhoretz, *The Present Danger*.

6. Given my view that too much significance has been placed on the Vance/Brzezinski split and the fact that many detailed accounts already exist in print, I have chosen to devote relatively little space to this issue in the discussion that follows. For a conventional account of the relationship between Vance and Brzezinski, see John Dumbrell, *The Carter Presidency: A Re-evaluation* (New York: Manchester University Press, 1993), pp. 194–99.

7. See, for instance, the first Trilateral Commission Task Force Report on North-South relations, which stressed that "we reject any idea of a 'rich man's club' forming defensive alliances against the poor. On the contrary, we seek a new international economic order based on cooperation between developed and developing countries, corresponding to the new balance of economic and political power, and responsive to growing demands for welfare and justice. We are convinced that an international economic system cannot successfully endure unless both rich and poor countries feel they have a stake in it"; Richard Gardner, Saburo Okita, and B. J. Udink, "A Turning Point in North-South Relations," in *Trilateral Commission Task Force Reports 1–7* (New York: New York University Press, 1977), p. 59. A later Trilateral Commission Task Force Report even contemplated redistributive policies toward the Third World: "The evolving order must focus explicitly on income distribution and on an adequate role for the developing countries if it is to attract them to constructive participation"; C. Fred Bergsten, Georges Berthoin, and Kinhide Mushakoji, "The Reform of International Institutions," *Trilateral Commission Task Force Reports 9–14* (New York: New York University Press, 1978), p. 97.

8. Frieden, "The Trilateral Commission."

9. Fred Block traces this thesis back to Karl Kautsky's writings on "ultra-imperialism." For

his critique of this position, see Block, "Trilateralism and Inter-Capitalist Conflict."

10. Samuel Huntington, "Coping with the Lippmann Gap," *Foreign Affairs: America and the World. 1987–88* 66, no. 3: 453–77.

11. Ibid., p. 455.

12. Kenneth Oye, "Constrained Confidence and the Evolution of Reagan Foreign Policy," in *Eagle Resurgent? The Reagan Era in American Foreign Policy*, 3d ed., ed. Kenneth Oye, Donald Rothchild, and Robert Lieber (Boston: Little, Brown, 1987), p. 22.

13. Kenneth Oye, "International Systems Structure and American Foreign Policy," in *Eagle Defiant: United States Foreign Policy in the 1980's*, ed. Kenneth Oye, Robert Lieber, and Donald Rothchild (Boston: Little, Brown, 1983), pp. 3, 4.

14. As, for instance, in Smith, *Morality. Reason and Power*.

15. Oye, "Constrained Confidence," pp. 3–4.

16. Francois Duchene, Kinhide Muchakoji, and Henry Owen, "The Crisis of International Cooperation," in *Trilateral Commission Task Force Reports 1–7* (New York: New York University Press, 1977), p. 38.

17. Ibid., p. 39.

18. Bergsten, Berthoin, and Mushakoji, "The Reform of International Institutions," p. 100.

19. Jimmy Carter, "Inaugural Address," January 20, 1977, reprinted in *American Foreign Relations. 1977: A Documentary Record*, ed. Elaine Adam (New York: New York University Press, 1979), p. 156.

20. Jimmy Carter, "United States–Soviet Relations," address before the 31st Annual Meeting of the Southern Legislative Conference, Charleston, South Carolina, July 21, 1977, reprinted in *American Foreign Relations. 1977*, p. 192.

21. Jimmy Carter, "Foreign Policy and the National Character," commencement address at the University of Notre Dame, May 22, 1977; reprinted in *American Foreign Relations. 1977*, p. 174.

22. Jimmy Carter, "Major Dimensions of Peace," address before the 32nd United Nations General Assembly, October 4, 1977; reprinted in *American Foreign Relations. 1977*, p. 201–2.

23. Ibid., p. 208.

24. Quoted in Jerel Rosati, *The Carter Administration's Quest for Global Community: Beliefs and Their Impact on Behavior* (Columbia: University of South Carolina Press, 1977), p. 69.

25. Duchene, Muchakoji, and Owen, "The Crisis of International Cooperation," p. 35.

26. Cyrus Vance, statement before Plenary Session of 33rd Regular Session of United Nations General Assembly, New York, Sept. 29, 1978; reprinted in *American Foreign Relations. 1978: A Documentary Record*, ed. Elaine Adam (New York: New York University Press, 1979), p. 496.

27. Carter, "United States–Soviet Relations," p. 190.

28. Carter, "Foreign Policy and the National Character," p. 177.

29. Zbigniew Brzezinski, "American Policy and Global Change," remarks before the Trilateral Commission, Bonn, October 30, 1977; reprinted in *American Foreign Relations 1977*, p. 455.

30. Ibid., p. 457.

31. Oye, "International Systems Structure" pp. 16–28.
32. Cyrus Vance, "Meeting the Challenges of a Changing World," address before the Association of Community and Junior Colleges, Chicago, May 1, 1979, in U.S. Department of State, *American Foreign Policy: Basic Documents. 1977–1980* (Washington, D.C.: U.S. Government Printing Office, 1983), document 12, p. 44.
33. Quoted in Rosati, *Carter Administration's Quest*, p. 54.
34. Carter, "United States–Soviet Relations," pp. 192–93.
35. Jimmy Carter, "Explaining United States Foreign Policy," address to representatives of United Nations Member States, New York, March 17, 1977; reprinted in *American Foreign Relations. 1978*, ed. Elaine Adam (New York: New York University Press, 1979), p. 159.
36. Carter, "United States–Soviet Relations," p. 195.
37. Rosati, *Carter Administration's Quest*, p. 52.
38. Walter LeFeber, *America. Russia and the Cold War. 1945–80*, 4th ed. (New York: John Wiley, 1980), p. 290.
39. Quoted in Rosati, *Carter Administration's Quest*, p. 62.
40. Ibid., p. 62.
41. Carter, "United States–Soviet Relations," p. 191.
42. Brzezinski, "American Policy and Global Change," p. 459.
43. Ibid., p. 456.
44. Jimmy Carter, "The State of the Union," address given before joint session of Congress, Washington, D.C., January 23, 1979; reprinted in *James E Carter*, ed. George Lankevich (Dobbs Ferry, N.Y.: Oceana Publications, 1981), p. 124.
45. Quoted in Rosati, *Carter Administration's Quest*, p. 44.
46. Jimmy Carter, interview with Leslie Gelb for the *New York Times* in June, 1976; cited in Leslie Gelb, "Beyond the Carter Doctrine," *New York Times Magazine*, Feb. 10, 1980, p. 26.
47. Carter, "Foreign Policy and the National Character," pp. 173–74.
48. Cyrus Vance, "The United States and Africa—Building Positive Relations," address before the Annual Convention of the National Association for the Advancement of Colored People (NAACP), St. Louis, July, 1, 1977; reprinted in *American Foreign Relations. 1977*, ed. Elaine Adam (New York: New York University Press, 1979), p. 312.
49. Cyrus Vance, "United States Policy Toward Africa 'Is Based on American Interests and African Realities,'" address before the annual meeting of the U.S. Jaycees, Atlantic City, New Jersey, June 20, 1978; reprinted in U.S. Department of State, *American Foreign Policy: Basic Documents. 1977–1980* (Washington, D.C.: U.S. Government Printing Office, 1983), document 611, p. 1148.
50. Carter, "Foreign Policy and the National Character," p. 173.
51. Ibid., pp. 173–74.
52. Hedrick Smith, "Carter's Foreign Policy: A Middle Course," *New York Times*, Feb. 21, 1979, p. A-l.
53. Quoted in Rosati, *Carter Administration's Quest*, p. 61.
54. David Newsom, "The Challenge of Political Change," address before the American Whig-Cliosophic Society, Princeton University, March 22, 1979, in U.S. Department of State, *American Foreign Policy: Basic Documents. 1977–1980* (Washington, D.C.: U.S. Gov-

ernment Printing Office, 1983), document 10, p. 34.

55. Kenneth Oye, "International Constraints and Carter Administration Foreign Policy," in *Eagle Entangled: U.S. Foreign Policy in a Complex World*, ed. Kenneth Oye, Donald Rothchild, and Robert Lieber (New York: Longman, 1979), p. 24. Emphasis in original.

56. For a discussion of the impact of the Angolan case on the early thinking of the administration, see Gerald Bender, "Angola, the Cubans, and American Anxieties," *Foreign Policy*, no. 31 (summer 1978): 3–30.

57. Quoted in Rosati, *Carter Administration's Quest*, p. 47.

58. Ibid., p. 46.

59. Carter, "Foreign Policy and the National Character," p. 177.

60. Brzezinski, "American Policy and Global Change," p. 461.

61. Harold Brown, "Challenges Confronting the National Security," address before the World Affairs Council of Northern California, San Francisco, July 29, 1977, in U.S. Department of State, *American Foreign Policy: Basic Documents. 1977–1980* (Washington, D.C.: U.S. Government Printing Office, 1983), pp. 12–13.

62. Larry Niksch, "U.S. Troop Withdrawal from South Korea: Past Shortcomings and Future Prospects," *Asian Survey* 27 (March 1981): 326.

63. Ibid.

64. Lucy Wilson Benson, "Controlling Arms Transfers: An Instrument of U.S. Foreign Policy," *Department of State Bulletin*, Aug. 1, 1977, p. 156.

65. All of the following figures and comparisons regarding the defense budget projections of the Ford and Carter administrations have been taken from Lawrence Korb, "The Policy Impacts of the Carter Defense Program," in *Defense Policy and the Presidency: Carter's First Years*, ed. Samuel Sarkesian (Boulder, Colo.: Westview, 1979), pp. 138–99.

66. Cyrus Vance, "Meeting the Challenges of a Changing World," address before the Association of Community and Junior Colleges, Chicago, May 1, 1979, in U.S. Department of State, *American Foreign Policy: Basic Documents. 1977–1980* (Washington, D.C.: U.S. Government Printing Office, 1983), document 12, p. 42.

67. Louis Kraar, "Yes, the Administration Does Have a Defense Policy (of Sorts)," *Fortune*, June 19, 1978, p. 129.

68. Ibid., p. 128.

69. Harold Brown, "Challenges Confronting the National Security," p. 13.

70. The most extensive and detailed source on the Carter administration policies toward the Soviet Union, discussed below, is Raymond Garthoff, *Détente and Confrontation: American-Soviet Relations from Nixon to Reagan* (Washington, D.C.: Brookings, 1984).

71. Andrew L. Pierre, *The Global Politics of Arms Sales*, (Princeton: Princeton University Press, 1982), p. 57.

72. Jerel Rosati, "The Impact of Beliefs on Behavior: The Foreign Policy of the Carter Administration," in *Foreign Policy Decision-Making: Perception. Cognition. and Artificial Intelligence*, ed. Donald Sylvan and Steve Chan (New York: Praeger, 1984).

CHAPTER THREE

1. Robert Tucker, "Reagan Without Tears: His 'Simple' World View is Truer than Carter's 'Complex' One," *New Republic*, May 17, 1980, p. 23.

2. This is a persistent theme, for instance, in Norman Podhoretz, *The Present Danger* (New York: Simon and Schuster, 1980).

3. Barry Posen and Stephen Van Evera, "Overarming and Underwhelming," *Foreign Policy*, no. 40 (fall 1980): 118.

4. This discussion will rely principally upon Robert Gilpin, *War and Change in World Politics* (Princeton, N.J.: Princeton University Press, 1981). Others have also discussed the rise and decline of hegemonic powers, reaching many of the same conclusions as Gilpin. Among these sources are George Modelski, "The Long Cycles of Global Politics and the Nation-State," *Comparative Studies in Sciety and History* 20 (April 1978): 214–35; Christopher Chase-Dunn, "International Economic Policy in a Declining Core State," in *America in a Changing World Political Economy*, ed. William Avery and David Rapkin (New York: Longman, 1982); and Paul Kennedy, *The Rise and Fall of the Great Powers: Economic Change and Military Conflict from 1500 to 2000* (New York: Random House, 1987).

5. Gilpin, *War and Change*, p. 168.

6. On the nature of collective goods in the international system, see Ibid., pp. 168–75. Also see Charles Kindleberger, *The World In Depression 1929–1939* (London: Allen Lane, 1973), pp. 291–308.

7. For a discussion of how the transfer of U.S. technology helped establish the Japanese semi-conductor industry, for instance, see Michael Borrus, James Millstein, and John Zysman, "Trade and Development in the Semi-Conductor Industry: Japanese Challenge and American Response," in *American Industry in International Competition*, ed. John Zysman and Laura D'Andrea Tyson (Ithaca, N.Y.: Cornell University Press, 1983), esp. pp. 177, 203, and 223. Also see Charles Ferguson, "America's High Tech Decline," *Foreign Policy*, no. 74 (1989): 123–44; B. R. Inman and Daniel F. Burton, "Technology and U.S. National Security," in *Rethinking America's National Security*, ed. Graham Allison and Gregory F. Treverton (New York: Norton, 1992) and Laura D'Andrea Tyson, *Who's Bashing Whom? Trade Conflict in High-Technology Industries* (Washington, D.C.: Institute for International Economics, 1992).

8. Joseph Nye, *Bound to Lead* (New York: Basic Books, 1990), p. 212.

9. Figures drawn from Table 5 titled "Structure of Demand" in World Bank, *World Development Report*, 1985, New York: Oxford University Press, 1985, pp. 182–83.

10. Kenneth Oye, "Constrained Confidence and the Evolution of Reagan Foreign Policy," in *Eagle Resurgent? The Reagan Era in American Foreign Policy*, ed. (Boston: Little, Brown, 1987), p. 11.

11. From 1975 to 1985, inclusive, the average annual rate of growth in economic productivity for the following five countries was: United States 0.73, West Germany 2.35, France 2.15, Great Britain 1.68, Italy 1.25. In other words, the average yearly rate of productivity growth among these other four countries was well over twice that of the United States during this period (1.83 vs. 0.73). For figures, see David Calleo, *Beyond American Hegemony: The Future of the Western Alliance* (New York: Basic Books, 1987), p.252.

12. Oye, "Constrained Confidence," p. 17. With regard to the Reagan defense buildup, take note of Paul Kennedy's comment: "Great Powers in relative decline instinctively respond by spending more on security, thereby diverting potential resources from investment and compounding their long-term dilemma." Paul Kennedy, "The (Relative) Decline of America," *The Atlantic Monthly* 260 (August 1987): 34.

13. A review of the literature on military spending and economic performance can be found in Michael D. Ward and David R. Davis, "Sizing Up the Peace Dividend: Economic Growth and Military Spending in the United States, 1948–1996," *American Political Science Review* 86 (September 1992): 748–55. Based upon their own empirical study, Ward and Davis conclude that high military spending has served as a drag on U.S. economic growth during the post–World War II period. For other discussions of this issue, see Steve Chan, "Military Expenditures and Economic Performance," in U.S. Arms Control and Disarmament Agency, *World Military Expenditures and Arms Transfers*, New Brunswick, N.J.: Transaction Books, 1986; Faye Duchin, "Economic Consequences of Military Spending," *Journal of Economic Issues* 17 (June 1983): 543–53; Robert DeGrasse Jr., *The Costs and Consequences of Reagan's Military Buildup* (New York: Council on Economic Priorities, 1982); and Kennedy, *Rise and Fall*, pp. 404–6.

14. Stephen Krasner, "American Policy and Global Economic Stability," in *America in a Changing World Political Economy* (New York: Longman, 1982), table 2.2, p. 38.

15. Central Intelligence Agency, *Handbook of Economic Statistics* (Washington, D.C.: U.S. Government Printing Office, 1986), table 109, p. 146.

16. David Blake and Robert Walters, *The Politics of Global Economic Relations*, 3rd ed. (Englewood Cliffs, N.J.: Prentice-Hall, 1987), figure 2–3, p. 17.

17. Robert Reich, *The Next American Frontier* (New York: Time Books, 1983), pp. 284–85.

18. This data is cited in Helen Milner, *Resisting Protectionism: Global Industries and the Politics of International Trade* (Princeton: Princeton University Press, 1988), p. 7.

19. Based upon William Thompson's calculations, cited in Nye, *Bound To Lead*, p. 76.

20. Laura D'Andrea Tyson, *Who's Bashing Whom? Trade Conflict in High Technology Industries* (Washington, D.C.: Institute for International Economics, 1992), p. 19,

21. Oye, "Constrained Confidence," p. 11.

22. This conclusion is not universally shared. A number of scholars have challenged the view that the United States is or has been a declining power. For examples, see Bruce Russett, "The Mysterious Case of Vanishing Hegemony, Or, Is Mark Twain Really Dead?" *International Organization* 39 (spring 1985): 207–32; Susan Strange, "The Persistent Myth of Lost Hegemony," *International Organization* 41 (autumn 1987): 551–74; Joseph Nye, "Short-Term Folly, Not Long Term Decline," *New Perspectives Quarterly* 5 (summer 1988): 33–35; and Stephen Gill, "American Hegemony: Its Limits and Prospects in the Reagan Era," *Millennium: Journal of International Studies* 15, no. 3 (1986).

The most extensive statement of the "anti-declinist" intepretation can be found in Nye, *Bound to Lead*. An extended discussion of the "declinism" debate is unnecessary for the purposes of the present study. But several relevent points should be made. First, the most important question from the standpoint of evaluating Carter's foreign policy strategy is whether the administration correctly perceived the trends in relative power that characterized the U.S. position through the mid-to-late seventies. On this issue, there is little disagreement between Nye's position and that presented here. Nye states that "there is no question that the slope of American decline was quite steep in the quarter century after the war." He argues, however, that "American decline has been much more difficult to discern from 1973 to the present" (p. 73). Even if Nye is right about the past two decades, the Carter administration found itself responding to the conditions created by the "steep" decline of the earlier postwar period. The operative problem facing decision makers was less declining power as such than the negative consequences of relative decline for the balance between internal resources and external commitments.

Second, the difficulties involved in meeting the array of U.S. external commitments during the seventies and eighties were not solely a product of declining relative international power. The tradeoffs facing policy makers were exacerbated by the fact that domestic demands on the federal coffers were growing rapidly over these decades (chiefly, via entitlements) while the political and economic constraints on the government's ability to raise tax levels were stronger than before. International burdens weighed more heavily in this period than, say, during the fifties, precisely because growing domestic demands combined with revenue constraints left less slack for financing external commitments without resorting to a rapid buildup of public debt.

23. In addition to the references cited below for specific topics, an excellent overall critique of the international-centered argument under examination here can be found in Ken Booth and Phil Williams, "Reagan's Myths About Détente," *World Policy* 3 (summer 1985): 501–32.

24. The case against Carter's defense policies is detailed in Colin Gray and Jeffrey Barlow, "Inexcusable Restraint: The Decline of American Military Power in the 1970s," *International Security* 10 (fall 1985): 27–69. A comparison of the Carter defense program with that of the early Reagan administration can be found in Samuel Wells, "A Question of Priorities: A Comparison of the Carter and Reagan Defense Programs," *Orbis* 27 (fall 1983): 641–66. Wells offers a generally critical evaluation of Carter's policies as compared with Reagan's.

25. See Arthur Macy Cox, "The CIA's Tragic Error," *New York Review of Books*, November 6, 1980; Leslie Gelb and Richard Halloren, "CIA Analysis Now Said to Find U.S. Overstated Soviet Arms Rise," *New York Times*, March 3, 1983, p. A-l; and Hedrick Smith, "CIA Report Says Soviet Arms Spending Slowed," *New York Times*, November 19, 1983, p. 6.

26. See Franklyn Holzman, "Are the Soviets Really Outspending the U.S. on Defense?" *International Security* 4 (spring 1980): 86–104; and Richard Stubbing, "The Imaginary Defense Gap: We Already Outspend Them," *Washington Post*, February 14, 1982, p. C-l.

27. See Barry Posen and Stephen Van Evera, "Overarming and Underwhelming," *Foreign Policy*, no. 40 (fall 1980):90–118. Also see Robert Komer, "What 'Decade of Neglect'?" *International Security* 10 (fall 1985): 70–83.

28. See the various essays in *Conventional Forces and American Defense Policy*, ed. Steven Miller (Princeton, N.J.: Princeton University Press, 1986), especially Barry Posen and Stephen Van Evera, "Defense Policy of the Reagan Administration: Departure From Containment"; Barry Posen, "Measuring the European Balance: Coping with Complexity in Threat Assessment"; John Mearsheimer, "Why the Soviets Can't Win Quickly in Central Europe"; and Benjamin Lambeth, "Uncertainties for the Soviet War Planner." Also see Warner Schilling, "U.S. Strategic Nuclear Concepts in the 1970's: The Search for Sufficiently Equivalent Countervailing Parity," in *Strategy and Nuclear Deterrence*, ed. Steven Miller (Princeton, N.J.: Princeton University Press, 1984).

29. This paragraph and the propositions listed below summarize arguments that, in whole or in part, can be found in the writings of a number of authors. In the interests of brevity, I

address the literature as a whole below rather than each author in turn. For a representative sampling, see Bayard Rustin and Carl Gershman, "Africa, Soviet Imperialism and the Retreat of American Power," *Commentary* 64 (October 1977): 33–43; Podhoretz, *Present Danger*; Jeane Kirkpatrick, "Dictatorships and Double Standards," *Commentary* 68 (November 1979): 34–45; and Keith Payne, "Are They Interested in Stability? The Soviet View of Intervention," *Comparative Strategy* Spring 1981). Also see a number of reports prepared by the Committee on the Present Danger in *Alerting America: The Papers of the Committee on the Present Danger*, ed. Charles Tyroler II (Washington, D.C.: Pergamon-Brassey's, 1984).

30. Samuel Huntington, "Renewed Hostility," in *The Making of America's Soviet Policy*, ed. Joseph Nye (New Haven: Yale University Press, 1984), p. 275.

31. Robert Legvold, "The Super Rivals: Conflict in the Third World," *Foreign Affairs* 57 (spring 1979): 761.

32. See Wayne Smith, "A Trap in Angola, " *Foreign Policy*, no. 62 (spring 1986): 61–74; John Stockwell, *In Search of Enemies: A CIA Story* (New York: Norton, 1978); and Raymond Garthoff, *Détente and Confrontation: American-Soviet Relations from Nixon to Reagan* (Washington, D.C.: Brookings, 1984), pp. 502–37.

33. Garthoff, *Détente and Confrontation*, pp. 623–30.

34. Ibid., pp. 630–53.

35. Ibid., pp. 699 and 716.

36. Fred Halliday, *Soviet Policy in the Arc of Crisis*, Washington D.C.: The Institute for Policy Studies, 1981, pp. 86–88; and Garthoff, *Détente and Confrontation*, pp. 894–95.

37. Legvold, "The Super Rivals, " p. 768.

38. Garthoff, *Détente and Confrontation*, p. 642.

39. Posen and Van Evera, "Overarming and Underwhelming," p. 116. Also see George Kennan, "The Soviet Threat: How Real?" *Inquiry*, March 17, 1980; Halliday, *Soviet Policy*, and "Soviet Geopolitical Momentum: Myth or Menace?" *The Defense Monitor* 9, no. 1 (1980).

40. Posen and Van Evera, "Overarming and Underwhelming," pp. 116–17.

41. Garthoff, *Détente and Confrontation*, p. 640. Garthoff notes that administration officials were concerned that Somalia was also pressing territorial claims against neighboring Kenya and had given support to ethnic Somalian insurgents in the northern part of the country. Kenya, not surprisingly, strongly supported Ethiopia in the Ogaden War.

42. Garthoff, *Détente and Confrontation*, p. 13.

43. Marshall Shulman, "Four Decades of Irrationality: U.S.-Soviet Relations," in *World Politics 88/89*, ed. Suzanne P. Ogden (Guilford, Conn.: Dushkin, 1988), pp. 24–25.

44. Michael Mandelbaum and William Schneider, "The New Internationalisms: Public Opinion and American Foreign Policy," in *Eagle Entangled: U.S. Foreign Policy in a Complex World*, ed. Kenneth Oye, Donald Rothchild, and Robert Lieber (New York: Longman, 1979).

45. Many of the early contributors to *Foreign Policy* later served as members of Carter's foreign policy team.

46. At the core of conservative internationalism, of course, lie attitudes toward the Soviet Union. Neither Vietnam war experience nor Nixon and Kissinger's policy of détente generated any thoroughgoing change in the public's fundamental distrust of the Soviets. Even when enthusiasm for Détente was at its peak during the early seventies, never did more that 19 per-

cent of the public hold a favorable view toward the Soviet Union. See Tom Smith, "The Polls: American Attitudes Toward the Soviet Union and Communism," *Public Opinion Quarterly* 47 (summer 1983): 280.

47. Thus a three-way division characterized both elite and public opinion: conservative internationalism, liberal internationalism, and noninternationalism. See Mandelbaum and Schneider, "The New Internationalisms," and Ole Holsti and James Rosenau, *American Leadership in World Affairs: Vietnam and the Breakdown of Consensus* (Boston: Allen & Unwin, 1984), pp. 141–43.

48. The literature on foreign policy opinion and beliefs is extensive. In addition to the sources cited elsewhere in this chapter, other pieces relevant to the Carter era include Allen Barton, "Consensus and Conflict Among American Leaders," *Public Opinion Quarterly* 38 (winter 1974): 507–30; Charles Kegley and Eugene Wittkopf, "Beyond Consensus: The Domestic Context of American Foreign Policy," *International Journal* 38 (winter 1982–83): 77–106; Michael Maggiotto and Eugene Wittkopf, "American Attitudes Toward Foreign Policy," *International Studies Quarterly* 25 (December 1981): 601–31; John Mueller, "Changes in American Public Attitudes Toward International Involvement," in *The Limits of Military Intervention*, ed. Ellen Stern (Beverly Hills, Calif.: Sage, 1977); Robert Oldendick and Barbara Ann Bardes, "Mass and Elite Foreign Policy Opinions," *Public Opinion Quarterly* 46 (fall 1982): 368–82; Alvin Richman, "Public Attitudes on Military Power, 1981," *Public Opinion* 4 (December/January 1982): 44–46; Bruce Russett and Donald DeLuca "'Don't Tread on Me': Public Opinion and Foreign Policy in the Eighties," *Political Science Quarterly* 96 (fall 1981):381–400; William Schambra, "More Bucks for the Bang: New Public Attitudes Toward Foreign Policy," *Public Opinion* 2 (January/February 1979): 47–51; William Watts and Lloyd Free, "Internationalism Comes of Age . . . Again," *Public Opinion* 3 (April/May 1980): 46–50; Eugene Wittkopf, "Elites and Masses: A Comparative Analysis of Attitudes Toward America's World Role," *Journal of Politics* 45, no.2 (1983): 303–34; Eugene Wittkopf and Michael Maggiotto, "The Two Faces of Internationalism: Public Attitudes Toward American Foreign Policy in the 1970's—And Beyond?," *Social Science Quarterly* 64 (June 1983): 288–304; Eugene Wittkopf, "Elites and Masses: Another Look at Attitudes Towards America's World Role," *International Studies Quarterly* 31 (June 1987): 131–59; Daniel Yankelovich "Farewell to 'President Knows Best,'" *Foreign Affairs: America and the World 1978* 57, no. 3: 670–93; and Daniel Yankelovich and Larry Kaagan, "Assertive America," *Foreign Affairs: America and the World 1980* 59, no. 3: 696–713.

49. For a report on CCFR survey findings, see *American Public Opinion and US Foreign Policy. 1975*, ed. John Rielly (Chicago: Chicago Council on Foreign Relations, 1975); and *American Public Opinion and US Foreign Policy. 1979*, ed. John Rielly (Chicago: Chicago Council on Foreign Relations, 1979).

50. For Holsti and Rosenau's analysis of their survey findings, see Holsti and Rosenau, *American Leadership in World Affairs*.

51. According to Schneider, the correlation between liberal internationalism and the net change in public support from 1974 to 1978 was $r=-.30$ (significant at $p=.02$). The correlation between conservative internationalism and net change in public support was $r=+.25$ (significant at $p=.05$). Since liberal internationalism and conservative internationalism share a common support for general internationalism, Schneider recalculated the correlation between

conservative internationalism and the net change in public support while controlling for internationalism. This provides a truer measure of ideological shifts, apart from changes in support for internationalism (which, incidentally, went down). This recalculation showed an even stronger correlation between the net change in public support and conservative internationalism at $r=.47$ (significant at $p=.01$). See William Schneider, "Conservatism, Not Interventionism: Trends in Foreign Policy Opinion, 1974–1982," in *Eagle Defiant: United States Foreign Policy in the 1980's*, ed. Kenneth Oye, Robert Lieber, and Donald Rothchild (Boston: Little, Brown, 1983), pp. 44–45.

52. *American Public and US Foreign Policy Opinion 1975*, and *American Public Opinion and US Foreign Policy 1979*.

53. Holsti and Rosenau, *American Leadership in World Affairs*.

54. From Walter Slocombe, Lloyd Free, Donald Lesh, and William Watts, "The Pursuit of National Security," *Policy Perspectives*.

55. From Daniel Yankelovich, "Cautious Internationalism: A Changing Mood Toward U.S. Foreign Policy," *Public Opinion* 1 (March/April 1978): 12–16.

56. Both items are cited in Daniel Yankelovich and Richard Smoke, "America's 'New Thinking,'" *Foreign Affairs* 67 (fall 1988): 4.

57. Commenting on the CCFR data, Wittkopf suggests that there may have been "a general turn toward conservatism even while the overriding structure of Americans' foreign policy beliefs remain undisturbed." In other words, the distance between the groupings remained roughly the same, while each segment of opinion became proportionately more conservative. Eugene Wittkopf, "On the Foreign Policy Beliefs of the American People: A Critique and Some Evidence," unpublished paper presented at the 1986 Annual Convention of the International Studies Association, Anaheim, Calif., March 25–29, 1986.

58. David Moore, "The Public is Uncertain, " *Foreign Policy*, no. 35 (summer 1979): 72.

59. Another critical factor was the consistently negative tone of most media and editorial coverage of Carter's foreign policy performance. For evidence on this point, see Mark Rozell, *The Press and the Carter Presidency* (Boulder, Colo.: Westview, 1989).

60. Samual Huntington, "Coping with the Lippmann Gap," *Foreign Affairs: American and the World 1987–88* 66, no. 3: 457.

61. See chapter 6 for an extensive discussion of the Panama Canal treaties case.

62. See chapter 6 for an extensive discussion of the SALT II treaty case.

63. For a discussion of the Carter administration' s China policies and the politics surrounding them, see Banning Garrett, "China Policy and the Constraints of Triangular Logic," in *Eagle Defiant*, pp. 245–51.

64. These differences were apparent in contrasting speeches given by Cyrus Vance and Zbigniew Brzezinski shortly after the decision to recognize the People's Republic of China was announced. See Bernard Gwertzman, "Vance and Brzezinski Differ Again on Peking Tie and Effect on Soviet," *New York Times*, Jan. 16, 1979, p. A-1.

65. On the development of an active constituency for the Carter administration's Africa policies, and those toward Zimbabwe in particular, see Andrew Young, "The United States and Africa: Victory for Diplomacy," *Foreign Affairs: America and the World 1980* 59, no. 3: 651–53.

66. Dimitri Simes, "The Anti-Soviet Brigade," *Foreign Policy*, no. 7 (winter 1979–80): 37.

CHAPTER FOUR

1. James Fallows, "The Passionless Presidency, I and II," *The Atlantic Monthly* 243 (May 1979): 33–46; (June 1979): 48.

2. Jimmy Carter, "Foreign Policy and the National Character," commencement address at the University of Notre Dame, May 22, 1977, reprinted in *American Foreign Relations. 1977: A Documentarv Record*, ed. Elaine Adam (New York: New York University Press, 1979), pp. 171–78.

3. See Katarina Brodin, "Belief Systems, Doctrines, and Foreign Policy," *Cooperation and Conflict* 7 no. 2 (1972): 97–112; Alexander George, "Domestic Constraints on Regime Change in US Foreign Policy: The Need for Policy Legitimacy," in *Change in the International System* (Boulder, Colo.: Westview Press, 1980), pp. 233–62; Theodore Lowi, *The End of Liberalism: The Second Republic of the United States,* 2d ed. (New York: Norton, 1979; and B. Thomas Trout, "Rhetoric Revisited: Political Legitimation and the Cold War," *International Studies Quarterly* 19 (September 1975): 251–84.

4. Leslie Gelb, "Dissenting on Consensus," in *The Vietnam Legacy: The War, American Society and the Future of American Foreign Policy*, ed. Anthony Lake (New York: New York University Press, 1976), pp. 113, 115.

5. Leslie Gelb, "National Security and the New Foreign Policy," *Parameters: Journal of the US Army War College* 7 (1977): 75.

6. Zbigniew Brzezinski, "American Policy and Global Change," address before the Trilateral Commission, Bonn, West Germany, Oct. 30, 1977; reprinted in *American Foreign Relations. 1977: A Documentarv Record*, ed. Elaine Adam (New York: New York University Press, 1979), p. 460.

7. Brodin, "Belief Systems," pp. 105–8.

8. George, "Domestic Constraints," p. 251.

9. Jimmy Carter, "Explaining U.S. Foreign Policy," address before representatives of United Nations member states, March 17, 1977; reprinted in *American Foreign Relations. 1977: A Documentarv Record*, ed. Elaine Adam (New York: New York University Press, 1979), p. 161.

10. The most revealing statement of the administration's approach toward the Third World can be found in an address by Undersecretary of State David Newsom, "The Challenge of Political Change," address before the American WhigCliosophic Society, Princeton University, March 22, 1979, reprinted in U.S. Department of State, *American Foreign Policy: Basic Documents. 1977–1980* (Washington, D.C.: U.S. Government Printing Office, 1983), document 10.

11. Anthony Lake, "Managing Complexity in U.S. Foreign Policy," speech before World Affairs Council of Northern California, San Francisco, March 14, 1978. Distributed by U.S. Department of State, Bureau of Public Affairs, Speech Series.

12. Carter, "Foreign Policy and the National Character," p. 174.

13. Brzezinski, "American Policy and Global Change," p. 465.

14. Richard Melanson, *Writing History and Making Policy: The Cold War, Vietnam, and Revisionism* (Lanham, Md.: University Press of America, 1983), p. 103.

15. George, "Domestic Constraints," p. 252.

16. Zbigniew Brzezinski, "America in a Hostile World," *Foreign Policy*, no. 23 (summer 1976).

17. Ibid., pp. 81–82.

18. Zbigniew Brzezinski, *Power and Principle: Memoirs of the National Security Adviser, 1977–81* (New York: Farror, Straus & Giroux, 1983), p. 3.

19. Brzezinski, "American Policy and Global Change," p. 456.

20. Gaddis Smith, Morality, Reason and Power: American Diplomacy in the Carter Years (New York: Hill and Wang, 1986) p. 50.

21. Quoted from internal memorandum in Burton Kaufman, *The Presidency of James Earl Carter, Jr.* (Lawrence: University of Kansas Press, 1993), p. 39.

22. Gelb, "National Security and the New Foreign Policy," p. 70.

23. See Michael Mandlebaum and William Schneider, "The New Internationalisms: Public Opinion and American Foreign Policy," *Eagle Entangled: U.S. Foreign Policy in a Complex World*, ed. Kenneth Oye, Donald Rothchild, and Robert Lieber (New York: Longman, 1979), p. 47.

24. John Rielly, *American Public Opinion and US Foreign Policy, 1979* (Chicago: Chicago Council on Foreign Relations, 1979), pp. 13–14.

25. Ibid., pp. 12–13.

26. Ibid., pp. 13–14.

27. Ibid., p. 8.

28. Lowi, *End of Liberalism*, pp. 145–48.

29. Destler, Leslie Gelb, and Anthony Lake, *Our Own Worst Enemy: The Unmaking of American Foreign Policy* (New York: Simon & Schuster, 1984), p. 73.

30. Quoted in Richard Burt, "In a Diplomatic Corner," *New York Times*, September 14, 1979.

31. See Raymond Garthoff, *Détente and Confrontation: American-Soviet Relations from Nixon to Reagan* (Washington, D.C.: Brookings, 1984), pp. 828–48; Smith, *Morality, Reason, and Power*, pp. 213–16; and David Newsom, *The Soviet Brigade in Cuba: A Study of Political Diplomacy* (Bloomington: Indiana University Press, 1987).

32. Leslie Gelb, "The Rightists' Brigade," *New York Times*, September 16, 1979.

33. Garthoff, *Détente and Confrontation*, p. 818.

34. Smith, *Morality, Reason and Power*, p. 168.

35. See C. Haberman and A. Krebs, "Arms Expert Resigns," *New York Times*, May 4, 1979, section III, p. 26.

36. Samuel Huntington, "Renewed Hostility," in *The Making of America's Soviet Policy*, ed. Joseph Nye (New Haven: Yale University Press, 1984), p. 282.

37. Garthoff, *Détente and Confrontation*, p. 946.

38. Jimmy Carter, "The State of the Union," address given before a joint session of Congress, January 23, 1980, reprinted in *James E. Carter*, ed. George Landevich (Dobbs Ferry, N.Y.: Oceana Publications, 1981), p. 135. Garthoff calls Carter's characterization "obviously a gross overstatement no matter how heinous or even potentially threatening the action." See Garthoff, *Détente and Confrontation*, p. 957.

39. Carter, "The State of the Union," p. 135.

40. Leslie Gelb, "Beyond the Carter Doctrine," *The New York Times Magazine*, February

10, 1980, p. 19.

41. Garthoff, *Détente and Confrontation*, pp. 951, 955–56, 958.

42. Ibid., pp. 891–98; and David Gibbs, "Does the USSR Have a 'Grand Strategy'? Reinterpreting the Invasion of Afghanistan," *Journal of Peace Research* 24 (December 1987): 367–71.

43. Garthoff, *Détente and Confrontation*, p. 939.

44. Ibid., pp. 895–965.

45. Ibid., p. 921.

46. Ibid., p. 928.

47. Ibid., pp. 927–37. Also see Gibbs, "Does the USSR Have a 'Grand Strategy,'" pp. 372–74.

48. Garthoff, *Détente and Confrontation*, pp. 938–65. For an interpretation of U.S. responses to the Afghan crisis that parallels that offered here, see David Gibbs, "The Military-Industrial Complex, Sectoral Conflict and the Study of U.S. Foreign Policy," in *Business and the State in International Relations*, ed. Ronald Cox (Boulder: Westview Press, 1996).

49. Garthoff, *Détente and Confrontation*, pp. 961–65.

50. Ibid., p. 957.

51. From CBS/New York Times surveys. Reported in "Opinion Roundup," *Public Opinion* 3 (Feb./March 1980): 21. It is important to emphasize that while Afghanistan raised the public salience of foreign policy issues, it did not represent as sharp a turning point in public opinion as is sometimes suggested. As Schnieder's analysis of the CCFR data (see chapter 4) clearly shows, the public had been moving in a more conservative direction, and one more given to distrust toward the Soviet Union, for several years prior to Afghanistan.

52. Cited in Kaufman, *The Presidency of James Earl Carter, Jr.*, p. 164.

53. George Gallup, *The Gallup Poll: Public Opinion 1980* (Wilmington, Del.: Scholarly Resources, 1981).

54. "Opinion Roundup," p. 27.

55. Gallup, *The Gallup Poll: Public Opinion, 1980*. The same pattern characterized public reactions to Carter's policies toward the Iranian hostage crisis. In a CBS/New York Times poll taken in January, 1980, only 1 percent thought that Carter's reaction to the taking of American hostages by Iran had been "too tough." Thirty six percent believed that Carter was doing enough to end the hostage crisis. By far the largest share of respondents, 63 percent, believed that Carter should have taken stronger actions against Iran. See "Opinion Roundup," p. 27.

56. Daniel Yankelovich and Richard Smoke, "America's 'New Thinking,'" *Foreign Affairs* 67 (Fall 1988): 4.

CHAPTER FIVE

1. See Lester Milbrath, "Interest Groups and Foreign Policy," in *Domestic Sources of Foreign Policy*, ed. James Rosenau (New York: Free Press, 1967), p. 240; and Joseph Nye, "The Domestic Environment of U.S. Policy-Making," in *U.S.-Soviet Relations: The Next Phase*, ed. Arnold Horelick (Ithaca, N.Y.: Cornell University Press, 1986), p. 116.

2. Aaron Wildavsky, "The Two Presidencies," *Transaction* 37 (December 1966): 10.

3. See, for instance, Charles Kegley and Eugene Wittkopf, *American Foreign Policy: Pat-*

tern and Process, 4th ed. (New York: St. Martins Press, 1991), pp. 267–77.

4. Bernard Cohen, "The Influence of Special Interest Groups and Mass Media on Security Policy in the United States," in *Perspectives on American Foreign Policy,* ed. Charles Kegley and Eugene Wittkopf (New York: St. Martin's Press, 1983), p. 224.

5. Lloyd Jensen, *Explaining Foreign Policy* (Englewood Cliffs, N.J.: Prentice Hall, 1982), pp. 137–38.

6. Barry Hughes, *The Domestic Context of American Foreign Policy* (San Francisco: W. H. Freeman, 1978), p. 217.

7. Milbrath, "Interest Groups and Foreign Policy," p. 250.

8. Stephen Krasner, *Defending the National Interest* (Princeton, N.J.: Princeton University Press, 1978); and Peter Katzenstein, "Domestic Structures and Strategies of Foreign Economic Policy," in *Between Power and Plenty: Foreign Economic Policy of Advanced Industrial States,* ed. Peter Katzenstein (Madison: University of Wisconsin Press, 1978).

9. Harold Mueller and Thomas Risse-Kappen, "From the Outside in and From the Inside Out," in *The Limits of State Autonomy: Societal Groups and Foreign Policy Formulation,* ed. David Skidmore and Valerie Hudson (Boulder, Colo.: Westview Press, 1992), pp. 33–36.

10. Theodore Lowi, *The End of Liberalism: The Second Republic of the United States,* 2d ed., (New York: Norton, 1979); Alexander George, "Domestic Constraints on Regime Change in U.S. Foreign Policy: The Need for Policy Legitimacy," in *Change in the International System,* ed. Ole Holsti, Randolph Siverson and Alexander George (Boulder, Colo.: Westview Press, 1980); Miroslav Nincic, "U.S.-Soviet Policy and the Electoral Connection," *World Politics* 42 (April 1990): 370–96.

11. Krasner, *Defending the National Interest,* p. 70.

12. It is worth noting, however, that recent studies have documented high degrees of interest group mobilization and influence during the Cold War era on some issues, thus suggesting that the conventional wisdom may require rethinking even for this period. See Ronald Cox, *Power and Profits: U.S. Policy in Central America* (Lexington: University of Kentucky, 1994) and David Gibbs, *The Political Economy of Third World Intervention: Mines, Money and U.S. Policy in the Congo Crisis* (Chicago: University of Chicago Press, 1991), both of which examine cases of business influence over U.S. foreign policy.

13. On business alignments toward U.S. foreign policy during the seventies, see Thomas Ferguson and Joel Rogers, "The Empire Strikes Back," *The Nation,* November 1, 1980.

14. On the Trilateral Commission, see Stephen Gill, *American Hegemony and the Trilateral Commission* (Cambridge: Cambridge University Press, 1990); and Holly Sklar, ed., *Trilateralism: The Trilateral Commission and Elite Planning for World Management* (Boston: South End Press, 1980).

15. For an overview of the growth of such groups during the seventies, see Dimitri K. Simes, "The Anti-Soviet Brigade," *Foreign Policy,* no.7 (winter 1979–80):28–42; and David Gibbs, "The Military-Industrial Complex, Sectoral Conflict and the Study of U.S. Foreign Policy," in *Business and the State in International Relations,* ed. Ronald Cox (Boulder, Colo.: Westview Press, 1996). The growth of conservative think tanks also played a critical role in providing ideas and credibility for the conservative movement on both domestic and foreign policy issues during the late seventies and early eighties. See Gregg Easterbrook, "'Ideas Move Nations': How Conservative Third Taks Have Helped to Transform the Terms of Political De-

bate," *The Atlantic* 257 (January 1986): 66–80.

16. See G. Peele, *Revival and Reaction: The Right in Contemporary America* (Oxford: Clarendon Press, 1984); A. Crawford, *Thunder on the Right: The "New Right" and the Politics of Resentment* (New York: Pantheon, 1980); and Thomas Edsall, *Chain Reaction* (New York: Norton, 1991).

17. Samuel Huntington, "Renewed Hostility," in *The Making of America's Soviet Policy*, ed. Joseph Nye (New Haven: Yale University Press, 1984), p. 274.

18. John Spanier, *American Foreign Policy-Making and the Democratic Dilemmas*, 4th ed.(New York: Holt, Rinehart, and Winston, 1985), p. 205.

19. On the origins, composition and political leanings of the Coalition for a Democratic Majority, see Jerry Sanders, *Peddlers of Crisis: The Committee on the Present Danger and the Politics of Containment* (Boston: South End Press, 1983), p. 150.

20. Quoted in George D. Moffett III, *The Limits of Victory: The Ratification of the Panama Canal Treaties* (Ithaca, N.Y.: Cornell University Press, 1985), p. 67. For a review of Carter's general Latin American policy written by a former Carter National Security Council staff member, see Robert Pastor, "The Carter Administration and Latin America: A Test of Principle," in *United States Policy in Latin America: A Quarter Century of Crisis and Challenge*, ed. John Martz (Lincoln: University of Nebraska Press), 1988.

21. Cyrus Vance, "Meaning of the Treaties," statement before the Senate Committee on Foreign Relations, September 26, 1977; reprinted in *American Foreign Relations. 1977: A Documentary Record*, ed. Elaine Adam (New York: New York University Press, 1979), p. 372.

22. Quoted in Moffett, *The Limits of Victory*, p. 107.

23. Martin Tolchin, "White House Woos Holdouts on Canal," *New York Times*, March 14, 1978.

24. In this study, I am primarily concerned with tracing the evolution of competing liberal and conservative interest group coalitions over time and across issues during the seventies. In my discussion of the Panama Canal treaties debate, therefore, I give greatest attention to groups that played an enduring role in one or the other of these coalitions while devoting little discussion to groups that were motivated by specific and particular ties to the Panama issue alone. A number of such groups, nevertheless, played significant roles in the treaties debate, including the American expatriates, or "Zonians," who lived in the Canal Zone and lobbied against the treaties, and various maritime and economic interests, whose positions varied. On the former groups, see William Jordan, *Panama Odyssey* (Austin: University of Texas Press, 1984), pp. 302–3, 456. On the latter, see Moffett, *The Limits of Victory*, pp. 181–202.

25. Michael Hogan, *The Panama Canal in American Politics: Domestic Advocacy and the Evolution of Policy* (Carbondale, Ill.: Southern Illinois University Press, 1986), p. 120.

26. William Lanouette, "The Panama Canal Treaties—Playing in Peoria and in the Senate," *National Journal*, November 8, 1977, p. 1556.

27. Ibid., p. 1560.

28. The information contained in this paragraph has been drawn from David Maxfield, "Panama Canal: Groups Favoring Treaties Fight to Offset Opponent's Massive Lobbying Effort," *Congressional Quarterly Weekly Report* 36 (January 21, 1978): 137; "Panama Canal Treaties Spurred Intense Lobby Effort as Supporters, Opponents Sought Senate Votes," *Congressional Quarterly Almanac* 4 (1978): 389; "Panama Canal Fight: Senators Feel the Heat,"

U.S. News and World Report, February 13, 1978, pp. 37–38; Hogan, *The Panama Canal in American Politics*, p. 119; and Moffett, *The Limits of Victory*, p. 171

29. John Opperman, "The Panama Canal Treaties: Legislative Strategy for Advice and Consent," in *Legislating Foreign Policy*, ed. Hoyt Purvis and Steven Baker (Boulder, Colo.: Westview Press, 1984), p. 88.

30. Graham Hovey, "Canal 'Truth Squad' Plans a 5-day Blitz," *New York Times*, January 10, 1978, p. A-ll.

31. Clyde Haberman and Caroline Rand Herron, "Truth Squad Marches," *New York Times*, January 22, 1978, section IV, p. 2. Also see "Panama Canal Treaties Spurred Intense Lobby Effort . . .," p. 389.

32. Lanouette, "The Panama Canal Treaties," p. 1560.

33. Terence Smith, "G.O.P. Committee Votes to Oppose Canal Treaties," *New York Times*, October 1, 1977, p. A-9.

34. Lanouette, "The Panama Canal Treaties," p. 1560.

35. Moffett, *The Limits of Victory*, pp. 172–73.

36. Ibid., p. 173, and Thomas Hollihan, "The Public Controversy Over the Panama Canal Treaties: An Analysis of American Foreign Policy Rhetoric," *Western Journal of Speech Communication* 50 (fall 1986): 371.

37. Quoted in Ibid. Thompson reportedly warned Democratic Senator Thomas J. McIntyre of New Hampshire that he, Thompson, would run against McIntyre in the 1978 election if McIntyre voted for the treaties. See "Panama Canal Fight," p. 37.

38. Quoted in Craig Allen Smith, "Leadership, Orientation, and Rhetorical Vision: Jimmy Carter, The 'New Right,' and the Panama Canal," *Presidential Studies Quarterly* 16 (spring 1986): 323.

39. Ken Bode, "Carter and the Canal," *New Republic*, January 14, 1978, p. 9.

40. Moffett, *The Limits of Victory*, p. 171.

41. Cecil V. Crabb, Jr., and Pat M. Holt, *Invitation to Struggle: Congress. the President and Foreign Policy* (Washington D.C.: Congressional Quarterly Press, 1980), p. 73.

42. Hogan, *The Panama Canal in American Politics*, p. 124.

43. Ibid.

44. Thomas Franck and Edward Weisband, *Foreign Policy by Congress* (New York: Oxford University Press, 1979), p. 198.

45. Bode, "Carter and the Canal," p. 8.

46. Hogan, *The Panama Canal in American Politics*, p. 121.

47. "Panama Canal Treaties Spurred Intense Lobby Effort . . .," pp. 388–89.

48. Hogan, *The Panama Canal in American Politics*, p. 110.

49. Ibid., p. 107.

50. Jimmy Carter, "The Treaties with Panama," radio-television address on February 1, 1978; reprinted in *American Foreign Relations. 1977*, ed. Elaine Adam (New York: New York University Press, 1979), p. 347.

51. Carter himself refused to "condemn my predecessors for having signed" the original Panama Canal Treaty and claimed that Theodore Roosevelt would have supported the new canal treaties. While rejecting the charge of colonialism against the United States, the Carter administration did argue that existing arrangements harmed America's image in many parts

of the world by creating the "perception of colonialism." This, however, was a pragmatic argument and not a moral judgment. See Hogan, *The Panama Canal in American Politics*, pp. 149–51.

52. Michael Hogan reports, "Many religious leaders reconsidered their early support for the treaties precisely because of the administration's refusal to indict the United States on charges of 'colonialism." See *The panama Canal in American Politics*, p. 151. For more on the role of pro-treaty religious groups in the campaign, see also Moffett, *The Limits of Victory*, pp. 140–44.

53. Hogan, *The Panama Canal in American Politics*, p. 102.

54. Ibid., pp. 102–3.

55. Ibid., p. 103.

56. It is perhaps significant that, unlike many conservative groups opposed to the treaties, COACT disbanded following the Senate vote, thus diluting the organizational momentum that liberals might have derived from the treaties victory. The above account of COACT's activities rests upon Hogan, *The Panama Canal in American Politics*, pp. 95–100; Moffett, *The Limits of Victory*, pp. 82–85; and "Panama Canal Treaties Spurred Intense Lobby Effort . . .," p. 388.

57. Terence Smith, "Carter Asks Democratic Leaders to Help Him on Panama Treaties," *New York Times*, October 8, 1977, p. A-24.

58. See Hogan, *The Panama Canal in American Politics*, pp. 92–95; and Moffett, *The Limits of Victory*, pp. 71–112.

59. Carter, "The Treaties with Panama," p. 348.

60. Harold Brown, "Challenges Confronting the National Security," address before the World Affairs Council of Northern California, San Francisco, July 29, 1977, in U.S. Department of State, *American Foreign Policy: Basic Documents. 1977–1980* (Washington, D.C.: U.S. Government Printing Office, 1983), document 4, p. 12.

61. David C. Jones, the Air Force Chief of Staff, called the Panama agreement "a treaty the Joint Chiefs can fully support" and pledged that "we will do what we can to help its ratification." James Wooten, "Joint Chiefs Pledge to Help Carter," *New York Times*, August 12, 1977, p. A-6.

62. Carter, "The Treaties with Panama," p. 349.

63. Moffett, *The Limits of Victory*, p. 90.

64. For discussions of the leadership amendments, see Ibid., pp. 87–92, and Hogan, *The Panama Canal in American Politics*, p. 192–96.

65. Moffett, *The Limits of Victory*, p. 97.

66. Ibid., p. 98.

67. Ibid., p. 103.

68. For a discussion of the DeConcini episode, see Ibid., pp. 96–106.

69. In addition to the sources cited above, information concerning congressional bargaining over the treaties can be found in William Furlong and Margaret Scranton, *The Dynamics of Foreign Policy-Making: The President. The Congress and the Panama Canal Treaties* (Boulder, Colo.: Westview Press, 1984) and Robert Strong, "Jimmy Carter and the Panama Canal Treaties," *Presidential Studies Quarterly* 21 (Spring 1991): 269–85.

70. Moffett, *The Limits of Victory*, pp. 114–55, 209.

71. Based upon Roper survey. For results, see Ibid., p. 212.

72. Hogan, *The Panama Canal in American Politics*, p. 207 and pp. 200–7. Moffett echoes Hogan's view that the turnabout in public opinion was more illusion than reality. See Moffett, *The Limits of Victory*, pp. 112–37. Also, for a survey of the public polling on the canal issue, see Bernard Roshco, "The Polls: Polling on Panama—Si; Don't Know; Hell, No!" *Public Opinion Quarterly* 42 (winter 1978): 551–62.

73. Jimmy Carter, *Keeping Faith: Memoirs of a President* (Toronto: Bantam Books, 1982), p. 166.

74. Franck and Weisband, *Foreign Policy by Congress*, p. 277.

75. "Carter's Panama Triumph—What It Cost," *U.S. News and World Report*, March 27, 1978. On Carter's efforts to win votes through pork barrel politics, see also Franck and Weisband, *Foreign Policy by Congress*, p. 278.

76. For an account, see Carter, *Keeping Faith*, pp. 175–77.

77. Quoted in Tolchin, "White House Woos Holdouts on Canal."

78. Gaddis Smith, *Morality. Reason and Power: American Diplomacy During the Carter Years* (New York: Hill and Wang, 1986), p. 115.

79. Moffett, *The Limits of Victory*, p. 107.

80. Hedrick Smith, "After Panama, More Battles," *New York Times*, April 20, 1978, p. 1.

81. Moffett, *The Limits of Victory*, p. 176.

82. "Carter's Panama Triumph—What It Cost."

83. Spanier, *American Foreign Policy-Making*, p. 211.

84. Moffett, *The Limits of Victory*, p. 176.

85. See Ibid., pp. 174–75.

86. Max Kampelman, "Introduction," in *Alerting America: The Papers of the Committee on the Present Danger*, ed. Charles Tyroler II (Washington, D.C.: Pergamon-Brassey's, 1984), p. xvi. For a review and analysis of the foreign policy views of the Committee on the Present Danger and similar groups, see Simon Dalby, *Creating the Second Cold War: The Discourse of Politics*, New York: Guilford Publishers, 1990.

87. Other familiar names among the committee's founders were Henry Fowler, Lane Kirkland, Charls Walker, Elmo Zumwalt, William Colby, John Connally, Arthur Dean, Douglas Dillon, Andrew Goodpaster, Leon Keyserling, Charles Burton Marshall, Matthew Ridgway, Paul Seabury, Maxwell Taylor, Edward Teller and Bertram Wolfe. For a full list of the CPD's initial membership, see Tyroler, *Alerting America*, pp. 5–9. On the earlier CPD, see Samuel Wells, "Sounding the Tocsin: NSC 68 and the Soviet Threat," *International Security* 4 (fall 1979): 141–51, and Sanders, *Peddlers of Crisis*, pp. 51–148.

88. "Common Sense and the Common Danger: Policy Statement of the Committee on the Present Danger," in Tyroler, *Alerting America*, p. 3.

89. Richard Pipes, "Team B: The Reality Behind the Myth," *Commentary* 82 (October 1986): 40. Also see Sanders, *Peddlers of Crisis*, pp. 197–204.

90. See Franklyn Holzman, "Are the Soviets Really Outspending the U.S. on Defense?" *International Security* 4 (spring 1980); Arthur Macy Cox, "The CIA's Tragic Error," *The New York Review of Books*, November 6, 1980; Leslie Gelb and Richard Halloren, "CIA Analysis Now Said to Find U.S. Overstated Soviet Arms Rise," *New York Times*, March 3, 1983; Raymond Garthoff, *Détente and Confrontation: American-Soviet Relations from Nixon to Reagan*

(Washington, D.C.: Brookings, 1984), pp. 794–800; and Hedrick Smith, "CIA Report Says Soviet Arms Spending Slowed," *New York Times*, November 19, 1983.

91. Among these were Paul Warnke (arms control), Marshall Shulman (Soviet Union), Andrew Young (U.N.), Leslie Gelb (Politico–Military Affairs), Richard Moose (Africa), Richard Holbrooke (East Asia), Anthony Lake (Policy Planning), and Patricia Derian (human rights). On Carter's rejection of the CPD list, see Sanders, *Peddlers of Crisis*, p. 180. On the critical reaction of conservative Democrats to Carter's appointments, see Rowland Evans and Robert Novak, "A Complaint from the Democratic Center," *Washington Post*, January 31, 1977.

92. Warnke was criticized, in particular, for two articles he authored (1975; 1976–77) during the mid-seventies in which he warned against exaggerating the Soviet threat. See Paul Warnke, "Apes on a Treadmill," *Foreign Policy*, no. 18 (spring 1975): 12–29; and Paul Warnke, "We Don't Need a Devil (To Make or Keep Our Friends)," *Foreign Policy*, no. 25 (winter 1976–77): 78–87.

93. Sanders, *Peddlers of Crisis*, pp. 209–10.

94. M. Destler, "Treaty Troubles: Versailles in Reverse," *Foreign Policy*, no. 33 (winter 1978–79): 48.

95. Murray Marder, "The Arms Muddle: Some Aides Feel U.S. Miscalculated," *The Washington Post*, April 2, 1977; and Strobe Talbott, *Endgame: The Inside Story of SALT II* (New York: Harper and Row, 1979), pp. 38–78.

96. Alan Platt, "The Politics of Arms Control and the Strategic Balance," in *Rethinking the U.S. Strategic Posture*, ed. Barry Blechman (Cambridge, Mass.: Ballinger, 1982), pp. 169–70.

97. Carter, *Keeping Faith*, p. 81. On the role of interest groups in the B-l debate, see William Lanouette, "The Battle to Shape and Sell the New Arms Control Treaty," *National Journal* 9 (December 31, 1977): 1991; Gordon Adams, "The Iron Triangle: Inside the Defense Policy Process," in *The Domestic Sources of American Foreign Policy: Insights and Evidence*, ed. Charles Kegley and Eugene Wittkopf (New York: St. Martin's Press, 1988), p. 76; Fred Hampson, *How America Buys Its Weapons* (New York: Norton, 1989), pp. 170–76; and Nick Kotz, *Wild Blue Yonder: Money, Politics, and the B-1 Bomber* (New York: Pantheon Books, 1988).

98. Hartung, William, *And Weapons for All* (New York: HarperCollins, 1994), pp. 63–69.

99. Among the firms represented in ALESA were General Dynamics, Lockheed, McDonnell Douglas, Raytheon, and Rockwell International. See Ibid., p. 64.

100. Ibid., pp. 69–70.

101. Ibid., pp. 70–76.

102. See Smith, *Morality. Reason. and Power*; and Sanders, *Peddlers of Crisis*, pp. 244–47.

103. Sanders, *Peddlers of Crisis*, p. 247.

104. "Countering the Soviet Threat," in Tyroler, *Alerting America*, p. 179.

105. "The 1980 Crisis and What We Should Do About It," in Tyroler, *Alerting America*, pp. 171–72.

106. "Opinion Roundup: Americans and the World," *Public Opinion* 2 (May/March, 1979): 29.

107. George Gallup, *The Gallup Poll: Public Opinion. 1978* (Wilmington, Del.: Scholarly

Resources, 1979), p. 213.

108. Sanders, *Peddlers of Crisis*, pp. 252–53.

109. Cyrus Vance, *Hard Choices: Critical Years in America's Foreign Policy* (New York: Simon and Schuster, 1983), pp. 128–30.

110. Quoted in Donald Spencer, *The Carter Implosion: Jimmy Carter and the Amateur Style of Diplomacy* (New York: Praeger, 1988), pp. 38–39.

111. Sanders, *Peddlers of Crisis*, p. 250.

112. Huntington, "Renewed Hostility," p. 279.

113. Marshall Shulman, "An Overview of U.S.-Soviet Relations," statement before the Subcommittee on Europe and the Middle East of the Committee on International Relations, House of Representatives, September 26, 1978 reprinted in *American Foreign Relations. 1977*, ed. Elaine Adam (New York: New York University Press, 1979), p. 223.

114. Garthoff, *Détente and Confrontation*, p. 741.

115. Hedrick Smith, "Poll Shows Belief Soviet Leads in Arms," *New York Times*, June 13, 1979.

116. Caddell's data is cited in Burton Kaufman, *The Presidency of James Earl Carter, Jr.* (Lawrence: University of Kansas Press, 1993), p. 151.

117. "What Is the Soviet Union Up To?," in Tyroler, *Alerting America*, pp. 1213.

118. Smith, "Poll Shows Belief Soviet Leads in Arms."

119. Quoted in Richard Burt, "Senator Nunn Sees U.S. Arms-Lag Peril," *New York Times*, May 1, 1979.

120. For general background on the SALT II ratification debate, see Dan Caldwell, *The Dynamics of Domestic Politics and Arms Control: The SALT II Treaty Ratification Debate* (Columbia: University of South Carolina Press, 1991).

121. Quoted in Adam Clymer, "G.O.P. Leaders Support Dissent in Foreign Policy," *New York Times*, February 4, 1979.

122. Bernard Weinraub, "U.S. Military Strength Dwindling, Republicans Say," *New York Times*, March 2, 1979.

123. For information on many of the groups discussed below, see Cynthia Watson, *U.S. National Security Policy Groups: Institutional Profiles* (New York: Greenwood Press, 1990).

124. Sanders, *Peddlers of Crisis*, p. 264.

125. Quoted in David Kurkowski, "The Role of Interest Groups in the Domestic Debate on SALT II," Ph.D. dissertation, Temple University, 1982, p. 153.

126. Quoted in Robert Scheer, *With Enough Shovels: Reagan. Bush and Nuclear War*, rev. ed. (New York: Vintage Books, 1983), p. 37.

127. Sanders, *Peddlers of Crisis*, p. 225.

128. See Fred Neal, "Inertia on SALT," *New York Times*, January 22, 1979; Kurkowski, "The Role of Interest Groups," p. 134; Sanders, *Peddlers of Crisis*, pp. 226, 264.

129. Neal, "Inertia on SALT."

130. "Excerpts From Criticism of Arms Pact," *New York Times*, April 12, 1979. Also see Richard Burt, "Ex-Aides Assail Soviet Arms Treaty," *New York Times*, April 12, 1979.

131. See L. Charlton, "Groups Favoring Strong Defense Making Gains in Public Acceptance," *New York Times*, April 4, 1977; Lanouette, "The Battle to Shape and Sell," p. 1991; Kurkowski, "The Role of Interest Groups," pp. 133, 136–39; and Sanders, *Peddlers*

of Crisis, pp. 264–65.

132. Kurkowski, "The Role of Interest Groups," pp. 126–32.

133. Sanders, *Peddlers of Crisis*, pp. 264–65.

134. Kurkowski, "The Role of Interest Groups," p. 244.

135. Quoted in Charles Mohr, "Senator Garn Guides Foes of Arms Treaty," *New York Times*, May 29, 1979.

136. Quoted in "Jackson Calls Approval of Pact 'Appeasement,'" *New York Times*, June 13, 1979.

137. Quoted in *Congressional Digest*, 58, 1979, p. 205.

138. John Spanier and Joseph Nogee, *Congress. the Presidency and American Foreign Policy* (New York: Pergamon Press, 1981), p. 212.

139. Quoted in Steven Roberts, "Arms Pact Friends and Foes Rally for Senate Battle," *New York Times*, April 13, 1979.

140. Richard Burt, "Money Is Already Starting to Flow From Both Sides in Treaty Debate," *New York Times*, January 23, 1979.

141. Quoted in Kurkowski, "The Role of Interest Groups," p. 81.

142. Ibid., p. 85.

143. Hallenberg, "The Image of the Soviet Union in American Politics: The Role of Public Interest Groups, 1977–1980," unpublished manuscript presented at the Annual Meeting of the International Studies Association held in Washington, D.C., April 10–14, 1990, p. 15.

144. Kurkowski, "The Role of Interest Groups," p. 73.

145. Quoted in Lanouette, "The Battle to Shape and Sell," p. 1987.

146. Ibid., p. 1977; and Kurkowski, "The Role of Interest Groups," pp. 73–74.

147. Lanouette, "The Battle to Shape and Sell," pp. 1985, 1990.

148. Quoted in Ibid., p. 1985.

149. Kurkowski, "The Role of Interest Groups," pp.101–8.

150. Quoted in Lanouette, "The Battle to Shape and Sell," p. 1985.

151. Kurkowski, "The Role of Interest Groups," p. 115; and Hogan, *The Panama Canal in American Politics*, p. 110.

152. As of March, 1979, one survey found that SALT opponents had outspent supporters by a margin of 15 to 1. See P. Stuart, "Anti-SALT Lobbyists Outspend Pros 15:1," *Christian Science Monitor*, March 23, 1979, pp. 1, 7.

153. Platt, "The Politics of Arms Control," pp. 162–63.

154. Richard Burt, "A New Approach to Selling the Arms Pact," *New York Times*, April 6, 1979. Also see Richard Burt, "At Arms Length: The Chances for SALT II May Improve with Time," *New York Times*, May 13, 1979.

155. Reprinted in *Congressional Digest* 58 (1979): 202.

156. Ibid., p. 208.

157. Gallup, *The Gallup Poll*, pp. 123, 195, 272. These results were confirmed by other surveys. See also William Lanouette, "The Senate's SALT II Debate Hinges on 'Extraneous' Issues," *National Journal*, September 22, 1979, p. 1564; Kurkowski, "The Role of Interest Groups," pp. 284–91; and "Opinion Roundup: SALT Support Shaky," *Public Opinion* 2 (October/November, 1979): 40.

158. Smith, "Poll Shows Belief Soviet Leads in Arms."

159. Platt, "The Politics of Arms Control," p. 159.

160. From 1977 through 1979, the Committee on the Present Danger or its spokespersons were mentioned 98 times in the *Washington Post, Christian Science Monitor,* and (New Orleans) *Times-Picayune*. These papers mentioned the American Committee on East-West Accord only twenty-three times during the same period. See Hallenberg, "The Image of the Soviet Union in American Politics," pp. 19–22.

161. Kurkowski, "The Role of Interest Groups," pp. 292, 288.

162. Richard Burt, "Vance Warns that Senate Changes Could Doom Arms-Limitation Pact," *New York Times*, May 14, 1979. Yet the administration took pains to consult with Congress while negotiations were under way. In one White House aide's view: "I don't believe there's another issue of foreign policy where there has been more consultation." Twenty-six Senators along with forty-six Representatives, drawn from both parties, attended the Geneva negotiations. In several instances, the administration held out for additional Soviet concessions as a result of pressure from key senators. The White House hoped, apparently in vain, that extensive Senate involvement in shaping U.S. negotiating positions would lessen opposition to the treaty's ratification. See Hedrick Smith, "Three Cornered Arms Talks," *New York Times*, April 14, 1979.

163. Garthoff, *Détente and Confrontation*, p. 818.

164. Franck and Weisband, *Foreign Policy by Congress*, pp. 190–291.

165. Spanier, *American Foreign Policy-Making*, p. 214.

166. Richard Burt, "Some U.S. Aides Fear a Directive by Carter Will Slow Arms Curbs," *New York Times*, September 21, 1979.

167. See also Garthoff, *Détente and Confrontation*, p. 746.

168. Burt, "Senator Nunn Sees U.S. Arms-Lag Peril"; and Richard Burt, "Are the Russians Outspending the U.S. on Weapons?" *New York Times*, September 23, 1979.

169. Burt, "Are the Russians Outspending the U.S. on Weapons?"; Richard Burt, "Carter Accepting Substantial Rise in Arms Budget," *New York Times*, November 29, 1979; Terrence Smith, "President Calls for 4.5% Increases in Military Budgets for Five Years," *New York Times*, December 13, 1979; and Terence Smith, "Carter's Plans for Arms Rise," *New York Times*, December 14, 1979.

170. Quoted in Smith, "Carter's Plans for Arms Rise."

171. Richard Burt, "Senate Panel Votes Anti-Treaty Report," *New York Times*, December 21, 1979.

172. Quoted in Ibid.

173. Dan Caldwell, "The SALT II Treaty Ratification Debate," unpublished manuscript presented at the Annual Meeting of the International Studies Association held in Washington D.C., April 10–14, 1990, p. 2.

174. See, for instance, Platt, "The Politics of Arms Control."

Chapter Six

1. On the possibilities for adjustment in U.S. foreign policy, see Kenneth Oye, "Beyond Postwar Order and the New World Order: American Foreign Policy in Transition," in *Eagle in a New World: American Grand Strategy in the Post–Cold War World*, ed. Kenneth Oye, Robert Lieber, and Ronald Rothchild (New York: HarperCollins, 1992).

2. Jerry Sanders, *Peddlers of Crisis: The Committee on the Present Danger and the Politics of Containment* (Boston: South End Press, 1983), pp. 287–88.

3. This perspective on the Reagan administration's foreign policies owes much to the valuable insights contained in Kenneth Oye, "Constrained Confidence and the Evolution of Reagan Foreign Policy," in *Eagle Resurgent? The Reagan Era in American Foreign Policy*, ed. Kenneth Oye, Ronald Lieber, and Donald Rothchild (Boston: Little, Brown, 1987).

4. A readable account of the Reagan administration's foreign policy experience can be found in Lou Cannon, *President Reagan: The Role of a Lifetime* (New York: Simon & Schuster, 1991).

5. For a useful discussion of the issues discussed in this paragraph and the next, see Miles Kahler, "The United States and Western Europe: The Diplomatic Consequences of Mr. Reagan," in *Eagle Resurgent? The Reagan Era in American Foreign Policy*, ed. Kenneth Oye, Ronald Lieber, and Donald Rothchild (Boston: Little, Brown, 1987).

6. Joseph Nye, *Bound to Lead* (New York: Basic Books, 1990), p. 217–18.

7. For supporting data and argumentation on these points, see Oye, "Constrained Confidence. . . ." Also see Joseph Nye, "U.S. Power and Reagan Policy," *Orbis* 26 (summer 1982): 391–411.

8. Nye, *Bound to Lead*, p. 204. For a critique of Reagan's economic policies and their impact on America's global position, see Michael Moffitt, "Shocks, Deadlocks, and Scorched Earth: Reaganomics and the Decline of U.S. Hegemony," *World Policy Journal* 4 (fall 1987): 553–82.

9. On the Reagan defense program, see Barry Posen and Stephen Van Evera, "Reagan Administration Defense Policy: Departure from Containment," in *Eagle Resurgent? The Reagan Era in American Foreign Policy*, ed. Kenneth Oye, Ronald Lieber, and Donald Rothchild (Boston: Little, Brown, 1987); and Robert DeGrasse Jr., *The Costs and Consequences of Reagan's Military Buildup* (New York: Council on Economic Priorities, 1982).

10. William Arkin, "The Buildup That Wasn't," *The Bulletin of the Atomic Scientists* 45 (January/February 1989): 3–10.

11. For a good summary of the case against SDI including elaboration on those points mentioned below, see Peter Clausen, "SDI in Search of a Mission," *World Policy Journal* 2 (spring 1985): 249–70. Also, for a treatment of the technical obstacles to space-based defense, see Hans Bethe, Richard Garwin, Kurt Gottfield and Henry Kendall, "Space-Based Missile Defense," *Scientific American* 251 (October 1984): 39–41.

12. The following account of the Reagan administration's Naval strategy and the criticisms we review are based upon Jack Beatty, "In Harm's Way," *The Atlantic* 259 (May 1987): 37–53.

13. Ibid., p. 52

14. The heavy losses such an attack might entail for the U.S. fleet prompted Admiral Stansfield Turner to comment that "it is hard to believe that thoughtful military planners would actually do this." Quoted in Ibid., p. 41. The principal rationale provided for this risky strategy was that it would be necessary in order to prevent Soviet attack submarines from crippling allied resupply convoys attempting to cross the North Atlantic. Yet one analyst estimated that the Soviets would be able to devote no more than sixty submarines to harass the 14,000 ships the allies would have had available to carry large military supply loads. Given the long odds facing the Soviet subs, critics argued that a traditional "defensive sea control"

strategy could offer adequate protection for allied shipping at far less cost and risk than the offensive means proposed by the Reagan administration.

15. Barry Rubin notes that "although the White House had courted a reputation for toughness, in fact it did not carry out reprisals, or even attempt missions to rescue hostages, in various terrorist incidents." Barry Rubin, "The Reagan Administration and the Middle East," in *Eagle Resurgent? The Reagan Era in American Foreign Policy,* ed. Kenneth Oye, Ronald Lieber, and Donald Rothchild (Boston: Little, Brown, 1987), p. 450.

16. Bruce Jentleson, "The Reagan Administration Versus Nicaragua: The Limits of 'Type C' Coersive Diplomacy," in *The Limits of Coersive Diplomacy,* ed. Alexander George and William Simons, 2d edition (Boulder, Colo.: Westeview Press, 1994).

17. Tim Zimmermann, "Coersive Diplomacy and Libya," in *The Limits of Coersive Diplomacy,* ed. Alexander George and William Simons, 2d edition (Boulder, Colo.: Westeview Press, 1994.

18. Richard Hermann, "Coersive Diplomacy and the Crisis over Kuwait," in *The Limits of Coersive Diplomacy,* ed. Alexander George and William Simons, 2d edition (Boulder, Colo.: Westeview Press, 1994.

19. For an overview of these efforts, see Bob Woodward, *Veil: The Secret Wars of the CIA, 1981–1987* (New York: Simon & Schuster, 1987).

20. For a discussion of these issues, see Richard Feinberg and Kenneth Oye, "After the Fall: U.S. Policy Toward Radical Regimes," *World Policy Journal* 1 (fall 1983): 201–15.

21. For a discussion of the Philippine case, see Raymond Bonner, *Waltzing with a Dictator: The Marcoses and the Making of American Foreign Policy* (New York: Vintage Books, 1988), pp. 295–456.

22. For a discussion, see Terry Deibel, "Why Reagan is Strong," *Foreign Policy,* no. 62 (spring 1986): 108–25.

23. See Daniel Yankelovich and Richard Smoke, "America's 'New Thinking,'" *Foreign Affairs* 67 (fall 1988): 4.

24. For an analysis of trends in public opinion during the Reagan years, see William Schneider, "'Rambo' and Reality: Having It Both Ways," in *Eagle Resurgent? The Reagan Era in American Foreign Policy,* ed. Kenneth Oye, Ronald Lieber, and Donald Rothchild (Boston: Little, Brown, 1987).

25. Terry Deibel, "Bush's Foreign Policy: Mastery and Inaction," *Foreign Policy,* no. 84 (fall 1991): 3–23.

26. For general discussions of the U.S. competitive position in the world economy, see Paul Kennedy, *Preparing for the Twenty-First Century* (New York: Random House, 1993); Lester Thurow, *Head to Head: The Coming Economic Battle among Japan, Europe and America* (New York: Morrow, 1992); Jeffrey Garten, *A Cold Peace: America, Japan, Germany, and the Struggle for Supremacy* (New York: Times Books, 1992); Clyde Prestowitz, *Trading Places: How We Allowed Japan to Take the Lead* (New York: Basic Books, 1988) and Wayne Sandholtz, et. al., *The Highest Stakes: The Economic Foundations of the Next Security System* (New York: Oxford University Press, 1992). For the case that the end of the Cold War will accelerate the relative decline of U.S. global power, see Aaron Friedberg, "The Future of American Power," *Political Science Quarterly* 109 (spring 1994): 1–22.

27. An excellent attempt to chart a roadmap for future adjustment in U.S. foreign and de-

fense policies can be found in Robert Art, "A Defensible Defense: American Grand Strategy After the Cold War," in *America's Strategy in a Changing World*, ed. Sean M. Lynn-Jones and Steven Miller (Cambridge: MIT Press, 1992).

28. For an argument that U.S. stakes in the Third World have been exaggerated, see Stephen Van Evera, "The United States and the Third World: When to Intervene," in *Eagle in a New World: American Grand Strategy in the Post–Cold War World*, ed. Kenneth Oye, Robert Lieber, and Ronald Rothchild (New York: HarperCollins, 1992) and David Callahan, "Saving Defense Dollars," *Foreign Policy* no. 96 (fall 1994): 94–112. For a rebuttal to Van Evera, see Steven David, "Why the Third World Still Matters," in *America's Strategy in a Changing World*, ed. Sean M. Lynn-Jones and Steven Miller (Cambridge: MIT Press, 1992).

29. For early overviews and assessments of Clinton's foreign policies, see Allen Tonelson, "Clinton's World," *Atlantic Monthly*, January, 1993, Charles William Maynes, "A Workable Clinton Doctrine," Foreign Policy, no. 93 (winter 1993–94): 3–21; Barry Schweid, "Warren's World," *Foreign Policy*, no. 94 (spring 1994): 137–47; and David Hendrickson, "The Recovery of Internationalism," *Foreign Affairs* 73 (September/October 1994): 26–43.

30. For a statement of the Clinton administration's foreign policy approach, see Warren Christopher, "America's Leadership, America's Opportunity," *Foreign Policy*, no. 98 (spring 1995): 6–27.

31. For overviews and evaluations of Clinton's defense program, see Dov Zakheim and Jeffrey Ranney, "Matching Defense Strategies to Resources: Challenges for the Clinton Administration," *International Security* 18 (summer 1993): 51–78; Callahan, "Saving Defense Dollars"; and Robert L. Borosage, "What to Do with Defense Spending: The Hungry Beast Growls," *The Nation*, October 3, 1994.

32. Ira Shorr, "Overkill," *In These Times*, January 23, 1995, p. 21.

33. See Borosage, "What to Do with Defense Spending," p. 337.

34. Eyal Press, "Arms Sales and False Economics: Prez Pampers Peddlers of Pain," *The Nation*, October 3, 1994, p. 340; Eric Schmidt, "Rulings on Foreign Arms Sales To Consider Economic Benefit," *New York Times*, November 16, 1994.

35. For a pessimistic appraisal, see Allan Nairn, "Occupation Haiti: The Eagle is Landing," *The Nation*, October 3, 1994.

36. Interestingly, Jimmy Carter, serving as an envoy of the Clinton administration, played a critical role in helping to negotiate the latter two diplomatic breakthroughs.

Chapter Seven

1. Alexander George's book on presidential decision making in foreign policy provides an excellent example of this approach. George examines how various impediments to effective "information processing" and the "rational calculation of policy" arise from the individual, small group and organizational contexts in which decisions are made. Rationality is defined according to five procedural criteria George specifies on page 10. This is, of course, a useful approach for examining many questions. It is less useful for understanding long term changes in underlying policy paradigms. See Alexander George, *Presidential Decision-making in Foreign Policy: The Effective Use of Information and Advice* (Boulder, Colo.: Westview Press, 1980).

2. For an innovative attempt to model foreign policy behavior based upon domestic in-

centives, see Douglas Van Belle, "Domestic Imperatives and Rational Models of Foreign Policy Decision-Making," in *The Limits of States Autonomy: Societal Groups and Foreign Policy Formulation*, ed. David Skidmore and Valerie Hudson (Boulder, Colo.: Westview Press, 1993).

3. See Theda Skocpol, "Bringing the State Back In: Strategies of Analysis in Current Research," in Bringing the State Back In, ed. Peter Evans, Dietrich Rueschemeyer and Theda Skocpol (Cambridge: Cambridge University Press, 1985).

4. On the interaction of domestic and international forces, see Peter Gourevitch, "The Second Image Reversed: The International Sources of Domestic Politics," *International Organization* 32 (autumn 1978): 881–912; Michael Mastanduno, David Lake, and G. John Ikenberry, "Toward a Realist Theory of State Action," *International Studies Quarterly* 33 (December 1989): 457–74; Robert Putnam, "Diplomacy and Domestic Politics: The Logic of Two Level Games," *International Organization* 42 (summer 1988): 427–60; and Harold Mueller and Thomas Risse-Kappen, "From the Outside In and From the Inside Out: International Relations, Domestic Politics and Foreign Policy," in *The Limits of States Autonomy: Societal Groups and Foreign Policy Formulation*, ed. David Skidmore and Valerie Hudson (Boulder, Colo.: Westview Press, 1993).

5. See Ernest May, *"Lessons" of the Past: The Use and Misuse of History in American Foreign Policy* (New York: Oxford University Press, 1973).

6. Stephen Krasner, "Approaches to the State: Alternative Conceptions and Historical Dynamics," *Comparative Politics* 16 (January 1984): 240–44.

7. Stephen Krasner, "Sovereignty: An Institutional Perspective," in *The Elusive State: International and Comparative Perspectives*, ed. James Caporaso (Newbury Park, Calif.: Sage, 1989), p. 74.

8. Jimmy Carter, *Keeping Faith: Memoirs of a President* (Toronto: Bantam, 1982), p. 21.

BIBLIOGRAPHY

The following bibliography lists the principal sources used in this study. For reasons of space, newspaper articles and individual speeches by members of the Carter administration have been omitted. The latter items are, however, included in the notes for each chapter.

Adam, Elaine, ed. *American Foreign Relations. 1977: A Documentary Record*. New York: New York University Press, 1979.
———, ed. *American Foreign Relations. 1978: A Documentary Record*, New York: New York University Press, 1979.
Adams, Gordon. "The Iron Triangle: Inside the Defense Policy Process." In *The Domestic Sources of American Foreign Policy: Insights and Evidence*, ed. Charles Kegley and Eugene Wittkopf. New York: St. Martin's, 1988.
Adelman, Kenneth. "The Runner Stumbles: Carter's Foreign Policy in the Year One." *Policy Review*, no. 3 (winter 1978): 89–115.
Ambrose, Stephen. *Rise to Globalism: American Foreign Policy, 1938–1976*. Rev. ed. New York: Penguin Books, 1976.
Arkin, William, "The Buildup That Wasn't," *The Bulletin of the Atomic Scientists* 45 (January/February 1989): 3–10.
Art, Robert. "A Defensible Defense: American Grand Strategy After the Cold War." In *America's Strategy in a Changing World*, ed. Sean M. Lynn-Jones and Steven Miller. Cambridge: MIT Press, 1992.
Barnet, Richard. "Carter's Patchwork Doctrine." *Harper's* (August 1977).
Barton, Allen. "Consensus and Conflict Among American Leaders." *Public Opinion Quarterly* 38 (winter 1974): 507–30.
Beatty, Jack. "In Harm's Way." *The Atlantic* 259 (May 1987): 37–53.
Bell, Coral. "Virtue Unrewarded: Carter's Foreign Policy at Mid-Term." *International Affairs* 54 (October 1978).
Bender, Gerald. "Angola, the Cubans, and American Anxieties." *Foreign Policy*, no. 31 (summer 1978):3–30.
Bethe, Hans, Richard Garwin, Kurt Gottfield, and Henry Kendall. "Space-Based Missile Defense." *Scientific American* 251 (October 1984): 39–49.

Bird, Kai. "Coopting the Third World Elites: Trilateralism and Saudi Arabia." In *Trilateralism: The Trilateral Commission and Elite Planning for World Management*, ed. Holly Sklar. Boston: South End, 1980.

Block, Fred. "Trilateralism and Inter-Capitalist Conflict." In *Trilateralism: The Trilateral Commission and Elite Planning for World Management*, ed. Holly Sklar. Boston: South End, 1980.

Bode, Ken. "Carter and the Canal." *New Republic*, January 14, 1978.

Bonner, Raymond. *Waltzing with a Dictator: The Marcoses and the Making of American Foreign Policy*. New York: Vintage Books, 1988.

Borosage, Robert L. "What to Do With Defense Spending: The Hungry Beast Growls." *The Nation*, October 3, 1994.

Booth, Ken, and Phil Williams. "Reagan's Myths About Detente." *World Policy* 3 (summer 1985): 501–32.

Borrus, Michael, James Millstein, and John Zysman. "Trade and Development in the Semi-Conductor Industry: Japanese Challenge and American Response." In *American Industry in International Competition*, ed. John Zysman and Laura Tyson. Ithaca, N.Y.: Cornell University Press, 1983.

Brawley, Mark. *Liberal Leadership: Great Powers and Their Challengers in Peace and War*. Ithaca: Cornell University Press, 1993.

Brodin, Katarina. "Belief Systems, Doctrines and Foreign Policy." *Cooperation and Conflict* 7, no. 2 (1972): 97–112.

Brzezinski, Zbigniew. "America in a Hostile World." *Foreign Policy*, no. 23 (summer 1976): 65–96.

———. *Power and Principle: Memoirs of the National Security Adviser, 1977–81*. New York: Farror, Straus & Giroux, 1983.

Caldwell, Dan. "The SALT II Treaty Ratification Debate." Unpublished manuscript presented at the Annual Meeting of the International Studies Association, Washington, D.C., April 10–14, 1990.

———. *The Dynamics of Domestic Politics and Arms Control: The SALT II Treaty Ratification Debate*. Columbia: University of South Carolina Press, 1991.

Callahan, David. "Saving Defense Dollars." *Foreign Policy*, no. 96 (fall 1994): 94–112.

Calleo, David. *Beyond American Hegemony: The Future of the Western Alliance*. New York: Basic Books, 1987.

Cannon, Lou. *President Reagan: The Role of a Lifetime*. New York: Simon & Schuster, 1991.

Carter, Jimmy. *Keeping Faith: Memoirs of a President*. Toronto: Bantam Books, 1982.

Chace, James, "Is a Foreign Policy Consensus Possible?" *Foreign Affairs* 57 (fall 1978): 1–16.

Chan, Steve. "Military Expenditures and Economic Performance." In U.S. Arms Control and Disarmament Agency, *World Military Expenditures and Arms Transfers*. New Brunswick, N.J.: Transaction Books, 1986.

Chase-Dunn, Christopher. "International Economic Policy in a Declining Core State." In *America in a Changing World Political Economy*, ed. William Avery and David Rapkin. New York: Longman, 1982.

Christopher, Warren. "America's Leadership, America's Opportunity." *Foreign Policy*, no. 98 (spring 1995): 6–27.

Cipolla, Carlos, ed. *The Economic Decline of Empires*, London: Methuen, 1970.
Clausen, Peter. "SDI in Search of a Mission." *World Policy Journal* 2 (spring 1985): 249–70.
Cohen, Bernard. "The Influence of Special Interest Groups and Mass Media on Security Policy in the United States." In *Perspectives on American Foreign Policy*, ed. Charles Kegley and Eugene Wittkopf. New York: St. Martin's, 1983.
Cox, Arthur Macy. "The CIA's Tragic Error." *New York Review of Books*, November 6, 1980.
Cox, Ronald. *Power and Profits: U.S. Policy in Central America*. Lexington: University of Kentucky, 1994.
Crabb, Jr., Cecil V., and Pat M. Holt. *Invitation to Struggle: Congress. the President and Foreign Policy.* Washington, D.C.: Congressional Quarterly Press, 1980.
Crawford, A. *Thunder on the Right: The "New Right" and the Politics of Resentment.* New York: Pantheon, 1980.
Dalby, Simon. *Creating the Second Cold War: The Discourse of Politics.* New York: Guilford Publishers, 1990.
David, Steven. "Why the Third World Still Matters." In *America's Strategy in a Changing World*, ed. Sean Lynn-Jones and Steven Miller. Cambridge: Cambridge University Press, 1992.
Davis, Vincent. "Carter Tries on the World for Size." In *The Post Imperial Presidency*, ed. Vincent Davis. New York: Praeger, 1980.
DeGrasse, Jr., Robert. *The Costs and Consequences of Reagan's Military Buildup.* New York: Council on Economic Priorities, 1982.
Deibel, Terry. "Why Reagan is Strong." *Foreign Policy*, no.62 (spring 1986): 108–25.
———. "Bush's Foreign Policy: Mastery and Inaction," *Foreign Policy*, no. 84 (fall 1991): 3–23.
Destler, I. M. "Treaty Troubles: Versailles in Reverse." *Foreign Policy*, no. 33 (winter 1978–79): 45–65.
Destler, I. M., Leslie Gelb, and Anthony Lake. *Our Own Worst Enemy: The Unmaking of American Foreign Policy.* New York: Simon & Schuster, 1984.
Duchin, Faye. "Economic Consequences of Military Spending." *Journal of Economic Issues* 17 (June 1983): 543–53.
Dumbell, John. *The Carter Presidency: A Re-evaluation.* New York: Manchester University Press, 1993.
Easterbrook, Gregg. "'Ideas Move Nations': How Conservative Think Tanks Have Helped to Transform the Terms of Political Debate." *The Atlantic* 257 (January 1986): 66–80.
Edsall, Thomas. *Chain Reaction.* New York: Norton, 1991.
Feinberg, Richard, and Kenneth Oye. "After the Fall: U.S. Policy Toward Radical Regimes." *World Policy Journal* 1 (fall 1983): 201–15.
Ferguson, Charles. "America's High Tech Decline." *Foreign Policy*, no. 74 (1989): 3–23.
Fallows, James. "The Passionless Presidency, I and II." *The Atlantic Monthly* 243 (May 1979): 33–48; (June 1979): 75–81.
Ferguson, Thomas, and Joel Rogers. "The Empire Strikes Back." *The Nation*, November 1, 1980.
Franck, Thomas, and Edward Weisband. *Foreign Policy by Congress.* New York: Oxford University Press, 1979.

Friedberg, Aaron. *The Weary Titan: Britain and the Experience of Relative Decline, 1895–1905*. Princeton: Princeton University Press, 1988.

———. "The Strategic Implications of Relative Economic Decline." *Political Science Quarterly* 104 (fall 1989): 401–32.

———. "The Future of American Power." *Political Science Quarterly* 109 (spring 1994): 1–22.

Frieden, Jeff. "The Trilateral Commission: Economics and Politics in the 1970's." In *Trilateralism: The Trilateral Commission and Elite Planning for World Management*, ed. Holly Sklar. Boston: South End, 1980.

Furlong, William, and Margaret Scranton. *The Dynamics of Foreign Policy-Making: The President. The Congress and the Panama Canal Treaties*. Boulder, Colo.: Westview, 1984.

Gaddis, John Lewis. *The United States and the Origins of the Cold War. 1941–1947*. New York: Columbia University Press, 1972.

Gallup, George. *The Gallup Poll: Public Opinion 1980*. Wilmington, Del.: Scholarly Resources, 1981.

Garthoff, Raymond. *Detente and Confrontation: American-Soviet Relations from Nixon to Reagan*. Washington, D.C.: Brookings, 1984.

Garten, Jeffrey. *A Cold Peace: America, Japan, Germany, and the Struggle for Supremacy*. New York: Times Books, 1992.

Garrett, Banning. "China Policy and the Constraints of Triangular Logic." In *Eagle Defiant: United States Foreign Policy in the 1980's*, ed. Kenneth Oye, Robert Lieber, and Donald Rothchild. Boston: Little, Brown, 1983.

Gelb, Leslie. "Dissenting on Consensus." In *The Vietnam Legacy: The War, American Society and the Future of American Foreign Policy*, ed. Anthony Lake. New York: New York University Press, 1976.

———. "National Security and the New Foreign Policy." *Parameters: Journal of the US Army War College* 7 (1977).

———. "Beyond the Carter Doctrine." *New York Times Magazine*, Feb. 10, 1980.

George, Alexander. "Domestic Constraints on Regime Change in U.S. Foreign Policy: The Need for Policy Legitimacy." In *Change in the International System*, ed. Ole Holsti, Randolph Siverson, and Alexander George. Boulder, Colo.: Westview, 1980.

———. *Presidential Decision-Making in Foreign Policy: The Effective Use of Information and Advice*. Boulder, Colo.: Westview, 1980.

Gershman, Carl. "The Rise and Fall of the New Foreign Policy Establishment." *Commentary* 70 (July 1980): 13–24.

Gibbs, David. *The Political Economy of Third World Intervention: Mines, Money and U.S. Policy in the Congo Crisis*. Chicago: University of Chicago Press, 1991.

———. "Does the USSR Have a 'Grand Strategy'? Reinterpreting the Invasion of Afghanistan." *Journal of Peace Research* 24 (December 1987): 365–79.

———. "The Military-Industrial Complex, Sectoral Conflict and the Study of U.S. Foreign Policy." In *Business and the State in International Relations*, ed. Ronald Cox. Boulder, Colo.: Westview, 1996.

Gill, Stephen. "American Hegemony: Its Limits and Prospects in the Reagan Era." *Millennium: Journal of International Studies* 15 (1986).

———. *American Hegemony and the Trilateral Commission*. Cambridge: Cambridge University Press, 1990.
Gilpin, Robert. *War and Change in World Politics*. Cambridge: Cambridge University Press, 1981.
Gould, Stephen Jay, and Niles Eldredge. "Punctuated Equilibria: The Tempo and Mode of Evolution Reconsidered." *Paleobiology*, 3 (spring 1977): 115–51.
Gourevitch, Peter. "The Second Image Reversed: The International Sources of Domestic Politics." *International Organization* 32 (autumn 1978): 881–912.
———. *Politics in Hard Times: Comparative Responses to International Economic Crises*. Ithaca: Cornell University Press, 1986.
Gray, Colin, and Jeffrey Barlow. "Inexcusable Restraint: The Decline of American Military Power in the 1970s." *International Security* 10 (fall 1985): 27–69.
Gutman, Roy. *Banana Diplomacy: The Making of American Foreign Policy in Nicaragua, 1981–1987*. New York: Simon & Schuster, 1988.
Haggard, Stephan. *Pathways from the Periphery*. Ithaca: Cornell University Press, 1990.
Hallenberg, J. "The Image of the Soviet Union in American Politics: The Role of Public Interest Groups, 1977–1980." Unpublished manuscript presented at the Annual Meeting of the International Studies Association, Washington, D.C., April 10–14, 1990.
Halliday, Fred. *Soviet Policy in the Arc of Crisis*. Washington, D.C.: Institute for Policy Studies, 1981.
Hampson, Fred. *How America Buys Its Weapons*. New York: Norton, 1989.
Hartung, William. *And Weapons for All*. New York: Harper Collins, 1994.
Hendrickson, David. "The Recovery of Internationalism." *Foreign Affairs* 73 (September/October 1994): 26–43.
Hermann, Richard. "Coersive Diplomacy and the Crisis over Kuwait." In *The Limits of Coercive Diplomacy*. 2d ed. Ed. Alexander George and William Simons. Boulder, Colo.: Westview, 1994.
Hermann, Charles. "New Foreign Policy Problems and Old Bureaucratic Organizations." In *The Domestic Sources of American Foreign Policy: Insights and Evidence*, ed. Charles Kegley and Eugene Wittkopf. New York: St. Martin's, 1988.
———. "Change Course: When Governments Choose to Redirect Foreign Policy." *International Studies Quarterly* 34 (March 1990): 3–21.
Hoffman, Stanley. "The Hell of Good Intentions." *Foreign Policy*, no.25 (winter 1977): 97–140.
———. "Carter's Soviet Problem." *New Republic*, July 29, 1978.
———. "A View from Home: The Perils of Incoherence," *Foreign Affairs: America and the World. 1978* 57, no. 3: 463–91.
———. "Reflections on the Present Danger." *The New York Review of Books*, March 6, 1980.
———. "Requiem." *Foreign Policy*, no. 42 (spring 1981): 3–26.
Hogan, Michael. *The Panama Canal in American Politics: Domestic Advocacy and the Evolution of Policy*. Carbondale, Il.: Southern Illinois University Press, 1986.
Hollihan, Thomas. "The Public Controversy Over the Panama Canal Treaties: An Analysis of American Foreign Policy Rhetoric." *Western Journal of Speech Communication* 50 (fall 1986): 368–87.

Holsti, Ole, and James Rosenau. *American Leadership in World Affairs: Vietnam and the Breakdown in Consensus.* Boston: Allen & Unwin, 1984.

Holzman, Franklyn. "Are the Soviets Really Outspending the U.S. on Defense?" *International Security* 4 (spring 1980):86–104.

Hughes, Barry. *The Domestic Context of American Foreign Policy.* San Francisco: W. H. Freeman, 1978.

Hughes, Thomas. "The Crack Up: The Price of Collective Irresponsibility." *Foreign Policy,* no. 40 (fall 1980): 33–60.

Huntington, Samuel. "Renewed Hostility." In *The Making of America's Soviet Policy,* ed. Joseph Nye. New Haven: Yale University Press, 1984.

Huntington, Samuel. "Coping with the Lippmann Gap." *Foreign Affairs: America and the World, 1987–88,* 66, no. 3: 453–77.

Ikenberry, G. John. "The State and Strategies of International Adjustment." *World Politics* 39 (October 1986): 53–77.

Inman, B. R., and Daniel F. Burton. "Technology and U.S. National Security." In *Rethinking America's National Security,* ed. Graham Allison and Gregory E. Treverton. New York: Norton, 1992.

Jensen, Lloyd. *Explaining Foreign Policy.* Englewood Cliffs, N.J.: Prentice Hall, 1982.

Jentleson, Bruce. "The Reagan Administration Versus Nicaragua: The Limits of 'Type C' Coercive Diplomacy." In *The Limits of Coercive Diplomacy.* 2d ed. Ed. Alexander George and William Simons. Boulder, Colo.: Westeview, 1994.

Jordan, William. *Panama Odyssey.* Austin: University of Texas Press, 1984.

Kahler, Miles. *Decolonization in Britain and France: Domestic Consequences of International Relations.* Princeton, N.J.: Princeton University Press, 1984.

———. "The United States and Western Europe: The Diplomatic Consequences of Mr. Reagan." In *Eagle Resurgent? The Reagan Era in American Foreign Policy,* ed. Kenneth Oye, Donald Rothchild, and Robert Lieber. Boston: Little, Brown, 1987.

Katznelson, Ira, and Kenneth Prewitt. "Constitutionalism, Class, and the Limits of Choice in U.S. Foreign Policy." In *Capitalism and the State in U.S.–Latin American Relations,* ed. Richard Fagen. Stanford, Calif.: Stanford University Press, 1979.

Katzenstein, Peter. "Domestic Structures and Strategies of Foreign Economic Policy." In *Between Power and Plenty: Foreign Economic Policy of Advanced Industrial States,* ed. Peter Katzenstein. Madison: University of Wisconsin Press, 1978.

———. *Small States in World Markets: Industrial Policy in Europe,* Ithaca: Cornell University Press, 1985.

Kaufman, Burton. *The Presidency of James Earl Carter, Jr.* Lawrence: University of Kansas, 1993.

Kegley, Charles, and Eugene Wittkopf. "Beyond Consensus: The Domestic Context of American Foreign Policy." *International Journal* 38 (winter 1982–83): 77–106.

———. *American Foreign Policy: Pattern and Process.* 4th ed. New York: St. Martin's, 1991.

Kennedy, Paul. *The Rise and Fall of the Great Powers: Economic Change and Military Conflict from 1500 to 2000.* New York: Random House, 1987.

———. "The (Relative) Decline of America." *The Atlantic,* August 1987.

Kennedy, Paul. *Preparing for the Twenty-First Century.* New York: Random House, 1993.

Kennan, George. "The Soviet Threat: How Real? " *Inquiry*, March 17, 1980.
Keohane, Robert. "Hegemonic Leadership and U.S. Foreign Economic Policy in the 'Long Decade' of the 1950's." In *America in a Changing World Political Economy*, ed. William Avery and David Rapkin. New York: Longman, 1982.
Keohane, Robert. *After Hegemony: Cooperation and Discord in the World Political Economy*. Princeton, N.J.: Princeton University Press, 1984.
Keohane, Robert. "Theory of World Politics: Structural Realism and Beyond." In *Neo-Realism and Its Critics*, ed. Robert Keohane. New York: Columbia University Press, 1986.
Kindleberger, Charles. *The World In Depression 1929–1939*. London: Allen Lane, 1973.
Kirkpatrick, Jeane. "Dictatorships and Double Standards." *Commentary* 68 (November 1979): 34–45.
Klunk, Brian. *Consensus and the American Mission*. Lanham, Md.: University Press of America, 1986.
Komer, Robert. "What 'Decade of Neglect'?" *International Security* 10 (fall 1985): 70–83.
Korb, Lawrence. "The Policy Impacts of the Carter Defense Program." In *Defense Policy and the Presidency: Carter's First Years*, ed. Samuel Sarkesian. Boulder, Colo.: Westview, 1979.
Kotz, Nick. *Wild Blue Yonder: Money, Politics, and the B-1 Bomber*. New York: Pantheon Books, 1988.
Kraar, Louis. "Yes, the Administration Does Have a Defense Policy (of Sorts)." *Fortune*, June 19, 1978.
Krasner, Stephen. "State Power and the Structure of Foreign Trade." *World Politics* 28 (April 1976): 317–47.
———. *Defending the National Interest: Raw Materials Investments and U.S. Foreign Policy*. Princeton, N.J.: Princeton University Press, 1978.
———. "United States Commercial and Monetary Policy: Unraveling the Paradox of External Strength and Internal Weakness." In *Between Power and Plenty: Foreign Economic Policies of Advanced Industrial States*, ed. Peter Katzenstein. Madison: University of Wisconsin Press, 1978.
———. "American Policy and Global Economic Stability." In *America in a Changing World Political Economy*, ed. William P. Avery and David P. Rapkin. New York: Longman, 1982.
———, ed. *International Regimes*, Ithaca, N.Y.: Cornell University Press, 1983.
———. "Approaches to the State: Alternative Conceptions and Historical Dynamics." *Comparative Politics* 16 (January 1984): 223–46.
———. "Sovereignty: An Institutional Perspective." In *The Elusive State: International and Comparative Perspectives*, ed. James Caporaso. Newbury Park, Calif.: Sage, 1989.
Kuhn, Thomas. *The Structure of Scientific Revolutions*. Chicago: University of Chicago Press, 1962.
Kupchan, Charles. *The Vulnerability of Empire*. Ithaca: Cornell University Press, 1994.
Kurkowski, David. "The Role of Interest Groups in the Domestic Debate on SALT II." Ph.D. dissertation, Temple University, 1982.
Lake, David. "International Economic Structures and American Foreign Economic Policy, 1887–1934." *World Politics* 35 (July 1983): 517–43.
———. "Leadership, Hegemony, and the International Economy: Naked Emperor or Tattered Monarch with Potential?" *International Studies Quarterly* 37 (December 1993):

459–89.

Lambeth, Benjamin. "Uncertainties for the Soviet War Planner." In *Conventional Forces and American Defense Policy*, ed. Steven Miller. Princeton, N.J.: Princeton University Press, 1986.

Lankevich, George, ed. *James E. Carter*. Dobbs Ferry, N.Y.: Oceana Publications, 1981.

Lanouette, William. "The Panama Canal Treaties: Playing in Peoria and in the Senate." *National Journal*, 9 (October 8, 1977): 1556–62.

———. "The Battle to Shape and Sell the New Arms Control Treaty." *National Journal* 9 (December 31, 1977): 1984–93.

———. "The Senate's SALT II Debate Hinges on 'Extraneous' Issues." *National Journal* 11 (September 22, 1979): 1564–67.

Layne, Christopher, and Benjamin Schwartz. "American Hegemony: Without an Enemy." *Foreign Policy*, no. 92 (fall 1993): 5–23.

LaFeber, Walter. *America. Russia and the Cold War. 1945–80*. 4th ed. New York: John Wiley, 1980.

———. "From Confusion to Cold War: The Memoirs of the Carter Administration." *Diplomatic History* (winter 1984).

Legvold, Robert. "The Super Rivals: Conflict in the Third World." *Foreign Affairs* 57 (spring 1979): 755–78.

Lowi, Theodore. *The End of Liberalism: The Second Republic of the United States*. 2d. ed. New York: Norton, 1979.

Maggiotto, Michael, and Eugene Wittkopf. "American Attitudes Toward Foreign Policy." *International Studies Quarterly* 25 (December 1981): 601–31.

Mandelbaum, Michael, and William Schneider. "The New Internationalisms: Public Opinion and American Foreign Policy." In *Eagle Entangled: U.S. Foreign Policy in a Complex World*, ed. Kenneth Oye, Donald Rothchild, and Robert Lieber. New York: Longman, 1979.

Mastanduno, Michael, David Lake, and G. John Ikenberry. "Toward a Realist Theory of State Action." *International Studies Quarterly* 33 (December 1989): 457–74.

Maxfield, David. "Panama Canal: Groups Favoring Treaties Fight to Offset Opponent's Massive Lobbying Effort." *Congressional Quarterly Weekly Report* 36 (January 21, 1978): 135–37.

May, Ernest. *"Lessons" of the Past: The Use and Misuse of History in American Foreign Policy*. New York: Oxford University Press, 1973.

———. "The Cold War." In *The Making of America's Soviet Policy*, ed. Joseph Nye. New Haven: Yale University Press, 1984.

Maynes, Charles William. "A Workable Clinton Doctrine." *Foreign Policy*, no. 93 (winter 1993–94): 3–21.

Mearsheimer, John. "Why the Soviets Can't Win Quickly in Central Europe." In *Conventional Forces and American Defense Policy*, ed. Steven Miller. Princeton, N.J.: Princeton University Press, 1986.

Melanson, Richard. *Writing History and Making Policy: The Cold War, Vietnam, and Revisionism*. Lanham, Md.: University Press of America, 1983.

Milbrath, Lester. "Interest Groups and Foreign Policy." in *Domestic Sources of Foreign Policy*, ed. James Rosenau. New York: Free Press, 1967.

Miller, Linda. "Morality in Foreign Policy: A Failed Consensus." *Daedalus* 109 (Summer 1980): 143–58.

Milner, Helen. *Resisting Protectionism: Global Industries and the Politics of International Trade.* Princeton: Princeton University Press, 1988.

Modelski, George. "The Long Cycles of Global Politics and the Nation-State." *Comparative Studies in Society and History* 20 (April 1978): 214–35.

Moffitt, Michael. "Shocks, Deadlocks, and Scorched Earth: Reaganomics and the Decline of U.S. Hegemony." *World Policy Journal* 4 (fall 1987): 553–82.

Moffett III, George D. *The Limits of Victory: The Ratification of the Panama Canal Treaties.* Ithaca, N.Y.: Cornell University Press, 1985.

Moore, David. "The Public is Uncertain." *Foreign Policy*, no. 35 (summer 1979): 68–73.

Morgenthau, Hans, and Kenneth Thomson. *Politics Among Nations: The Struggle for Power and Peace.* 6th ed. New York: Knopf, 1985.

Mueller, John. "Changes in American Public Attitudes Toward International Involvement." In *The Limits of Military Intervention*, ed. Ellen Stern. Beverly Hills, Calif.: Sage, 1977.

Mueller, Harold, and Thomas Risse-Kappen. "From the Outside in and From the Inside Out: International Relations, Domestic Politics and Foreign Policy." In David Skidmore and Valerie Hudson (eds.), *The Limits of State Autonomy: Societal Groups and Foreign Policy Formulation*, Boulder, Colo.: Westview, 1993.

Nairn, Allen, "Occupation Haiti: The Eagle is Landing," *The Nation*, October 3, 1994.

Nettl, J. P. "The State as a Conceptual Variable." *World Politics* 20 (July 1968): 559–92.

Newsom, David. *The Soviet Brigade in Cuba: A Study of Political Diplomacy.* Bloomington: Indiana University Press, 1987.

Niksch, Larry. "U.S. Troop Withdrawal From South Korea: Past Shortcomings and Future Prospects." *Asian Survey* 27 (March 1981): 325–41.

Nincic, Miroslav. "U.S.-Soviet Policy and the Electoral Connection." *World Politics* 42 (April 1990): 370–96.

Nisbet, Robert. *Social Change and History: Aspects of the Western Theory of Development*, New York: Oxford University Press, 1969.

Nye, Joseph. "U.S. Power and Reagan Policy," *Orbis* (summer 1982).

———. "The Domestic Environment of U.S. Policy-Making." In *U.S.-Soviet Relations: The Next Phase*, ed. Arnold Horelick. Ithaca: Cornell University Press, 1986.

———. "Short-Term Folly, Not Long Term Decline." *New Perspectives Quarterly* 5 (summer 1988): 33–35.

———. *Bound to Lead.* New York: Basic Books, 1990.

Oldendick, Robert, and Barbara Ann Bardes. "Mass and Elite Foreign Policy Opinions." *Public Opinion Quarterly* 46 (fall 1982): 368–82.

Olson, Mancur. *The Rise and Decline of Nations: Economic Growth. Stagflation. and Social Rigidities*, New Haven: Yale University Press, 1982.

"Opinion Roundup: Americans and the World." *Public Opinion* 2 (March/May 1979): 21–40.

"Opinion Roundup: SALT Support Shaky." *Public Opinion* 2 (October/November 1979): 40.

Opperman, John. "The Panama Canal Treaties: Legislative Strategy for Advice and Consent." In *Legislating Foreign Policy*, ed. Hoyt Purvis and Steven Baker. Boulder, Colo.: Westview,

1984.

Osgood, Robert. "Carter Policy in Perspective." *SAIS Review* 25 (winter 1981).

Oye, Kenneth. "International Constraints and Carter Administration Foreign Policy." In *Eagle Entangled: U.S. Foreign Policy in a Complex World*, ed. Kenneth Oye, Donald Rothchild, and Robert Lieber. New York: Longman, 1979.

———. "International Systems Structure and American Foreign Policy." In *Eagle Defiant: United States Foreign Policy in the 1980's*, ed. Kenneth Oye, Robert Lieber, and Donald Rothchild. Boston: Little, Brown, 1983.

———. "Constrained Confidence and the Evolution of Reagan Administration Foreign Policy." In *Eagle Resurgent? The Reagan Era in American Foreign Policy*, ed. Kenneth Oye, Donald Rothchild, and Robert Lieber. Boston: Little, Brown, 1987.

———. "Beyond Postwar Order and the New World Order: American Foreign Policy in Transition." In *Eagle in a New World: American Grand Strategy in the Post–Cold War World*, ed. Kenneth Oye, Robert Lieber and Ronald Rothchild. New York: Harper Collins, 1992.

"Panama Canal Treaties Spurred Intense Lobby Effort as Supporters, Opponents Sought Senate Votes." *Congressional Quarterly Almanac* 4 (1978): 388–89.

Pastor, Robert. "The Carter Administration and Latin America: A Test of Principle." In *United States Policy in Latin America: A Quarter Century of Crisis and Challenge*, ed. John Martz. Lincoln: University of Nebraska Press, 1988.

Payne, Keith. "Are They Interested in Stability? The Soviet View of Intervention." *Comparative Strategy* (spring 1981).

Peele, G. *Revival and Reaction: The Right in Contemporary America*. Oxford: Clarendon, 1984.

Petras, James. "U.S. Foreign Policy: The Revival of Interventionism." *Monthly Review* (February 1980).

Pierre, Andrew L. *The Global Politics of Arms Sales*. Princeton: Princeton University Press, 1982.

Pipes, Richard. "Team B: The Reality Behind the Myth." *Commentary* 82 (October 1986): 25–40.

Platt, Alan, "The Politics of Arms Control and the Strategic Balance." In *Rethinking the U.S. Strategic Posture*, ed. Barry Blechman. Cambridge, Mass.: Ballinger Publishing Co., 1982.

Podhoretz, Norman. "The Culture of Appeasement." *Harper's,* October 1977.

———. *The Present Danger*, New York: Simon & Schuster, 1980.

Posen, Barry. "Measuring the European Balance: Coping with Complexity in Threat Assessment." In *Conventional Forces and American Defense Policy*, ed. Steven Miller. Princeton, N.J.: Princeton University Press, 1986.

Posen, Barry, and Stephen Van Evera. "Overarming and Underwhelming." *Foreign Policy*, no. 40 (fall 1980):90–118.

———. "Defense Policy of the Reagan Administration: Departure From Containment." In *Conventional Forces and American Defense Policy*, ed. Steven Miller. Princeton, N.J.: Princeton University Press, 1986.

Press, Eyal. "Arms Sales and False Economics." *The Nation*, October 3, 1994.

Clyde Prestowitz. *Trading Places: How We Allowed Japan to Take the Lead*. New York: Basic Books, 1988.

Putnam, Robert. "Diplomacy and Domestic Politics: The Logic of Two Level Games." *Inter-

national Organization 42 (summer 1988): 427–60.

Quester, George. "Consensus Lost." *Foreign Policy*, no. 40 (fall 1980): 18–32.

Rapkin, David, ed. *World Leadership and Hegemony*. Boulder, Colo.: Lynne Rienner Publishers, 1990.

Raskin, Marcus. "The National Security State (Carter Style)." *Inquiry*, April 3, 1978.

Reich, Robert. *The Next American Frontier*. New York: Time Books, 1983.

Reichard, Gary. "Early Returns: Assessing Jimmy Carter." *Presidential Studies Quarterly* 20 (summer 1990): 603–20.

Richman, Alvin. "Public Attitudes on Military Power, 1981," *Public Opinion* 4 (December/January 1982): 44–46.

Rielly, John, ed. *American Public Opinion and US Foreign Policy. 1975*. Chicago: Chicago Council on Foreign Relations, 1975.

———, ed. *American Public Opinion and US Foreign Policy. 1979*. Chicago: Chicago Council on Foreign Relations, 1979.

Rosati, Jerel. "The Impact of Belief on Behavior: The Foreign Policy of the Carter Administration." In *Foreign Policy Decision-Making: Perception. Cognition. and Artificial Intelligence*, ed. Donald Sylvan and Steve Chan. New York: Praeger, 1984.

———. *The Carter Administration's Quest for Global Community: Beliefs and Their Impact on Behavior*. Columbia: University of South Carolina Press, 1987.

———. "Human Needs and the Evolution of U.S. Foreign Policy." In *The Power of Human Needs in World Society*, ed. Roger A. Coate and Jerel A. Rosati. Boulder, Colo.: Lynne Rienner Publishers, 1988.

Rosati, Jerel A., Joe D. Hagan, and Martin W. Sampson III, eds. *Foreign Policy Restructuring: How Governments Respond to Global Change*. Columbia: University of South Carolina Press, 1994.

Rosenau, James. *The Study of Political Adaptation: Essays on the Analysis of World Politics*. New York: Nichols, 1981.

Roshco, Bernard. "The Polls: Polling on Panama—Si; Don't Know; Hell, No!" *Public Opinion Quarterly* 42 (winter 1978): 551–62.

Rozell, Mark. *The Press and the Carter Presidency*. Boulder, Colo.: Westview, 1989.

Rubin, Barry. "The Reagan Administration and the Middle East." In *Eagle Resurgent? The Reagan Era in American Foreign Policy*, ed. Kenneth Oye, Donald Rothchild, and Robert Lieber. Boston: Little, Brown, 1987.

Russett, Bruce. "The Mysterious Case of Vanishing Hegemony; or Is Mark Twain Really Dead?" *International Organization* 39 (spring 1985): 207–32.

Russett, Bruce, and Donald DeLuca. "'Don't Tread on Me': Public Opinion and Foreign Policy in the Eighties." *Political Science Quarterly* 96 (fall 1981):381–400.

Rustin, Bayard, and Carl Gershman. "Africa, Soviet Imperialism and the Retreat of American Power." *Commentary* 64 (October 1977): 33–43.

Sanders, Jerry. *Peddlers of Crisis: The Committee on the Present Danger and the Politics of Containment*. Boston: South End, 1983.

Sandholtz, Wayne, et. al. *The Highest Stakes: The Economic Foundations of the Next Security System*. New York: Oxford University Press, 1992.

Schambra, William. "More Bucks for the Bang: New Public Attitudes Toward Foreign Pol-

icy." *Public Opinion* 2 (January/February 1979): 47–51.
Scheer, Robert. *With Enough Shovels: Reagan. Bush and Nuclear War*. Rev. ed. New York: Vintage Books, 1983.
Schilling, Warner. "U.S. Strategic Nuclear Concepts in the 1970's: The Search for Sufficiently Equivalent Countervailing Parity." In *Strategy and Nuclear Deterrence*, ed. Steven Miller. Princeton, N.J.: Princeton University Press, 1984.
Schlesinger, Arthur. "The Great Carter Mystery." *New Republic*, April 12, 1980.
Schneider, William. "Conservatism, Not Interventionism: Trends in Foreign Policy Opinion, 1974–1982." In *Eagle Defiant: United States Foreign Policy in the 1980's*, ed. Kenneth Oye, Robert Lieber, and Donald Rothchild. Boston: Little, Brown, 1983.
———. "'Rambo' and Reality: Having It Both Ways." In *Eagle Resurgent? The Reagan Era in American Foreign Policy*, ed. Kenneth Oye, Donald Rothchild, and Robert Lieber. Boston: Little, Brown, 1987.
Schweid, Barry, "Warren's World." *Foreign Policy*, no. 94 (spring 1994): 137–47.
Shalom, Stephen. "Remembering the Carter Administration." *Zeta Magazine*, October, 1988.
Shorr, Ira. "Overkill." *In These Times*, January 23, 1995.
Shoup, Lawrence. *The Carter Presidency and Beyond: Power and Politics in the 1980's*. Palo Alto, Calif.: Ramparts, 1980.
Shulman, Marshall. "Four Decades of Irrationality: U.S.-Soviet Relations." In *World Politics 88/89*, ed. Suzanne P. Ogden. Guilford, Conn.: Dushkin, 1988.
Simes, Dimitri K. "The Anti-Soviet Brigade." *Foreign Policy*, no. 7 (winter 1979–80):28–42.
Sklar, Holly. "Trilateralism and the Management of Contradictions." In *Trilateralism: The Trilateral Commission and Elite Planning for World Management*, ed. Holly Sklar. Boston: South End, 1980.
Skowronek, Stephen. *Building a New American State: The Expansion of National Administrative Capacities*. New York: Cambridge University Press, 1982.
Slocombe, Walter, Lloyd Free, Donald Lesh, and William Watts. "The Pursuit of National Security." *Policy Perspectives*.
Smith, Craig Allen. "Leadership, Orientation, and Rhetorical Vision: Jimmy Carter, The 'New Right', and the Panama Canal." *Presidential Studies Quarterly* 16 (spring 1986): 317–28.
Smith, Gaddis. *Morality, Reason and Power: American Diplomacy in the Carter Years*. New York: Hill and Wang, 1986.
Smith, Tom. "The Polls: American Attitudes Toward the Soviet Union and Communism." *Public Opinion Quarterly* 47 (summer 1983): 277–92.
Smith, Wayne. "A Trap in Angola." *Foreign Policy*, no. 62 (spring 1986): 61–74.
Snidal, Duncan. "The Limits of Hegemonic Stability Theory." *International Organization* 39 (autumn 1985): 579–614.
Snyder, Jack. *Myths of Empire: Domestic Politics and International Ambition*. Ithaca: Cornell University Press, 1991.
"Soviet Geopolitical Momentum: Myth or Menace?" *The Defense Monitor* 9, no. 1 (1980).
Spanier, John, and Joseph Nogee. *Congress. the Presidency and American Foreign Policy*. New York: Pergamon, 1981.
Spanier, John. *American Foreign Policy-Making and the Democratic Dilemmas*. 4th ed. New

York: Holt, Rinehart, & Winston, 1985.
Spencer, Donald. *The Carter Implosion: Jimmy Carter and the Amateur Style of Diplomacy*. New York: Praeger, 1988.
Stein, Arthur. "The Hegemon's Dilemma: Great Britain, the United States, and the International Economic Order." *International Organization* 38 (spring 1984): 355–86.
Stockwell, John. *In Search of Enemies: A CIA Story*. New York: Norton, 1978.
Strange, Susan. "The Persistent Myth of Lost Hegemony." *International Organization* 41 (autumn 1987): 551–74.
Strong, Robert. "Jimmy Carter and the Panama Canal Treaties." *Presidential Studies Quarterly* 21 (spring 1991): 269–85.
Talbott, Strobe. *Endgame: The Inside Story of SALT II*. New York: Harper & Row, 1979.
Thornton, Richard. *The Carter Years: Toward a New Global Order*. New York: Paragon House, 1991.
Thurow, Lester. *Head to Head: The Coming Economic Battle among Japan, Europe and America*. New York: Morrow, 1992.
Tonelson, Allen. "Clinton's World." *The Atlantic* 271 (February 1993): 70–74.
Trilateral Commission Task Force Reports 1–7. New York: New York University Press, 1977.
Trilateral Commission Task Force Reports 9–14, New York: New York University Press, 1978.
Trout, B. Thomas. "Rhetoric Revisited: Political Legitimation and the Cold War." *International Studies Quarterly* 19 (September 1975): 251–84.
Tucker, Robert. "America in Decline: A Foreign Policy of 'Maturity.'" *Foreign Affairs: America and the World 1979* 58, no. 3: 449–84.
———. "Reagan Without Tears: His 'Simple' World View is Truer than Carter's 'Complex' One." *New Republic*, May 17, 1980.
Tyroler, II, Charles, ed. *Alerting America: The Papers of the Committee on the Present Danger*. Washington, D.C.: Pergamon-Brassey's, 1984.
Tyson, Laura D'Andrea, *Who's Bashing Whom? Trade Conflict in High-Technology Industries*. Washington, D.C.: Institute for International Economics, 1992.
U.S. Department of State. *American Foreign Policy: Basic Documents. 1977–1980*. Washington, D.C.: U.S. Government Printing Office, 1983.
Van Belle, Douglas. "Domestic Imperatives and Rational Models of Foreign Policy Decision-Making." In *The Limits of State Autonomy: Societal Groups and Foreign Policy Formulation*, ed. David Skidmore and Valerie M. Hudson. Boulder, Colo.: Westview, 1993.
Van Evera, Stephen. "The United States and the Third World: When to Intervene." In *Eagle in a New World: American Grand Strategy in the Post–Cold War World*, ed. Kenneth Oye, Robert Lieber, and Ronald Rothchild. New York: Harper Collins, 1992.
Vance, Cyrus. *Hard Choices: Critical Years in America's Foreign Policy*. New York: Simon and Schuster, 1983.
Waltz, Kenneth. *Theory of International Politics*. Reading, Mass.: Addison-Wesley, 1979.
Wander, Phillip. "The Rhetoric of American Foreign Policy." *The Quarterly Journal of Speech* 70 (November 1984): 339–61.
Ward, Michael D., and David R. Davis. "Sizing Up the Peace Dividend: Economic Growth and Military Spending in the United States, 1948–1996." *American Political Science Review* 86 (September 1992): 748–55.

Warnke, Paul. "Apes on a Treadmill." *Foreign Policy*, no. 18 (spring 1975): 12–29.
———. "We Don't Need a Devil (To Make or Keep Our Friends)," *Foreign Policy*, no. 25 (winter 1976–77): 78–87.
Watson, Cynthia. *U.S. National Security Policy Groups: Institutional Profiles*. New York: Greenwood, 1990.
Watts, William, and Lloyd Free. "Internationalism Comes of Age . . . Again." *Public Opinion* 3 (April/May 1980): 46–50.
Wells, Samuel. "Sounding the Tocsin: NSC 68 and the Soviet Threat." *International Security* 4 (fall 1979): 116–58.
———. "A Question of Priorities: Comparison of the Carter and Reagan Defense Programs." *Orbis* (fall 1983).
Wildavsky, Aaron. "The Two Presidencies." *Transaction* (December 1966).
Wittkopf, Eugene. "Elites and Masses: A Comparative Analysis of Attitudes Toward America's World Role." *Journal of Politics* 45, no.2 (1983): 303–34.
———. "On the Foreign Policy Beliefs of the American People: A Critique and Some Evidence." Unpublished paper presented at the 1986 Annual Convention of the International Studies Association, Anaheim, Calif., March 25–29, 1986.
———. "Elites and Masses: Another Look at Attitudes Towards America's World Role," *International Studies Quarterly* 31 (June 1987): 131–59.
Wittkopf, Eugene, and Michael Maggiotto. "The Two Faces of Internationalism: Public Attitudes Toward American Foreign Policy in the 1970's—And Beyond?" *Social Science Quarterly* 64 (June 1983): 288–304.
Wolfe, Alan. "Trilateralism and the Carter Administration: Changed Realities and Vested Interests." In *Trilateralism: The Trilateral Commission and Elite Planning for World Management*, ed. Holly Sklar. Boston: South End, 1980.
Woodward, Bob. *Veil: The Secret Wars of the CIA, 1981–1987*. New York: Simon & Schuster, 1987.
World Bank. *World Development Report*, 1985. New York: Oxford University Press, 1985.
Yankelovich, Daniel. "Farewell to 'President Knows Best.'" *Foreign Affairs: America and the World 1978* 57, no. 3: 670–93.
———. "Cautious Internationalism: A Changing Mood Toward U.S. Foreign Policy." *Public Opinion* (March/April 1978).
Yankelovich, Daniel, and Larry Kaagan. "Assertive America." *Foreign Affairs: America and the 1980* 59, no. 3: 696–713.
Yankelovich, Daniel, and Richard Smoke. "America's 'New Thinking.'" *Foreign Affairs* 67 (fall 1988): 1–17.
Yoffie, David. *Power and Protectionism*. New York: Columbia University Press, 1983.
Young, Andrew. "The United States and Africa: Victory for Diplomacy." *Foreign Affairs: America and the 1980* 59, no. 3: 648–66.
Zakheim, Dov, and Jeffrey Ranney. "Matching Defense Strategies to Resources: Challenges for the Clinton Administration." *International Security* 18 (summer 1993): 51–78.
Zimmermann, Tim, "Coercive Diplomacy and Libya." in *The Limits of Coercive Diplomacy* 2d ed. Ed. Alexander George and William Simons. Boulder, Colo.: Westview, 1994.

INDEX

adjustment, strategy of, xix–xxii, 20, 52–53, 55, 60, 66, 68, 81, 83–87, 102, 105, 149–153, 164, 166–167, 169–170, 175–178; and theoretical models, 3–14; and Carter's foreign policy, xvi, 26, 28, 31–32, 50

Afghanistan, 27, 47–48, 50, 62, 64–65, 74, 76, 80, 146, 165; Soviet occupation of, 97–101; and the Reagan Doctrine, 159–160

AFL-CIO, 118

Africa, 41–42, 49–50, 62, 64–65, 126, 162

Alvor Accords, 63

Ambrose, Stephen, 17

American Committee on East-West Accord, 140, 143

American Conservative Union, 113–115, 117, 139

American League for Exports and Security Assistance, 132

American Legion, 113

American Security Council (ASC), 113–114, 138–139

Americans for Democratic Action, 118

Americans for SALT, 149, 146

Amin, Hefizullah, 99, 100

Angola: normalization of relations with, 30, 32, 43, 49; Soviet-Cuban involvement in, 47, 63–64; civil war in, 63, 65, 165; and Katanga, 63; and Reagan Doctrine, 159–161

anti-communism, 17, 69, 90–93

Aristide, Jean-Bertrand, 170

arms sales, xii, 32, 44, 48–49, 132–133

Asia, 43–44, 46–47, 49, 62

B-1 bomber, 46, 49, 132, 154

Baker, Howard, 137; and Panama Canal debate, 79–80, 117, 127; and SALT II debate, 146

Bartholomew, Reginald, 97

Benson, Lucy Wilson, 44

Blumenthal, Michael, 126

Boer War, 23

Brammer, Robert, 141

Brazil, 46

Brock, William, 137

Brodin, Katarina, 15

Brown, Harold: and South Korea, 44; and burden sharing, 47; and Panama Canal, 121; and arms sales, 132–133; and the Committee on the Present Danger, 134; and SALT II debate, 142–143, 145

Brzezinski, Zbigniew, 135; and clash with Vance, 29, 95, 97; and U.S. leadership, 35; and East-West relations, 39, 135; and U.S. attitude toward change, 40; and U.S. China policy, 43; and rapid deployment force, 50; and global complexity, 87–88; and human rights, 90–91; and Afghanistan, 98; and Panama Canal debate, 126; and arms sales, 132–133; and the Committee on the Present Danger, 134; and SALT II, 144

burden-sharing, xx, 31–32, 47, 155, 168–169

Bush, George, xxii, 151, 170; and Team B episode, 130; and Persian Gulf War,

229

158–159; presidency of, 164–166
Business and Professional Committee for a New Panama Canal Treaty, 119
Business Roundtable, 119

Caddell, Patrick, 136
Cambodia, 63–65, 159–161
Camp David Accords, 32, 49, 65, 78, 80–81, 95
Campus Republican Action Organization, 113
Canada, 57–58
Cape Verde, 64
Carter Doctrine, 98
Carter, James E. (Jimmy), xi–xii, xix–xxii, 22, 25, 66–68, 77–83, 105, 149–151, 167, 169, 173, 176–177, 180; and strategy of adjustment, xv–xvii, 30–47; and competing interpretations of his foreign policies; 26–30, 52–55, 59–66; and U.S.-Soviet relations, 37–39, 47–48; and U.S.–Third World relations, 39–44, 48–49; and U.S. defense policy, 44–47, 49–50, 57, 155; and abandonment of policy reform, 47–51; views on U.S. power, 30–36, 58; and public opinion, 68–77, 92–93, 101–102; and policy legitimation, 84–103; and human rights, 90–94; and Panama Canal Treaties, 111–129; and SALT II, 129–147
Carter, Rosalyn, 125
Castro, Fidel, 116
Central Intelligence Agency (CIA), 32, 70, 72, 163; and Team B episode, 130
Chamber of Commerce, 119
Chamberlain, Joseph, 23
Chamberlain, Neville, 137
Chammaro, Violetta, 160
Chicago Council of Foreign Relations (CCFR), 70–71, 92–94
China, Peoples Republic of, xi, 61, 64–65, 85; normalization of relations with, 30–32, 43–44, 47–50, 78, 80, 95
Christopher, Warren, 169
Citizens for the Republic, 113
Clifford, Clark, 17
Clinton, William (Bill), xx, xxii, 150–151, 161, 166–167, 169–173
Coalition for a Democratic Majority (CDM), 110
Coalition for a New Foreign and Military Policy, 128, 141
Coalition for Peace Through Strength, 138
Cold War, 52, 79–81, 84, 98, 104–105, 108, 111, 129, 148, 151; and domestic legitimation; xvi, xxii, 16–18, 67–69, 85–86, 88–89, 91, 107, 177; end of, xx, 150, 164, 166–170, 174, 181
Committee for Ratification of the Panama Canal Treaties, 118
Committee for the Survival of a Free Congress, 113
Committee of Americans for the Canal Treaties (COACT), 120
Committee on the Present Danger, 129–130, 134, 136–137, 140, 143, 157
Committee to Save the Panama Canal, 113–115
Common Cause, 118, 141
communism, xi, 16–17, 39, 41, 70, 98, 100, 116, 163–166, 174, 181
Conservative Caucus, 113–114, 116–117, 139, 147
containment doctrine, 39, 69, 153
Conventional Arms Transfer (CAT) talks, 133
Costa Rica, 153
Council for Inter-American Security, 113–114
Council for National Defense, 113
Council of the Americas, 119, 128
Crabb, Cecil, 117
Crane, Phillip, 116
Cranston, Alan, 146
cruise missile, 46
Cuba, 30, 32, 43, 49, 126, 146; and Angola, 63, 160; and Ogaden War, 63–65; Soviet brigade in, 96; and Grenada, 158

Danforth, John, 117
DeConcini, Dennis, 122–123
defense spending, 32; under Carter Administration, 44–50; and U.S. decline, 57–58; U.S. and Soviet levels compared, 60–61, 82; domestic bargaining over, 79, 97, 145; under Reagan Administration, 154–157, 162; under Clinton Administration, 169–170

INDEX

Democratic Party, 109–110, 120
Denmark, 57
Destler, I. M., 95
detente, xi, 43–45, 50, 60, 62, 66, 75–76, 88–89, 92, 95, 98, 108–110, 142, 146, 152
Disarmament Working Group, 141
distributive coalitions, 12–13
doctrine, foreign policy: 15–18, 86–88, 168
Doud Khan, Mohammad, 99
Dulles, John Foster, 17

Ecumenical Program for Inter-American Communication and Action, 118–119
Egypt, 78, 100
Eisenhower, Dwight, 17
El Salvador, 161, 165
Emergency Coalition Against Unilateral Disarmament, 131
Emergency Coalition to Save the Panama Canal, 113
Equatorial Guinea, 64
Ethiopia, 63–64, 89
Europe, Western, 21, 33–34, 46–47, 49, 56, 62, 73, 153–155
evolutionary model, 4, 6–8

Federation of American Scientists, 141
FNLA, 63
Ford, Gerald, 31, 45–46, 57, 110, 130
Foreign Affairs, 69
Foreign Policy Leadership Project, 70, 73–74
Foreign Policy, 69
Franck, Thomas, 125
Friedberg, Aaron, 23–24

Gaddis, John Lewis, 17
Galbraith, John, Kenneth, 140
Garn, Jake, 139
Garthoff, Raymond, 66, 98–101
Gelb, Leslie, 87, 92, 95–98
General Agreement on Tariffs and Trade (GATT), 162
George, Alexander, 14, 16, 88–89
Gilpin, Robert, 4, 22, 56
Gorbachev, Mikhael, 164
Graham, Daniel, 115, 139
Great Britain, 44, 57–58, 80; decline of, 22–24

Greece, 16–17
Grenada, 64, 158
Guinea, 64

Haiti, 161, 170–171
Haskel, Floyd, 115
Hayakawa, S. I., 126
hegemony, xv, xvi–xviii, xxi, 3–14, 16, 19–20, 22–24, 26, 28, 55–57, 68, 175–178, 180
Hermann, Charles, 18–19
Hogan, Michael, 113, 117–118, 125
Holsti, Ole, 70
Holt, Pat, 117
Hoopes, Townscend, 140
human rights, xii, 51, 85; and domestic legitimation, 86, 90–93, 135
Huntington, Samuel, 31, 62, 78, 97, 135
Hussein, Saddam, 159

Indonesia, 64
institutionalism, 7–8, 12, 180
interest groups, xvi–xvii, xxii, 7, 12–13, 18–19, 76–77; and the foreign policy making process, 104–108, 147–148; liberal groups, 108, 118–120, 128–129, 140–142, 147; conservative groups, 108–111, 113–117, 127–140, 147; and Panama Canal debate, 113–120, 127–129; and SALT II debate, 129–142, 146–147
Intermediate Nuclear Forces (INF) Treaty, 161
Iran, 62, 64–65, 76, 160
Iran-Contra scandal, 164
Iraq, 64
Iraq, 158, 159
isolationism, 70
Israel, 48
Italy, 57–58

Jackson, Henry: and the Coalition for a Democratic Majority, 110; and SALT II, 131, 139, 146
Japan, 21, 33–34, 56, 58, 73, 106, 167
Jarmin, Gary, 115
Jordan, Hamilton, 114, 135

Kampelman, Max, 129

Katangan separatists, 63
Keegan, George, 139
Kendall, Donald, 140
Kennan, George, 17, 140
Kennedy, Paul, 22
Keohane, Robert, 6, 10, 11, 22
Khadafy, Muammar, 158
Khymer Rouge, 64–65, 161
Kissinger, Henry, 110, 126, 145
Kraar, Louis, 45–46
Krasner, Stephen, 7, 13, 106, 180
Kreisberg, Paul, 89
Kurkowski, David, 143
Kuwait, 158–159, 165

Lake, Anthony, 88, 95, 169
Laos, 64
Latin America, 43, 78, 121, 157
Laxalt, Paul, 115, 138
Lebanon, 158
legitimacy, foreign policy, xiv–xv, xxi, 14–17, 28, 66–67, 84–87, 90, 102–103, 177, 179
Legvold, Robert, 65
Lehman, John, 156
liberal internationalism, xi, xvi–xviii, xxi, 36, 50–51, 68–69, 77–78, 95, 108, 110; Carter's retreat from, 84; and conservative internationalism, 68; demise of under Carter administration, xii, xvi, 53, 55, 60, 62, 66, 74; as doctrine, 88; and human rights, 90; public support for, 69; and strengths in the Carter administration, 77–78; and Trilateral Commission, 33
Libya, 64, 158
Linowitz, Sol, 112, 125
Lippman Gap, 31, 78
Lowi, Theodore, 14, 15, 95

Mandelbaum, Michael, 69
Marcos, Ferdinand, 161
Marcy, Carl, 140
Marshall Plan, 17
McGovern, George, 109–110
Melanson, Richard, 89
Middle East, 62, 85, 98, 153, 157, 162, 171
Milbrath, Lester, 104
Moffett, George, 116, 126–127

Mondale, Walter, 126, 163
Moore, David, 74
Moore, Thomas, 115, 116
Morgenthau, Hans, 6
MPLA 42, 62, 160
MX missile, 46, 49–50, 144, 154

National Association of Manufacturers, 119
National Conservative Political Action Committee, 113–114
National Council of Churches, 118
Neal, Fred Warner, 140
New Directions; and Panama Canal debate, 118, 128; and SALT II debate, 141–142
New Right, 108–109, 111
Newsom, David, 42
Nicaragua, 62, 65; and Reagan Doctrine, 153, 158–161, 165
Nigeria, 46
Niksch, Larry, 44
Nitze, Paul, 129, 140, 145
Nixon, Richard, xi, xvii, 31, 37, 57, 85, 90, 109
Noriega, Manuel, 158–159
North Atlantic Treaty Organization (NATO), 32, 46–49, 61, 134, 143, 155, 165, 172
North Korea, 44, 171
Northern Ireland, 171
Nunn, Samuel, 145
Nye, Joseph, 104

Olson, Mancur, 12
Opinion Research Corporation, 124
Organization of Petroleum Exporting Countries (OPEC), 31
oversell, 14–18, 86, 95–96
Oye, Kenneth, xix–xx, 31, 32, 36, 42

Packard, David, 129
Palestinian Liberation Organization (PLO), 97
Panama Canal Treaties, xxii, 32, 48, 65, 77–79, 81, 103, 105, 111–129, 136, 142
Panama, 158, 165
Partnership for Peace, 171
Persian Gulf, 50; and Soviet occupation of Afghanistan, 98; and Iraqui war, 158–159

INDEX

Philippines, 161
Phillips, Howard, 116
Poland, 157
Portugal, 63
Posen, Barry, 55, 65
Powell, Jody, 92
Presidential Decision 13 (PD-13), 132
Presidential Decision 18 (PD-18), 45–46
Presidential Decision 50 (PD-50), 144–145
Presidential Decision 59 (PD-59), 50
Presidential Review Memorandum 10 (PRM 10), 133
preventive diplomacy, 32, 40–41, 50, 62, 82, 167
public opinion, xv–xvi, 19, 89, 106, 134–136; conservative shift in, 69–77; and human rights, 92–94; and Carter response to Afghanistan, 101–102; and Panama Canal Treaties, 124–125; and SALT II, 143–144; and Reagan's foreign policies, 163–164
punctuated equilibrium, 7, 13, 180

Rapid Deployment Forces, 49–50
Reagan Doctrine, 159–161
Reagan, Ronald, xii, xix–xx, xxii, 22, 58; and 1976 presidential campaign, 110; and Panama Canal debate, 115; and B-1 bomber, 132; and foreign policy as president, 149–164, 166, 176, 180
realism, xv, xvii, xix, 6–10, 13, 24, 32, 52, 55, 175, 178–179
Republican Party: and conservative resurgence, 109–110; and Panama Canal Treaties, 115; and Carter's foreign policy, 137; and unilateralism, 172
resistance, strategy of, xix–xxi, 3, 5, 9, 20, 22, 26, 52, 177–178; and Reagan's foreign policies, 151–152
Rosati, Jerel, 38, 51
Rosenau, James, 70
Rowney, Edward, 131–132
Rusk, Dean, 129

Sadat, Anwar, 48, 100
Saudi Arabia, 46, 159
Savimbi, Jonas, 160
Schmidt, Robert, 140
Schneider, William, 69–71

Shulman, Marshall, 66, 135
Siegnious, George, 97, 144
Simes, Dimitri, 82
Smith, Gaddis, xi, 91,126
Smith, Hedrick, 126
Smith, Terrance, 115
Solidarity, 157
Somalia, 63–65, 170
Somoza, Anastasio, 62
Sorensen, Theodore, 131
South Africa, 63, 85, 92, 160
South Korea, 44, 49, 134–135
South Yemen, 62, 64–65, 76, 160
Soviet Union, 29, 32, 34, 43–44, 78, 82, 108–109, 152–154, 156–157, 165, 171; U.S. relations with, x, xii, 16–17, 37–39, 47–48, 54, 88, 110, 134, 141; military capabilities of, 21, 31, 45–46, 59, 61, 130; and occupation of Afghanistan, 27, 48, 50, 80, 97–102, 145, 160; and Third World, 40, 42, 60, 62–66, 89, 126, 161; U.S. public attitudes toward, 68–76, 134, 143–144, 163–164; and human rights, 92, 135; and brigade in Cuba, 96; and SALT II, 130, 142, 146; and arms sales, 133; collapse of, 150, 174
Spain, 57
sporadic model, 4, 7
state weakness, xiv, xvi, xviii, xxi, 4, 8–10, 12–16, 18–20, 24, 68, 106, 147–148, 172, 176, 180
Stone, Jeremy, 140–141
Strategic Arms Limitation Treaty II (SALT II), xxii, 48, 77–80, 96–97, 103, 105, 110–112, 114, 127; and ratification battle, 128–147
Strategic Defense Initiative (SDI), 154, 156, 162
Strout, Richard, 112
Sudan, 64

Taiwan, 78
Taraki, Jur Mohammad, 99, 100
Team B, 130, 133
Thompson, Meldrum, 116
Torrijos, Omar, 116, 122
Trident II, 49–50
Trilateral Commission, 27, 30, 33, 35, 108, 128

Trout, B. Thomas, 15
Truman, Harry, 16
Tucker, Robert, 54
Turkey, 16–17

UNITA, 63, 160
United Auto Workers, 118
United Nations (UN), 93, 159–160, 169
United States Catholic Conference, 118

Van Evera, Stephen, 55, 65
Vance, Cyrus; and clash with Brzezinski, 29, 95, 97; and U.S. leadership, 34–36; and U.S.-Soviet relations, 37–38; and preventive diplomacy, 40–41, 112; and nuclear balance, 45; and Panama Canal Treaties, 112, 126; and U.S. withdrawal from South Korea, 135; view of Committee on the Present Danger, 138; and SALT II, 142; resignation, 146
Vandenberg, Arthur, 17, 137
Veterans of Foreign Wars, 113
Vietnam, 22, 130; domestic legacies of U.S. involvement in war in, xi, xv, 31, 33, 41–42, 69–70, 76, 85, 90, 92, 94, 104, 107–109, 116, 148, 157, 163; normalization of relations with, 30, 32, 43, 49; occupation of Cambodia by, 63–65, 160–161
Viguerie, Richard, 114–116

Waltz, Kenneth, 10
Warnke, Paul, 97, 131, 144
Washington Office on Latin America, 118
Watergate, 109–110
Weisband, Edward, 125
West Germany, 57–58
Weyrick, Paul, 115
Wiesner, Jerome, 140
Wilson, F. Raymond, 141

Yom Kippur War, 76
Yost, Charles, 140
Young Americans for Freedom, 113–115
Young Republicans, 113
Young, Andrew, 38, 97
Yugoslavia, 158, 170

Zaire, 47, 63
Zimbabwe, 32, 49, 65, 78, 80, 81
Zorinsky, Edward, 125–126

REVERSING COURSE

was electronically composed in 10 on 12 Adobe Garamond
with display type in RadiantBoldExtraCondensed;
printed on 55-pound, acid-free, Glatfelter Sebago paper,
with 80-pound endsheets and dust jackets printed in 3 colors,
notch case bound over 88-point binder's boards
in Roxite B-grade cloth,
by Donnelley & Sons Company.
Both book and jacket design are the work of Gary Gore.
Published by Vanderbilt University Press,
Nashville, Tennessee 37235.